# The Auth

Bruce Kinloch was born in India in 1919. Coming from a long line of soldiers and hunter-naturalists, he was educated at Berkhamsted and trained at Sandhurst. In 1939 he was commissioned into the Indian Army and saw active service with the 3rd Gurkha Rifles, first on the North West Frontier and then during the greater part of the Burma campaign, where he was awarded the Military Cross for his part in the battle of the Sittang River in 1942. Later he ran some of the first jungle warfare courses and also commanded a 'Chindit' battalion.

Retiring, with the rank of Major, on the break-up of the old Indian Army in 1947, he joined the Colonial Service. His first post was that of District Officer at Kilifi, on the Kenya coast, where he became closely involved with the control of elephants and the pursuit of ivory poachers.

In 1949, he transferred to the Uganda Game and Fisheries Department as Assistant to the Chief Game Warden whom he succeeded less than a year later. During the next ten years he re-organised and expanded the Department and was one of the chief architects of Uganda's National Parks.

In 1960, Kinloch accepted another transfer to become Chief Game Warden of Tanganyika; here, he again re-organised and expanded the Department after studying modern wildlife techniques in the U.S.A. and Canada on a United Nations Fellowship. His greatest achievement was the creation of the College of African Wildlife Management, to train Africans to become the game and national park wardens of the newly independent African countries. He retired in 1964 when his own post was 'Africanised'.

Two subsequent short-term assignments as Wildlife adviser to the Governments of Botswana and Rwanda ultimately led to his appointment, in 1969, as the Chief Game Warden of Malawi, where he built up an independent Department of National Parks and Wildlife Management.

Bruce Kinloch is now retired and living in Herefordshire, in the attractive village of Fownhope, overlooking the River Wye.

*The Conversion of St Hubert*

# Tales from a Crowded Life

by

Bruce Grant Kinloch (Major, M.C.)

Librario

Other books by the author

*Sauce for the Mongoose*
*The Shamba Raiders*
*Game Wardens in Africa*

Published by

**Librario Publishing Ltd.**

ISBN: 978-1-906775-05-6

Copies can be ordered via the Internet
www.librario.com

or from:

Brough House, Milton Brodie, Kinloss
Moray IV36 2UA
Tel/Fax No 00 44 (0)1343 850 178

Printed and bound in the UK

Typeset by 3btype.com

*This book is dedicated to Elizabeth, my beloved wife, who,*
*for 64 selfless years, endured, without complaint,*
*not only the high spots but also the bad periods of*
*our exciting life together.*

*Wedding Day*

# Contents

Preface                                                                                    9

Chapter I        The Formative Years                                13
Chapter II       The Formative Years *(continued)*        31
Chapter III      The Birth of a Wildfowler                       45
Chapter IV       The Making of a Rifleman                      53
Chapter V        The Way of a Transgressor                     61
Chapter VI       The Tale of the Dulikhet Panther          71
Chapter VII      The Final Test                                       81
Chapter VIII     A Christmas Camp in India                   91
Chapter IX       Frontier Flash-back                              101
Chapter X        To the High Himalayas                          115
Chapter XI       Tiger, Tiger                                           123
Chapter XII      The Mule Saga                                     133
Chapter XIII     The Elusive Sambar                             141
Chapter XIV      The Battle for the Sittang Bridge         151
Chapter XV       Suicide Mission                                    169
Chapter XVI      A Battery on a Shoestring                    181
Chapter XVII     The Lure of the Elephant                     189
Chapter XVIII    The Elephants of Knysna                     193
Chapter XIX      A Truly Royal Fish                               203
Chapter XX       Stalking the Scottish Stag                    211
Chapter XXI      Desert Lake                                         235
Chapter XXII     Kismet                                                263
Chapter XXIII    In Search of the Fish God                   289

Appendix I                                                                  305
Appendix II                                                                 315
Appendix III                                                                323

# Preface

As the tales in this book unfold, it will rapidly become apparent, even to the least discerning reader, that the author of this book (myself) must certainly be a dedicated follower of the centuries old cult of St Hubert, the patron saint of hunters. Furthermore, it was the discernment of those earlier dedicated hunters who, through their pursuit of the policy of controlled hunting as an essential part of practical wildlife management, later became recognised as also being true conservationists.

For the sake of the uninitiated, let me explain, as briefly as possible, what little is known about St Hubert, who lived in the border area between modern France and Germany, as long ago as the 7th Century AD.

Hubert (or Hubertus) who was alleged to have been, in his younger days, a wealthy and dissolute nobleman, had an all-consuming passion for hunting, his quarry being the red deer and wild boar that abounded in the dense forests of his native Ardennes. Furthermore, although he was a devout and practicing Christian, Hubert did not permit his religious beliefs to interfere, in any way, with his overriding love of the chase. So, according to legend, it was on a Good Friday that an event occurred which changed the course of Hubert's life for ever.

On that particular Friday, while the faithful were at prayers, Hubert had set out early, with two of his favourite hounds, in pursuit of a red deer stag whose deep tracks he had found, that very morning, close to his forest home. The chase that followed was long and arduous, but near sunset he finally entered a wide clearing where, revealed before him he saw, in the dying rays of the setting sun, the figure of a mighty stag with, between its spreading horns, a shining cross of gleaming gold.

Dropping to his knees, beside his whimpering hounds, Hubert heard a clear but distant voice, which said … "Hubert, unless you turn to the Lord, and lead a holy life, you shall quickly fall into the abyss of Hell". Hubert then fell prostrate on the ground and asked, "Lord, what would you have me do?" whereupon he received the reply, "Go and seek Lambert, and he will instruct you".

Lambert, who at that time was the Bishop of Maastricht, received Hubert kindly and became his spiritual adviser. Following Lambert's guidance, Hubert first abandoned his patronage and then gave all his worldly goods to the poor and needy, before beginning to study for the priesthood. Following his Ordination, Hubert continued to be guided by Bishop Lambert and quickly became famous and widely respected, both for the power of his preaching and for the extent of his tireless work for the poor.

Eventually, Bishop Lambert sent Hubert on a pilgrimage to Rome and, according to legend, it was while Hubert was actually attending an audience with the Pope, that the latter had a vision of Bishop Lambert being murdered in Maastricht. Immediately and without hesitation, so the legend relates, the Pope appointed Hubert to replace Lambert as Bishop of the Diocese of Maastricht.

In Hubert's time, idolatry was not only prevalent but deeply entrenched and widely practiced in the Ardennes. However, such was the power of Hubert's preaching that a great many heathen were converted to Christianity. This, coupled with a number of minor miracles that Hubert performed during his priesthood, led him, on his death, to being beatified. From then on, St Hubert became recognised as being the Patron Saint not only of hunters, but also of all those whose profession is, in any way, associated legitimately with the chase.

For the first ten years of my active life, my own career followed closely in the footsteps of both my grandfathers. Like them I was trained at the Royal Military College, Sandhurst, and also like them I became a commissioned officer in a famous Rifle Regiment. From then on, however, the similarity ends abruptly for, whereas both my grandfathers served on to become generals – one with the added accolade of a Victoria Cross – I myself was faced with little option but to resign my regular commission when, on the partition of India in August 1947, the famous Imperial Indian Army was divided between Pakistan and the newly independent India.

Although I had not even heard of St Hubert as being the Patron Saint of hunters until after I returned to India, the land of my birth, in 1939, by faithfully following, from then on, the ethics ideals and principals of St Hubert, finally led me to becoming, for 25 years of my crowded life, the Chief Game Warden of three different countries in Africa. Ultimately, it also led to the creation, at Mweka, near Moshi, on the slops of 19,340 foot snow-capped Mount Kilimanjaro, the highest mountain in Africa, of my brain child, The College of African Wildlife Management.

Conceived initially to meet the wildlife management needs of the English speaking countries of East and Central Africa, and promptly copied by the creation of a carbon copy of the College at Garua, in Cameroon, for the French speaking countries of West Africa, and then by South Africa, also, 42 years later Mweka is still flourishing after having trained students from all four continents. However, what few people now know and what those who did know have long forgotten, is that had it not been for an extraordinary coincidence, the College of African Wildlife Management at Mweka would never have come into existence – the hand of fate indeed!

The story of that part of my life – including a detailed account of the extraordinary coincidence that finally led to the creation of The College of African Wildlife Management – has already been told in the best selling and twice re-printed book 'The Shamba Raiders', copies of which are still available from Librario Publishing Limited, of Elgin, who are also the publishers of this, my current book.

Now, in this book, I have attempted to narrate some tales of the most interesting and/or exciting events that occurred during the other years of my crowded life. Furthermore, since most of these tales are associated, directly or indirectly, with the teachings of St Hubert in his role as the patron saint of hunters, I decided that, for the frontispiece of the book, it would be most appropriate to use a copy of a German lithograph entitled 'The Conversion of Saint Hubert', a picture, now hanging in the St Hubert Club of Great Britain, but one which I once held in my own possession for many years.

**Bruce Kinloch**

*My grandfather's fascinating book was the size and weight of a large family bible,
difficult for a small boy to even lift*

# Chapter I

# The Formative Years

*The Child is father of the Man*

WILLIAM WORDSWORTH
*My Heart Leaps Up* 1804

The little, dusty cantonment town of Saharanpur, in what was then the United Provinces of British Imperial India, is not the most salubrious spot to make one's debut in this troubled world, particularly on the hottest day of the hot weather; but I had no say in the matter. My father was stationed there; it was the twenty-seventh day of the sweltering month of August, in the year following the close of the First World War; the mercury in the thermometer stubbornly refused to drop below the 110° mark; I was on schedule and that was that.

I was born with the taste of a silver spoon still lingering in my mouth, but what was left of the substance had been removed, finally and irrevocably, by my paternal grandfather, a tough, adventurous but somewhat eccentric character with little business acumen – common traits in the Kinloch family, I fear.

I never knew my grandfather for he died the year I was born, but he exerted

*Logie House*

*The author's grandfather Major-General A.A.A. Kinloch, C.B.*
*late of the 'King's Royal Rifle Corps' (60th rifles)*

a profound influence on my early life. On his death the family estate of Logie, in the Scottish county of Angus, had to be sold. All I inherited from him were the genes of a compulsive and dedicated hunter-naturalist and a book which became my bible. It was a massive, olive-green tome, which a small boy could only lift with an effort. On the front cover was an imposing, gold-embossed picture of the head of a fierce-looking gaor (or Indian 'bison') and the impressive title – *'Large Game Shooting in Thibet, the Himalayas, Northern and Central India'*, by Brigadier-General Alexander A.A.Kinloch.

My grandfather had a facile pen and the eye of a keen observer. He was a noted authority on Indian and Himalayan big game and his book is enriched by vivid descriptions of the country, and of the habits and natural history of the elusive animals that he pursued, with such determination, tenacity and unflagging energy, in the dense Indian jungles and the wild and inhospitable regions of the greatest mountain range in the world. Frequently, for weeks on end, he would search for an outstanding specimen of some particularly coveted species, letting nothing stand in his way. He even resorted to disguise to enable him to enter the forbidden country of Thibet, the mysterious land of the 'roof of the world', long banned to Europeans. When caught and summarily ejected by the Tartar guards, he merely bided his time and tried again.

In those days there was no motor transport and virtually all hunting had to be done on foot. Even the initial journey to some remote hunting ground often involved weeks of hard foot-slogging, sometimes assisted by porters, mules or pack ponies to carry out the basic essentials for spartan living. Weapons were also primitive by modern standards. Their short range and limited accuracy necessitated as close an approach to the chosen quarry as that dictated by the light miniature camera and telephoto lens of the present day wildlife photographer. The latter moreover, does most, if not all, of his camera hunting in the ease and safety of a modern, cross-country vehicle, having first reached his intended area in the speed and comfort of an aeroplane or high-powered car, in place of a long and arduous march.

I often think of these facts when I read or listen to the sanctimonious vapourings of well meaning but ill-informed people who, in their ignorance of the truth, vilify the old time big-game hunters, branding them one and all, without exception, as mendacious butchers pure and simple. That such critics existed even in my grandfather's time is made abundantly clear in the course of the introduction to his famous book, which soon became a classic and is now a collector's piece.

Beginning the introduction he wrote in his first paragraph:

'The love of the chase is an instinct which centuries of civilisation have been unable to eradicate; the pursuit which was a necessity to the savage, and in fact the business of his life, being now followed as a relaxation by those whose means place them in a position where physical toil and hardships are totally unnecessary'.

These words were written more than one hundred years ago, when people's ideas of what constituted relaxation, physical toil and hardship differed considerably from the modern concept of these terms. Most people in these soft-living and somewhat decadent times would hardly classify my grandfather's arduous hunting exploits as 'relaxation', but they would certainly regard them as the acme of quite unnecessary physical toil and hardship! Admittedly, he was an exceptionally hardy and spartan character, even for his day. He held a commission in the King's Royal Rifle Corps (60th Rifles) and his predominantly cockney troops called him 'old iron 'ead', for throughout his long service in India, he steadfastly refused to wear either a solar topee[1], or a spine-pad, as protection against what were then regarded as the death-dealing rays of the tropical sun.

From his pictures he was a tall, fine-looking man with a neat imperial beard which, despite army regulations, he was allowed to wear as a special dispensation. With a height of six foot four inches he towered above most of his little riflemen who stood in awe of this tough and eccentric officer.

Although he bothered little about creature comforts, he did occasionally take some medical precautions to reduce the risk of his hunting activities being in any way curtailed. Describing one of his elephant hunts, about which I have never tired of reading since I was a very small boy, he writes in his book about the dangers of 'jungle fever' – in other words malaria.

"Early in September of the same year (i.e. 1863)," he says in his chapter on the Asiatic elephant, "I disregarded all warnings about jungle fever, and set out to have another try for elephant in the Siwalikhs[2]. I took the precaution of swallowing a glass of sherry with a *good dose* of quinine every morning when I got out of bed, and I never had a touch of fever".

The italics above are mine, for one's imagination boggles at the nauseating

---

[1]  A pith sun-helmet.

[2]  A very old and densely forested range of hills in Northern India, close to the foothills of the Himalayas.

thought of a massive dose of gall-bitter quinine, inadequately camouflaged by a large glass of sherry, descending on an empty stomach in the dim, grey light of a jungle dawn. But Alexander, Airlie Angus was a man of iron. In fact, he refused to admit that there was such a thing as pain! It was this erroneous belief, a yogi-like mastery of mind over matter that finally led to his death as an old man. Sitting by the fire one night, dozing, his tweed trousers were set alight by a falling ember. Since he refused to acknowledge the existence of pain, he did not notice the fact until one of his legs was very badly burnt. Gangrene finally set-in and, indestructible almost to the last, the old warrior moved on to the happy hunting grounds.

The remainder of the introduction to my grandfather's classic treatise on big game shooting reveals that he was a true hunter-naturalist of the old school. He was opposed to wasteful and excessive killing and was only interested in hunting which provided a real challenge to his skill and endurance. In many ways his ideas were ahead of his time and his opinions of the views held by the misguided sentimentalists of his day, as well as of the less creditable activities of a certain school of vain, avaricious and thoughtless sportsmen, were caustic and to the point. Had he been alive now he would have made an outstanding game warden!

Continuing from the first pointed paragraph of his introduction his comments become steadily more pungent. Expanding on his dissertation on man's natural hunting instinct he goes on to say – "That this instinct, like most of the promptings of healthy Nature, is a pretty safe guide to follow, is generally admitted; and there are few who question the advantages to be derived from field sports, among the votaries of which may be numbered some of the greatest names in history".

If the old man had been alive now, he could truthfully have added to his latter statement – 'and the majority of the leaders of the powerful, world-wide wildlife conservation movement of today!'

Turning to the opponents of field sports he wrote:

'There is indeed a limited school who talk of the immorality and cruelty of all field sports; but it will be found that the professors of such doctrines have very peculiar views on other subjects, and seem to make it the business of their lives to prove that the world has been going on a wrong system, and that they have fortunately been born to set it right. If they had their own way, men would become effeminate, and women would lose much that now gives dignity and charm to their sex.

So general is the instinct which leads to the love of the chase in its many forms, that it may almost be said to be universal; and when the taste is not developed, it will generally be found that the want of early initiation, or lack of opportunity, are the causes to which its absence may be ascribed."

At this point the old man switched his aim to criticise and condemn those who, by their attitude and actions, bring field sports into disrepute:

"It is unnecessary to write a defence of field sports;" he wrote, "but it must be admitted that of late years there has been some foundation for the assertion that many man shoot for the love of slaughter and not for healthy excitement.

…nothing can possibly be said in favour of the practice of turning down pheasants, and even hares and rabbits, the day before a grand shooting party. It is hard to imagine what pleasure anyone can find in butchering animals under such circumstances, and the introduction of the system can only be attributed to a vulgar and childish desire to show a long list of slain at the end of the day, and obtain the cheap (in one sense only) notoriety of the heaviest bag of the season".

As I have already said, this book was written more than a hundred years ago, but the sentiments that the old General expressed in it are as valid today as they were then. It is nearly seventy-five years since my father first began to read chapters of the book to me as bed-time stories – at my earnest and pleading request. Later I read them and re-read them for myself. The stories fascinated me, particularly the tales of elephant hunting in the dense hill jungles of the Siwalikhs (to which I myself was destined to return not many years after) and the pursuit of the cunning rharkhor and the wily mountain sheep in the mighty Himalayas, in the foothills of which I was eventually to start my own career as a professional soldier.

The famous naturalist and brilliant wildlife artist, the late J. G. Millais, in this biography of one of the greatest hunter-naturalists of all time, the late Captain Frederick, Courtenay Selous, D.S.O., wrote:

*The author's mother: Mary Eva nee Channer, daughter of General G.N. Channer, V.C., C.B. late of the 1st King George V's Own Gurkha Rifles*

*The author's father: Ronald Kinloch, Commissioner, Imperial Indian Police*

'There are few of us whose early inspirations and subsequent acts are not influenced by literature. Some book comes just at the time of our life when we are most impressionable and seems exactly to fit in with our ideas and temperament'.

No truer words were ever penned. In the case of Selous the vital book that sent him off to Africa was Baldwin's *'African Hunting from Natal to the Zambesi'*. Many other famous hunters and pioneers tell a similar story. In my own more humble case it was my grandfather's book on the hunting of Indian and Himalayan big game that steered my uncertain feet back to India, the land where I had been born.

My grandfather had devoted so much of his time, energy and interest to the pursuit of big game that I often wondered how he found any time at all for soldiering. But it is clear that he was also a successful professional soldier, for he eventually retired with a C.B and the rank of Major General. In fact, from my own experience of campaigning against the Japanese Imperial Army,

*Thibetian Antelope*

in the jungles of Burma, during the Second World War, those men who had had some experience of big game hunting started off with a distinct advantage. At the beginning the Japanese soldiers ran rings round the bewildered Allied troops, for the tough and fanatical 'Sons of Nippon' had been specially trained in jungle warfare in Formosa. They were at home in the jungle while to the Allied soldiers, schooled in the tactics of more conventional battle grounds, the forest was a strange and hostile place, mysterious, dark and menacing – an enemy in itself. The few exceptions (of which I was lucky enough to be one) were those officers and men who had regularly lived and hunted in the jungle. To them the jungle was a friend. They understood it and through this understanding many of them not only survived but lived to turn the tables on the ant-like yellow hordes from the 'Land of the Rising Sun'.

In the days before the cavalry were forced to trade their beloved horses for clanking mechanical monsters, it used to be said that the fox-hunting field in England was the finest peace-time training for war in the jungle, the real infantryman's war which is often decided at close quarters, man to man, as in days of yore.

My own decision to become a professional soldier was long delayed and by no means a slavish adherence to family traditions. From a very early age I was as shy and as wild as the animals and birds which were my main interest in life. The fascination of wild things and wild places held me in thrall to such an extent that any idea of an ordered, restricted or disciplined existence filled my with revulsion and dread. "In any case, we haven't got the money!" I would cry triumphantly, whenever some officious relation eyed me disapprovingly and said to my kindly and indulgent parents – "The boy needs discipline. You should put him in the army."

My grandfather's single-minded, determined and life-long dedication to the hunting of an endless variety of obscure wild beasts, in the depths of the Indian jungles and the most remote fastnesses of the Himalayas and Thibet, resulted in neglect of his family and estates and the dissipation of what remained of the Kinloch family fortunes. Left to the tender mercies of a kindly but strict aunt (a determined character who even hammered all traces of a Scottish accent out of them) my father and his brothers were thus denied the opportunity of following in my grandfather's footsteps. Instead, one became a tea-planter in Southern India, where he was eventually killed by a wild boar – a fate which my grandfather himself narrowly escaped when, one day on the Indian plains, armed only with a spear, he was charged and cut to ribbons by a mighty boar. Another became a rubber-planter in Malaya. A third wandered off to Australia. And my father joined the Indian police.

The long history of the Kinloch family is full of vicissitudes, with many violent ups and downs over the centuries. Yet, in these days when inverse snobbery is the fashion I have always retained a quiet pride and interest in the fact that the family of Kinloch is one of the oldest in Scotland, tracing its origins back for over a thousand years, to AD 900, when a Bishop Killoch was Archbishop of St Andrews, in the County of Fife, between the Firths of Forth and Tay.

It is more than likely that the Bishop was the first educated and law-abiding Kinloch, and an astute as well as a holy man, for his immediate descendants, bearing the name of 'de Kinloch' or 'de Kindeloch', were big landowners in Fife in the twelfth and thirteenth centuries, under charters conferred by William the Lion. During the next two or three hundred years the surplus sons appear to have moved north of the Tay into the counties of Perth and Angus, and my father's branch of the family seemed to have blossomed in Dundee where, in 1515, James Kinloch established himself firmly as Town Treasurer.

Few of the subsequent Kinlochs were as righteous and as law-abiding as one must suppose His Holiness, the Bishop must have been, nor as astute as the Town Treasurer. In fact they were a colourful lot who developed a penchant for adventure and an unhappy knack of espousing lost causes. To this day they have always appeared to be rebels by nature, an attribute which has regularly landed them in serious trouble. From time to time their lands have been confiscated, their titles forfeited, and their freedom lost by banishment to a foreign land – when they have been lucky enough to escape the hangman's noose, that is. It is therefore hardly necessary to add that they were staunch and enthusiastic Jacobites, who played a leading part in the risings of the '15 and the '45, the gallant but finally abortive attempts to restore the 'auld Stuarts' to the throne of Scotland – first James, the 'Old Pretender', in 1715, and then, in 1745, his son, Prince Charles Edward, 'Bonnie Prince Charlie', the 'Young Pretender'.

Although they sometimes backed the wrong side, when the Kinlochs took up soldiering, as a good many of them did over the years, they appeared to have an aptitude for it. In the family conspiracy to impress me in the Army I was never allowed to forget this and, among other family tales, I was frequently regaled with romantic stories of the gallant deeds of Sir James Kinloch and his two brothers, Charles and Alexander, in the bloody campaign of the '45, tales of daring-do which were enough to excite the interest and imagination of any adventurous minded Scottish lad.

According to family records, which my father used to quote, it was in the autumn of 1745, that Sir James apparently received a letter headed 'Blair in Atholl' and dated 'September 2nd, 1745'. It said – 'You cannot fail to have heard before this of my arrival in Scotland, with a firm resolution never to abandon the Island, but to assert His Majesty's right to the utmost. I am now at the head of a good body of His Majesty's loyal subjects, and intend with all convenient speed to march South, and now think fit to acquaint you of my design, and require that you may immediately repair to the Royal Standard, when you won't fail to meet with suitable marks of my favour.' – The letter was signed 'CHARLES, P. R.'

What could a loyal Scot do?

Sir James helped Lord Ogilvie to raise the 1st Battalion of the Angus Regiment, and together they joined Prince Charles at Edinburgh. Having received a Commission as Lieutenant Colonel, Sir James returned to raise and command the 2nd Battalion of the Angus Regiment.

History relates that the Angus men were the best equipped and best disciplined in the Prince's Army. They fought with particular gallantry and distinction at the battles of Falkirk and Culloden, at both of which Sir James Kinloch's Battalion carried Prince Charlie's Colours. Clear proof of their orderly and fighting withdrawal, when the final battle was lost and with it the last lingering hope of the Jacobite cause, was their gallant and successful defence of the Colours, which they carried with them, in deep snow, over the

Grampians. The banner, bearing the motto – *'Nemo Me Impune Lacessit,'*[3] is the only one in existence, for all the others, taken by the Duke of Cumberland ('The Butcher') were burned by the Common Hangman at the Cross of Edinburgh in 1746. For nearly two hundred years it remained in the possession of the Kinlochs of Logie, until the sad day in April, 1920, when my father's old home was sold, after the death of the General, and the historic Colours found a new resting place in the Museum at Dundee.

Sir James Kinloch's reward for his gallant indiscretion was confiscation of his estates, forfeiture of his baronetcy, and a sentence of death for high treason. His only good fortune was an eleventh hour reprieve and banishment!

Sir James's brothers, Charles and Alexander, shared his fate. With him and their brother-in-law, Major James Rattray of Ranalgulzion, they had fought desperately at Culloden, being among the last to leave the bloody carnage on the field of battle that fateful night. Together they had accompanied Prince Charles to the Bridge of Faillie, where, torn and bloodstained, they had bade their Prince a sorrowful farewell. "Is there yet any way in which we can serve you Royal Highness?" they had asked. Despairingly the Prince had answered – "There is now no favour you can do me equal to saving yourselves and your friends, and by forgetting my ruined cause. Let me live in your recollection, but save yourselves and your followers." Thereupon he turned to his aide-de-camp John Kinloch, Sir James's youngest brother, who was a Captain in Lord Ogilvie's Regiment and the person mainly responsible for rescuing the Colours, saying – as he felt in his doublet to produce a diamond studded locket containing a lock of his own fair hair – "Take this, I had it inscribed after Falkirk. Keep it in memory of me and our lost cause."

My father was a romantic. There was a far away look in his eyes whenever he related this and other colourful episodes of family history. On his retirement he lived more and more in the past. As I grew older and more understanding, I came to realise that, subsisting on an inadequate pension in an English country village and later in a small suburban house, he was a soul in exile, his heart in his beloved Scotland where he was raised and his ancestors before him for a thousand years.

My father's boyhood had been spent at Logie, the family estate which marched with that of Glamis Castle, the seat of the Earls of Strathmore, the

---

3   'No one provokes me with impunity'.

*Logie House*
*The home of the Kinloch family for nearly 200 years.*

scene of Shakespeare's *'Macbeth',* and the birthplace of Queen Elizabeth, Britain's late Queen Mother. Inevitably, as a young man he had mixed with the highest in the land, yet in his retirement he was no more than a small ratepayer with his name on the voter's list in a rural Essex constituency.

Logie had been sold on my grandfather's death, a few years before my father retired. The old General had been a brilliant hunter and a fine soldier, but when it came to money matters he had been as naïve and irresponsible as a child. On his demise the whole estate had to be sold to meet accumulated debts and death duties. My father had been in India at the time and all that he had managed to salvage from the wreck of his old home were a few trinkets and items of furniture, every one of which he had had to bid for in the sale. This, I think, broke his heart. Once, before he died, I returned to Scotland with him to visit Logie. All that was left of the Kinlochs was a sadly decaying family mausoleum, desecrated by vandals. It was crammed with marble memorial slabs to the numerous Kinlochs who had passed on over the years. Many of the names were hardly decipherable. Even the most recent were blurred by thick, green mould. But the whole added up to a picture of a family which had roamed the world, many of its members losing their lives in the process, in the utmost corners of the globe, the majority of them while fighting for Britain's once great Empire. I am a great believer in the strong influence of heredity, often confused with family tradition, and I do not think it is at all surprising therefore, that my elder brother and I were also destined to become wanderers on the face of the earth.

Both my brother and I spent the early years of our childhood in India and my earliest conscious recollections are of animals – memories of swaying through the beautiful sal forests of the northern United Provinces on the back of a majestic and well-trained elephant; the grunting, bubbling camels that formed the protesting baggage train when we accompanied my father on tour; and an unexpected encounter with a pair of ill-tempered sloth bears which spread panic among the plodding column. All these I can still recall, although the pictures are blurred by the mists of time.

My father himself was a keen shikari, but nothing like so fanatical as the old General. I can just remember running inquisitive fingers through the thick orange, black and white ruff of a magnificent cold-weather tiger, a very dead cattle-killer, anxiously watched by one Haidar Khan, my father's bearded and turbanned police orderly. I was three and a half years old at the time. And when my parents retired, the place of honour in the small entrance hall of our house in England was filled by the massive head and horns of a mighty Indian bison. Even in death, staring from the gloomy shadows at the foot of the stairs, it had a look of savage malevolence that startled sensitive old ladies and timorous children. In life it had charged and injured my father, who was only saved by his gallant dog, a black retriever which hurled itself into the fray and seized the enraged bison by the nose, thus enabling my dazed parent to crawl to his fallen rifle. From that day on dogs, and particularly retrievers, had a respected place in the Kinloch family.

When my brother Ian was thirteen and I was just six, our parents decided to return to England for good. My father was really too young to retire, but after surviving the rigours of thirty, sweltering hot weathers in the plains of India he felt he had had enough. Moreover, he was a kindly, thoughtful man who remembered his own sad childhood. Shy and reserved, he had married rather late in life, and he was determined that my brother and me should be spared the unhappiness of the long family separations that had always been the major drawback of any career in British Imperial India.

The early days of retirement were happy ones for all of us. I remember our first home with affection and nostalgia. It was in the little rural village of Bulmer, in Essex, close to the Suffolk county border; a sunny cheerful house with what estate agents call – 'a southern aspect'. In fact, apart from the bathroom and kitchen, all the rooms faced squarely south.

In the day-time the house was filled with light and sunshine. At night it was lit by the soft but uncertain glow of oil lamps that flickered and smoked in the slightest draught. The water supply was primitive. It came from a tall hand-pump in the garden, fed by a deep, cool well. The bath water was heated in an enormous copper that hissed, boiled and bubbled like the witches' cauldron in Macbeth. The toilet had been an earth closet in a battered shed at the bottom of the garden, but my father would have none of that. Instead he installed a modern convenience in the bathroom, a chemical contrivance that was rather more hygienic but presented problems of disposal, besides filling the house with an overpowering odour of creosote if the back door was left open when the wind was in the north. The year was 1925.

On one side of the house, but separated from it by a high, brick wall, was a farm-yard with a big barn and hay-ricks, densely populated by a thriving colony of large, fierce and fertile brown rats and a multitude of equally prolific squeaking mice – a rich and rewarding hunting ground for a small boy with an air-gun. On the other side, discreetly screened by an apple orchard and two small cottages, was a popular local establishment called the 'Cock and Blackbirds Inn', the scene of rural revelry on most normal Saturday nights.

The house faced onto a wide expanse of grassy meadows containing a green, odiferous pond covered with duck-weed and full of multi-coloured newts, tadpoles and other mysterious and exciting aquatic creatures. The fields were bisected by a long avenue of fine plane trees, leading up to an old, weathered stone church, the square tower of which housed the belfry, the guaranteed source of an endless supply of young and vocal jackdaws to swell the ranks of the Kinloch family menagerie.

The countryside around teemed with rabbits and wood pigeons that waxed fat and lazy on the rich variety of crops. The farmers welcomed any assistance to deal with these pests, a task that my brother and I tackled with vigour and enthusiasm. Day after day, during the holidays, Ian and I would sally forth; he armed with a .22 rifle or a .410 shotgun; myself acting as retriever and game carrier, with an occasional shot as a reward for my labours. We would then cycle in six miles to the local market town of Sudbury, where healthy rabbits would fetch a shilling a piece and a plump wood-pigeon ninepence. The proceeds paid for our ammunition, with a comfortable surplus to swell our pocket money, in turn required for such essentials as sweets, books, fishing-tackle and catapult elastic.

All together it was an idyllic existence for the budding hunter and naturalist, but like all good things in life it had to come to an end. It lasted four years.

I learnt a lot during this period, but the knowledge I gained was mainly about the birds, the beasts and the fishes of the unspoilt East Anglian country-side. I learnt their habits and, in the case of those which were listed as fair quarry for the hunter, I also learnt how best to outwit them. For the rest I discovered the joys of being a watcher. My tutors were the sons and the gamekeepers of the big landowners, who were tolerant of my activities as long as I did not disturb their partridges and pheasants. My classrooms were the fields, the hedgerows and the woods. My playgrounds were the slow, quiet rivers of Suffolk; the still, calm lakes of Essex; and the great marshes of East Anglia.

By the time I was ten years old I had been thoroughly schooled in the care and safe-handling of firearms. I was a good shot with a miniature rifle and small-bore shotgun. And I had learnt the importance of patience in the art of hunting.

Frequently, for the greater part of an evening, I would squat in ambush behind a barricade of boards in the barn next door, waiting for the twitching whiskers of an old buck rat to appear from a hole in the granary wall. And often in the early mornings I would lie hidden in the dew-soaked grass for half an hour or more at a time, until a careless rabbit hopped out of a hedgerow to nibble the fresh green corn. My weapon was usually an air-gun, but with my brother's growing interest in motor-cycles and all things mechanical, on occasions, as a great concession, or in return for services rendered, I was allowed to borrow his .22 rim-fire rifle or .410 shotgun. At such carefully chosen times I would slide quietly out before Ian could change his mind, usually leaving him bathed in a thick emulsion of oil, dirt and sweat, as he struggled with the fitting of a recalcitrant piston-ring or the complex intestinal coils of a stubborn magneto.

Nevertheless, I sometimes actually preferred using my old, but trusty air-rifle, because it was so silent. Even at that early, thoughtless age I did not go hunting merely for the purpose of killing something. I also liked to watch and listen, and the advantage of my air-rifle was that it caused no noise or disturbance when fired. In any case, I did not fire over-many shots, for it had been drummed into me from a very early age that no true sportsman, and certainly no true naturalist, would ever dream of killing anything, bird or animal, unless it was either a nuisance, or a danger, or good to eat, or a specimen particularly coveted for scientific study or to fill a gap in a prized collection. However, I was a born collector and as all animals fascinated me I seldom missed a chance to 'rescue' any bird or beast that appeared to me to be sick, or injured, or abandoned when too young to fend for itself.

Despite the entirely humanitarian nature of my intentions, I never ceased to be surprised, and not a little hurt, that my patients seldom, if ever, appeared to recognise in me the noble attributes and the pure and selfless intentions of a true 'good Samaritan'. In fact, they usually objected strongly to any interference on my part and, in consequence, as often as not, my rescue operations had to be carried out forcibly in the face of considerable physical and vocal resistance on the part of the rescued. Disappointed at their puzzling lack of perception, and convinced that I knew better than they did what was good for them, I used to ignore their violent struggles and angry protestations. Such noisy outbursts I put down to sheer ignorance and stupidity on their part and, perhaps surprisingly, most of my unwilling patients finally settled down happily enough in their new and certainly strange surroundings.

The old stable, which sheltered the family car – a vintage, 'Austin Seven' tourer of uncertain temperament – also provided the necessary sanctuary for this odd assortment of mammals and birds, wild and domestic, young and old. Fledgling jackdaws and rooks, mixed up with immature hedgehogs and rabbits, were always resident in fluctuating numbers. Occasionally there would be an exciting new arrival such as a sleepy dormouse or an agile, chittering young squirrel, or a raucous juvenile magpie or jay. And of course there were the domestic regulars – 'Jock', the elderly retriever; a half-bred, wriggling black spaniel, 'Mac'; and the assorted, multi-coloured kittens, 'Lanoline', 'Glycerine', 'Tangerine', and 'Margerine', whose mother was a 'gypsy' and whose father was a 'travelling man'. But my prized possession was 'Dopey', an outsize polecat ferret, who was really more of a status symbol than an asset to rabbiting as he invariably laid-up when released in a burrow.

'Dopey' had been given to me by a friendly gamekeeper during a long summer holiday. At the time I had been almost overwhelmed by the keeper's apparent generosity. Later, after several lengthy sessions of weary, back-breaking labour, excavating labyrinthine tunnels, many of them ending in heavy clay and no ferret, I began to have uneasy doubts as to the purity of his motives. My suspicions were finally confirmed one dark evening in late autumn, when I overheard my keeper friend say to a professional rabbit catcher, as he was emerging from the 'Blackbird Inn' – 'Every time I used that bloody ferret I had to dig him out. I'm mighty glad to be rid of him'. From that day on 'Dopey' (as I had renamed him) was put on the retired list, a prize exhibit and no more.

When the weather proved too foul even for my brother and I to sally forth, there was always the playroom which was a haven for any nature loving boy. Besides our collection of birds' eggs and my early attempts at taxidermy, it housed an ever-growing assortment of books on natural history, hunting and fishing. These books gave me intense vicarious pleasure. Often, with the rain pelting against the windows, I would bury myself in some classic of chase and imagine myself tracking elephants through dense tropical jungles, or stalking the wily ibex in the high Himalayas.

These were happy and rewarding times. They had a profound influence on my subsequent life and outlook, and I could not imagine them changing, let alone coming to an end. Then the blow fell and my world tumbled about my ears, for my parents reluctantly decided that the family would have to move to the busy city of Rochester, in the county of Kent, for the sake of my brother's future.

My brother had made up his mind that he wanted to go into civil aviation. After much discussion it was arranged that he would join the firm of Short Brothers, the famous aircraft manufacturers who built sea-planes and flying-boats at their factory on the River Medway at Rochester. Since Ian was only seventeen, there seemed no reasonable alternative to the family setting up a new home close to his place of work. The state of my parents' finances and the problem of my future schooling were the final deciding factors. I had been at preparatory school near Bournemouth, but the time had come for me to go to a public school. Rochester could meet this need in the shape of its old and venerated King's School, which I should be able to attend as a day-boarder.

So, our happy Essex home was sold and we moved into a tall, narrow and ugly terrace house, high on a hill in Rochester, with a commanding view of tramways, houses and still more houses. I felt like a wild animal that had been lured into a cage. My only consolation was that the nightmare house was only rented, and to this thin thread of comfort I pinned my hopes that my exile to this alien and hostile environment would be short-lived. In fact, it lasted far too long for my peace of mind.

After three years of what, to me, was penal servitude, I was rescued by 'the slump' – the sad economic depression that hit Great Britain in the early nineteen thirties. The aircraft industry being in the doldrums, my brother searched for pastures new and finally joined the head office of the Hong Kong and Shanghai Bank, in London, prior to being posted to the Far East. From that moment the need for us to live in the restricted confines of a busy industrial city no longer existed. My parents breathed sighs of relief almost as loud as my own, and, after some months of searching, the family moved house again, this time to Hertfordshire, so that I could attend my brother's old school of Berkhamsted, while he could commute daily to London.

At last we were back in the country, between Boxmoor and Berkhamsted, but the year before we moved, there occurred one of those twists of fate that seem to be pre-arranged staging posts on the path of life, in this case of mine.

# Chapter II

# The Formative Years

## *(continued)*

For me, the year 1932 began badly, for, in the early spring of that year, I became very ill. A severe attack of measles, coupled with acute gastric trouble and other complications, left me weak, limp and listless. I was long, lanky, and out-growing my strength. The doctor looked serious and advised a protracted holiday in new surroundings despite the loss of school time. My mother thought hard and remembered her elder brother who, after many years service in India, had retired to live in an old farmhouse in the county of Devon. Urgent letters resulted in a warm and kindly invitation for my father and I to stay as long as we wished. With my brother at work and still living at home, my mother was tied to the house, but kind and unselfish as always, she was happy to see what even the promise of a holiday in the country had done to me. I was like a prisoner who has just been told that he is to be released on parole.

George Kendall Channer, Lieutenant Colonel, D.S.O., had served in the Indian Army. Almost from the first moment we met he became my favourite uncle, I think because he was a true countryman and himself still a boy at heart. He was a short, stocky, tough little man, his skin tanned to the colour of very old, brown parchment from years of campaigning in tropical climes. His round, sun-tanned face, weathered and slightly wrinkled, reminded me forcibly of a newly ripened walnut. This, together with his bullet-shaped head, close-cropped grizzled hair and neat greying moustache, his pointed, puck-like ears and his small, twinkling brown eyes, all combined to give him a distinctly Mongolian appearance. In fact, his regiment had been the 3rd Gurkha Rifles ('Queen Alexandra's Own') and it often occurred to me that he could easily have doubled for one of his own veteran Gurkha soldiers. He had the look of some grizzled old Subadar or Subadar Major with many years service on India's North West Frontier, and he shared the Gurkha's impish sense of humour and youthful delight in earthy practical jokes.

With my Aunt Gertrude, a tall, kindly woman who towered over him, and a happy, bouncing, black cocker-spaniel dog named 'Don', my uncle lived in a rambling old farm house called 'Tadworthy', close to the village of Northam, which lies to the seaward side of Bideford, the market town that clusters round the head of the estuary of that famous North Devon salmon river, the Torridge.

'Tadworthy' was a warm and friendly house, full of real old world charm and the relics of my uncle's long service in India. It looked straight on to green fields, bordered by low thorn hedges atop typical grassy Devon banks that were alive with primroses and wild violets in season. The fields led on to the famous 'Burrows' of Westward Ho! and the long pebble ridge that divided them from the cold Atlantic waters of Bideford Bay. On a clear day, twenty miles away in the open Atlantic, one could see the low, dark outline of the rocky cliffs of Lundy Island, the 'Isle of Puffins', the home of wild goats, great grey seals, countless sea birds and the restless spirits of the smugglers, the wreckers and the pirates who haunted the wild north coast of Devon in days gone by.

This was Rudyard Kipling's country, the scene of his school days, for the old United Services College, immortalised in his classic story 'Stalky and Co', had been at Westward Ho! It was on these very same 'Burrows' and gorse-covered cliffs that Kipling himself (as 'Beetle'), with his two compatriots and partners in crime, 'Stalky' and "M'Turk', poached rabbits, broke bounds, and generally defied scholastic authority. Their contempt for petty discipline, their poaching achievements with the long-barrelled saloon pistols that they concealed down their trouser legs, their proficiency with their 'tweakers' (the traditional Devon name for a home-made catapult), their dislike of organised school games, and their general antipathy to meekly following the herd, all these things struck an eager and sympathetic chord in me.

These three were individualists. All of them became famous men. 'Stalky', their leader, was my boyhood hero. He became an unorthodox but renowned soldier – because, in the military sense, he was an imaginative nonconformist, as well as being an individualist and a born leader, traits common to many if not most of the great men of history. Ever since I had read the book, I had been inspired to emulate 'Stalky's' example and here I was making a pilgrimage to the very shrine of my chosen prophet!

My Uncle Ken fitted well into my youthful Kiplinesque philosophy. A well-worn catapult hung on a hook above the desk in his study; below it, on a shelf, was an old tobacco tin full of buckshot; engines of war all ready to discourage the nocturnal serenadings of the virile and amorous, semi-wild tom-cats whose hideous wailings so often disturbed the sleeping household.

On several occasions during my visit, I was awakened by the ghastly feline symphony of two rival, battle-scarred toms, crouched on the roof, silhouetted against the waning moon, singing lustfully to the wide, yellow eyes of their eager paramours. From my uncle's room would come a sleepy mumbled curse, the creak of a stealthily opened window, the unmistakable 'flick' of a catapult, and the 'zipp' of a well-aimed buckshot ending, as often as not, in a muffled 'thock' that signalled a direct hit. Cut rudely short at the peak of his performance, with a wild and anguished scream the smitten virtuoso would hurl himself from the roof, while his alarmed feline audience scattered frantically over the clattering tiles. A grunt of satisfaction from the Colonel, the 'click' of a firmly closed window, and the moon-lit Devon night would return to its normal peace, broken only by the muted hooting of an out-raged barn-owl, perched, with ruffled feathers, in the old yew tree at the foot of the garden.

Like the majority of officers of the old Indian Army, George Kendall Channer had been a keen shikari during his service overseas. He was an artist with a fly rod and a very competent shot. In his retirement he fished the cold, clear, rippling waters of the rocky moorland streams and tinkling, tree-lined brooks of Devon for the small but lively brown trout, golden sided, red-spotted, and pink of flesh. At dusk he matched his cunning with the wily sea-trout; heavier and stronger; leaping, flashing bars of savagely fighting quicksilver. All this he showed me, together with the poachers' trick of 'guddling' – as Devonians have it, the art of 'tickling' trout; the technique of sliding a quiet hand under a rock or overhanging bank to stroke the belly of a resting fish, lulling its suspicions until, with a lightning, treacherous flick of hand and arm, the poacher whips the startled trout out of the water onto the greasy bank.

"Only when they won't take a fly, my boy," my uncle said severely, the twinkle in his eye belying the tone of his voice as he climbed stiffly to his feet, brushing the dirt and twigs from his knees, while the third plump trout lay gleaming where it had fallen in the grass behind him.

It was spring, and when we were not fishing we strolled along the top of the cliffs where Don, the black cocker spaniel, happily and noisily chased the

*'... A lone Ghurka Rifleman,*
*in one hand a gleaming Kukri, in the other hand a lump of rock'*

*A picture which hung in the Officer's Mess of the 3rd Q.A.O. Gurkha Rifles*
*in Almora and later in Dehra Dun*

contemptuous rabbits through the yellow gorse, while, with quiet pride, the Colonel pointed out an inaccessible ledge where a pair of peregrines had nested regularly for many years – "Magnificent birds, my boy, *magnificent* birds!" he kept repeating as, through our binoculars, we watched, in the distance, the tercel stoop and bind on a half-grown rabbit that had been basking, happily but carelessly, in the warm spring sun.

In the dining room at 'Tadworthy', over the sideboard, there hung a picture that fascinated me; every morning, as I dug my spoon into a large bowl of steaming oatmeal porridge, I stared at it, wondering. It was a sketch of a Gurkha soldier in a battle-worn khaki uniform. His shorts and puttees were grimy and covered with ominous stains. His tunic, soaked with sweat, was open to the waist. His ammunition pouches gaped empty. Around his head was a torn, blood-stained bandage. In his right hand was the gleaming, curved blade of a drawn *kukri*; in his left a heavy lump of rock, poised for throwing. He stood defiant, legs firmly apart, a broken, twisted rifle at his feet, silhouetted against the erupting dust and smoke of a bursting shell. Underneath was the cryptic inscription:

'NEBI SAMWIL, November 22nd, 1917'.

One day I could stand it no longer. Swallowing a spoonful of near scalding porridge, I gulped and blurted out – "What *is* that picture, Uncle Ken?"

The Colonel paused in his task of lovingly paring wafer-thin slices off the cold ham. Lowering the carving knife he cocked a professional eye at the sketch on the wall. – "That, my boy, was at the battle of Nebi Samwil in the Palestine campaign."

"Yes, but what *happened*?"

My uncle looked thoughtful. "I was commanding the third battalion (of the 3rd Gurkha Rifles) at the time," he mused. "We had captured a large mosque with a high minaret which is meant to cover the grave of the prophet Samuel. It stood on a hill nearly three thousand feet high. The Turks didn't like us having it, *at all!*" He paused again to collect his thoughts while the carving knife resumed its unerring course through the succulent, pink ham.

"They shelled us heavily throughout the day, attacking repeatedly with their infantry. Our casualties were heavy and our ammunition soon began to run low; but we managed to hold out till dusk when the mosque was surrounded by a strong force of Turks. By then nearly half my men were dead or wounded. There was only one thing left for us to do."

"What was that?" I whispered with bated breath.

"Counter-attack, of course", snorted the Colonel scornfully, fixing me with a pitying glance. "We crept out of the back of the mosque and caught the Turks on the flank. When my Gurkhas ran out of ammunition they finished the job with their kukris and lumps of rock. The Turk is a tough fighter, but they ran that night!" – My uncle chuckled. "The ones that were still able to run, that is!"

He failed to add that he himself had been wounded in the head the day before, but had refused to be evacuated. Nor did he mention that this particular exploit had earned him the D.S.O.

I returned to my porridge, saying no more but thinking much. Was this the example that I was meant to follow? If so, it seemed highly dangerous and like all young animals the instinct of self-preservation was strong in me. With a shock, I remembered that my maternal grandfather, the father of the tough little man now ferociously attacking a piled plate of ham and eggs as if it was a strongly defended enemy position, had also served in the Gurkha Rifles with the same sort of reckless distinction. In fact, he had gone one better, for, in the Malay Peninsula campaign of 1875–76, he and his Gurkha orderly, entirely alone and unsupported, had captured three stockaded, bandit-held villages, one after the other, in rapid succession. Pistol and kukri in hand, and shouting 'Ayo Gorkhali!' (The Gurkhas are upon you!), the Gurkha war-cry, they had leapt the walls, scattering the surprised enemy like chaff in a high wind. Bewildered by this sudden and audacious assault, and bluffed into thinking that they were being attacked by a greatly superior force, the well-armed dacoits fled, panic-stricken, into the jungle. This daring exploit earned him Britain's highest award for military valour, the Victoria Cross, while his gallant Gurkha orderly was decorated with the Indian Order of Merit, at that time the highest decoration for which the Gurkhas were eligible.

Like my paternal grandfather, my maternal grandfather also had been a fine shikari, a keen hunter-naturalist, and had ended his spectacular career with a C.B. added to his Victoria Cross; but in his case he had retired with the rank of *full* General.

Surrounded by these overpowering examples of valour and success, my youthful mind confused, awe-struck and groping blindly for an easy way out,

I stared gloomily at the plate of ham and eggs that my kindly aunt had placed before me – but the seeds of my future had been sown.

Like most boys of my age I had begun to wonder rather vaguely about what I should do when I grew up. It was a nuisance that I would have to earn my own living, but I was determined that this unfortunate necessity should not debar me from enjoying the only kind of life that I felt I could tolerate. I shuddered when I saw the office workers commuting daily by train to London, burdened by bulging brief-cases and regimented by rigid time-tables and the traditional civilian uniform of dark suit, hard bowler hat and neatly rolled umbrella long dictated by custom. In later years I learnt to admire these men for their patience, doggedness and determination, attributes which have enabled Britain to survive many a crisis and have saved the country in two world wars when these same nameless, faceless men have answered the call to arms. But in my youth and prejudice I recoiled from their way of life. Not knowing whether they had adopted it from choice or necessity, I pitied them and said – "This is not the life for me." Yet, what *were* the feasible alternatives?

Of one thing I was certain, I was resolved that whatever kind of career I followed it must be one that required me to spend most of my time out-of-doors and enabled me to enjoy a surfeit of shooting and fishing. Clearly, the Indian Army was one possible solution; it also had the advantage of being strongly favoured by my parents and relations, who clung fondly to the hope that I would follow family traditions. However, the army meant strict discipline, which did not appeal to a natural rebel like myself. Moreover, after listening to my uncle's vivid stories, it appeared to me that service in the *Indian* Army in particular, laid an unhealthy emphasis on the adjective 'active', and I was not at all sure that I was cut out to be a hero. I didn't mind the idea of shooting at other people. In fact, I thought it might be rather exciting – like a glorified form of big-game hunting. But, I was far from certain that I would feel quite the same way if anyone had the temerity to shoot back at me! Ethologists, in their wisdom, now tell us that aggression is a more potent force in man than even the sex urge, but since I had not yet reached the age of puberty, I felt that, as a vulnerable school-boy, I was justified in adopting a rather more defensive attitude to life.

If not India, then where else? That night, as I lay drowsing in bed, lulled by the distant, muffled roar of the Atlantic waves breaking on the Pebble Ridge, I thought of my uncle's description of the battle of Nebi Samwyl and his father's exploits in the jungles of Malaya. Then suddenly I remembered. My uncle's son Vivian, my first cousin but a generation older than me, was in East Africa, the hunter's 'Utopia'. I had books about hunting in East Africa which I had read and re-read avidly, but for some strange reason it had always seemed to me to be a country beyond my reach. I would ask my uncle in the morning. And with this resolve I rolled over happily and drifted into a restless sleep in which Gurkhas, mounted on trumpeting African elephants, waving their kukris and shouting 'Ayo Gorkhali!', chased an oddly assorted crowd of bewildered Turkish soldiers and frightened Malay dacoits across the Pebble Ridge into the storm-lashed waters of Bideford Bay.

* * *

In the years immediately following the First World War, the future of the British in India appeared to be in doubt and the likelihood of a young British

*Elephants in author's dream*

officer being able to look forward to a full and rewarding career in the Indian Army seemed problematical. Later, the situation ostensibly settled down and on the face of it prospects brightened. But when the time came for my cousin Vivian to leave the Royal Military College, Sandhurst, this temporary improvement in the political climate had not yet occurred. Regretfully, my uncle Ken was forced to advise his son against following in his own footsteps and the long tradition that linked the family with the Brigade of Gurkhas, an elite mercenary force which, at that time, still formed part of the *Indian* Army only. Instead, Vivian joined a famous West Country regiment, the 'Duke of Cornwall's Light Infantry'; but he had inherited the family urge to travel and see service in wild places, so, as soon as he decently could, he applied for secondment to the 'King's African Rifles'.

Until independence came to the British Colonial Territories of Africa, the 'King's African Rifles' were officered by secondments from the British Regular Army. Kenya, Uganda, Tanganyika and Nyasaland each had its own battalion, recruited from its most soldierly and warlike tribes, who provided the *askaris*, the rank and file of the fighting men. Most of the officers were attracted to the K.A.R. by the spectacular wildlife of East Africa and the exceptional opportunities for sport that was offered them through military service in that fascinating part of the world. Competition for such postings was therefore very keen.

Secondments were for limited periods of a few years at a time. Normally, if he was lucky, an officer could hope for two such terms of attachment; occasionally, in exceptional cases, he might achieve three. In the case of Vivian Channer, fate took a hand at a crucial moment. Using every known strategy, he had managed to prolong his secondments, and postpone his final return to the British Army at home, to the very limit possible. Then the Second World War broke out and there was no longer any doubt that his knowledge and experience were of greatest value in command of East African troops. So, he completed a long and distinguished military career with the 'Kings African Rifles', retiring to Kenya after the war, as a Brigadier and Colonel-in-Chief of 'The Uganda Rifles', formerly the old 4th (Uganda) Battalion of the K.A.R.

Here was the link that finally led me to East Africa; but fate works in strange and devious ways. Before I was to reach the 'Dark Continent' much was to happen and my uncertain feet were to take me to the high ranges of the Himalayas; to the arid, hostile hills of the North West Frontier; and to the dense, steaming jungles of India and Burma.

\* \* \*

The next day, with an understanding smile, my uncle listened attentively to my excited questions about East Africa and what my cousin Vivian was doing. Then it was my turn to listen. With his back to the fire the old Colonel proudly told me of his son's life in the 'King's African Rifles'; about his *askaris*, whose cheerful character and simple, happy-go-lucky attitude to life reminded him greatly of the Gurkha; his hunting experiences – he had been ambushed by a belligerent buffalo, charged by angry elephants, chased by irritable rhinos, and badly mauled and nearly killed by an enraged lioness; and finally his marriage to the daughter of one, Jack Lucy, a famous Kenya Professional Hunter – or 'White Hunter' as they were called in those days. To me it revealed an exciting new world, but as far as I could see the big snag still remained – it seemed that, yet again, the only feasible gateway to this paradise was the army! I sighed and switched my thoughts to more immediate problems. For the moment the future would have to look after itself.

Two days later my uncle drove my father and I to Bideford Station in his old Armstrong Siddleley. We left the house early, as he wanted to make a detour to show me some of his favourite woodcock coverts. By dint of guile and blandishments he enjoyed the privilege of over a thousand acres of rough shooting, scattered throughout a number of small North Devon farms. Every year it cost him three bottles of Scotch whisky, three large boxes of chocolates, and the exercise of his persuasive tongue.

Cruising slowly and sedately, we followed the narrow Devon lanes, winding and twisting between high grassy banks yellow with primroses, until we reached the head of a deep, wooded coomb.

"Something I want to show you here," grunted my uncle, as he halted the car at a broken farm gate. He led the way across a field and down a narrow path that slanted through dense bramble thickets and clumps of high, green ferns that sprouted luxuriantly from the rich, red soil. In the bottom of the coomb he pushed his way, quietly, and carefully, through a small hazel spinney that clustered at the foot of a low cliff of gravel and sand. Suddenly he halted and with a dramatic flourish swept aside a tangled screen of low branches. There, in front of me, was an old badger sett, the first I had ever seen.

"They've been here ever since I was a boy," said my uncle proudly. "Fine animals. *Fine* animals," he repeated. "But some ignorant fools don't like 'em," he added belligerently. "One vicious idiot tried to kill the whole family last month. Dropped a poisoned rabbit here. Two of the cubs died. I'd like to poison *him*.

"Yes, I know who did it," he continued fiercely, answering my unspoken query, "but I can't prove it. If I could I'd have his guts for a necktie." Looking at my uncle's flushed face and bristling moustache I was glad that I was not the culprit.

Back at the car the Colonel felt behind the squab of the rear seat, took out his old, double, solid leather gun-case, opened it, and removed a pair of well-oiled, Damascus-barrelled shotguns; beautiful old weapons, made by Stephen Grant, with thumb-levers and great dog-eared hammers, handmade by craftsmen and chastened with almost loving care. My uncle was a staunch traditionalist and something of a snob. "His Majesty[1] still uses guns like these," my uncle had said proudly when he had first shown me his treasured shotguns. But now more serious things were afoot.

"Come on Bruce, we've a job to do before you catch the train," he said grimly, handing me one of the guns and two shiny twelve-bore cartridges; their glistening green cases and gleaming, deep-brass heads seemed to wink at me sardonically as they lay in my still open hand. I stared at them, puzzled.

"About turn!" said the Colonel quietly. Instinctively I obeyed and found myself facing two large, glass-fronted notice boards raised imperiously on the top of the high bank across the narrow road. They were so high that I had not noticed them before. In bold, four-inch letters, one of them commanded:

"REPENT! THE DAY OF JUDGEMENT IS NIGH."

The other, even more menacing, thundered –

"BE SURE YOUR SINS WILL FIND YOU OUT."

I just had time to get the message when the Colonel ordered – 'LOAD!'

---

[1]  King George V at that time

Automatically, I opened the gun, slipped the gleaming cartridges into the welcoming chambers, closed the weapon with a smooth click, cocked the mighty hammers, and waited.

"When I give the word," said my uncle, slowly and distinctly, as if he was addressing a parade of timid recruits, "*you* take the one on the left. I'll deal with the other."

"PRESENT" he snapped, raising his weapon. Bewildered, I lifted the shotgun to my shoulder and saw the printed words dancing mockingly just above the end of the wavering barrels.

'Be sure your sins will find you out!' they jeered at me.

"FIRE!" barked the Colonel. With the roar of his gun in my ears I jumped and tugged at the front trigger. The gun leapt in my hands and the glass covering the mocking notice shattered into a thousand fragments.

"FIRE!" came the staccato order again, followed by the crash of my uncle's gun as I shut my eyes and pulled at the second trigger.

"UNLOAD!" snapped the Colonel, and for the fifth time I obeyed automatically, sniffing the exciting smell of burnt powder from the empty cartridge cases before slipping them discreetly into my pocket.

"Not bad," said my uncle, surveying the damage with keen satisfaction. My notice board was leaning at a drunken angle for my second shot had gone a bit low, cutting the supporting upright almost in half. My first shot had not only shattered the glass but destroyed some of the lettering, leaving a tattered and misleading message, torn and pock-marked with pellet holes. All its aggressiveness had gone:

'BE SURE YOU… … …FIND … OUT,' it now read, rather pathetically.

The other board had received two direct hits, accurately placed, right in the centre. The top notice had disappeared, along with the glass, and now drooped limply from its frame, stirring gently in the breeze. Revealed beneath was the previous triumphant and demanding message:

'LIFT UP THE BANNER…' (the rest was obliterated.)

Uncle Ken stared at it thoughtfully for a long moment; by the side of the lane was a pile of gravel, a shovel and a road-worker's warning flag; with a quick movement he picked up the faded red flag and with a flourish, planted it firmly on top of the battered notice board. Then with a sardonic glance and a grunt of satisfaction he climbed back into the car.

As we drove off he turned to my astonished father with a grin.

"I owe you an explanation, Ronald!" he said apologetically. "The chap who put up those notices is a bad hat. Lay preacher or something. Damned hypocrisy *him* trying to dictate and preach to *us*. The farmers hereabouts swear he dabbles in black magic. Don't know about that but he was the fellah who tried to poison my badgers. Said they were stealing his scrofulous chickens." My uncle snorted. "Probably only keeps his damn birds to cut their throats at a 'Black Mass'!"

I listened open-mouthed and fascinated. I had learnt a lot on this holiday.

"If I had the chance I'd have him defrocked and drummed out of the county!" the Colonel exploded. "Meanwhile I'm not having him hoisting his revolting notices on *my* shoot, like a lot of regimental daily orders, *and* without my permission." He lapsed into a grim silence, relieved after a few moments by his infectious chuckle. I hugged myself in sheer delight. This tough little ex-officer of the Gurkha Rifles, with his love of the wild, his exciting record as a gallant soldier, his courteous and kindly understanding of boys, and his mischievous puck-like sense of humour, really was my favourite uncle. What I could not know then was that his influence on my subconscious mind had already steered me onto the road ahead.

As the London train puffed fussily away from Bideford station, I leant out of the window sadly to wave goodbye to the stocky little figure standing on the near-deserted platform. His right hand raised his green Tyrolean hat in a typically courteous gesture of farewell; I could still see the trout flies stuck in the brim and the woodcock pin-feathers clustered in the ribbon. There was a familiar impish grin accentuated by the flash off a gold-crowned tooth. Above the hiss of steam from the carriage brakes I could hear his brisk, cheerful voice. "Come back in the autumn, my boy, and we'll have a go at the woodcock!" I then realised how much he missed his own son, far away in Africa.

While our train thundered steadily eastwards, heading in the direction of the Home Counties, my father settled himself comfortably in a corner window seat, with that morning's '*Daily Telegraph*' spread across his lap. I took the seat opposite to him and as I idly watched the ever-changing patterns of the colourful Devon countryside sliding past the carriage windows, my thoughts drifted back over all the exciting things that had happened during the previous few weeks … and, yet, again, I hugged myself with delight! I did not realise it at the time, but, for me, my first ever visit to my favourite uncle had sown firmly in my mind the seeds of an exciting idea, an idea which, if it finally germinated, would shape the whole course of my life for the foreseeable future.

# Chapter III

# The Birth of a Wildfowler

*The door to memory lane ... and the birth of a wildfowler*

Inspired by the particularly colourful example of my paternal grandfather[1], some of whose genes I'm sure I have inherited, as well as the examples of both my father and my favourite uncle, for as long as I can remember – and that is now a very long time – I have been a dedicated devotee of all field sports.

Now, looking back over the four score years of my own active life, it has made me realise that you don't necessarily need to have reached the age of Methuselah to have built up a rich treasure trove of your own sporting memories, nor does this call for the financial resources of a Rockefeller. In fact, a near bottomless purse can well prove to be as much a hindrance as an advantage, since experiences too easily gained are inevitably devalued and thus often soon forgotten. What is needed to keep the highlights on one's sporting memories fresh and untarnished is time, time to recollect and then to reflect.

Sadly, in this frenetic day and age, time for quiet reflection is a luxury which few of us can often afford, but even so there are occasional times when one has little to do but think. For instance, when you nave been lying out at the edge of a saltmarsh, in an icy January dawn, patiently waiting for the wigeon to flight; or standing at the covert side listening idly for the first distant taps of the beaters' sticks; or half dozing on a sunlit river bank dreamily watching your pike float bobbing gently in the glittering ripples; or when – like me – you have been crouching at the edge of an African maize field in the gathering dusk, tensely waiting for that single sharp crack in the nearby forest, the

---

[1]  Major-General Alexander A.A. Kinloch, C.B., – late of the King's Royal Rifle Corps and of the Rifle Brigade

breaking branch which heralds the almost wraith-like night approach of a herd of crop-raiding elephants; it has been then, I'll wager, that from time to time your concentration will have wavered and your thoughts will have wandered to other times, other places, other events.

And what did you think about on those occasions? Problems at work or family crises? I doubt it, for your mind, like a built in computer, will have been locked into the natural scene, and it is my guess that your thoughts will have been of previous but allied experiences with gun or rod, or with horse and hound. Further more, since the human mind is a strange but normally kindly machine, with a happy knack of brushing painful memories firmly under the carpet and highlighting recollections of happy events and minor triumphs, I am equally sure that many of your thoughts will have been of unrepeatable and therefore unforgettable happy first experiences.

As your thoughts have wandered at those times, you may well have re-lived – for instance – your first wildfowling foray, your first stalk of a Scottish stag; your first covert shoot, your first goose, your first woodcock, your first big pike and of course your first salmon, even – at an early age – your first wood-pigeon, rabbit and trout; all these and more will have been carefully stored away in your memory bank, mental treasure trove to be savoured at leisure. These are what I call 'Glorious Firsts!'

Thinking back, I would say that my own list of 'Glorious Firsts' probably commenced with my first, full bloodied wild fowling expedition, but there was an important preliminary to that very special event, a happening which in itself is worthy, I think, of being labelled a 'Glorious First'. I was not quite fourteen years old at the time and I was living with my parents and my elder brother Ian, in a house between Boxmoor and Berkhamsted in Hertfordshire. Our house was partly surrounded by a broad expanse of open farmland, while to the front it faced over open, grassy fields, dotted with large trees, which sloped down to a long, fish-filled stretch of the Grand Union Canal. On the near side of the canal was a sprawling, ready marsh and a small, clear brook full of small trout. The marsh had a resident population of moorhens, and numerous rabbits and the occasional hare in the drier patches, while in winter it harboured numbers of snipe and a few itinerant duck.

On the further side of the canal was a sizeable, reed-edged lake – and old flooded gravel pit – rich in fish life from pike to roach and perch, and a haven for moorhens, coot and a variety of wild duck. Woodpigeons abounded and, all in all, this small, compact area – an unkeepered no-man's land – was a paradise for a small boy who thought of little else but shooting and fishing and natural history.

So far as shooting was concerned, I had cut my teeth on a 'Daisy' airgun, a puny and inaccurate weapon the use of which had at least taught me the rudiments and importance of fieldcraft – how to stalk and get close to my quarry, the sharp-eyed sparrows, starlings and rats which swarmed in the stock yard and granary of a nearby farm. Before long however, I had been promoted to a B.S.A. air-rifle, a present from a kindly uncle; it was an old but serviceable weapon and its power and accuracy delighted me. At last, with careful stalking and selected head shots, I had been able to get on terms with the local rabbit population and even with a few of the fatter and more careless wood-pigeons which cooed complacently in the big trees near our house.

Finally, after much pleading and saving of pocket money, I had graduated to a shotgun. It was not much of a shotgun – a Belgian made, double-barrelled, hammer, side-lever, folding .410 – but to me it was my pride and joy. At last I had got my foot on the first rung of the real shooting ladder, and after much reading of theory, and at the expense of a dwindling population of slow flying moorhens on the marsh and lake, I had taught myself the rudiments of wing shooting. But I still lacked something – I did not have a proper gundog.

The family dog was an elderly, blue roan cocker spaniel by the name of Jock, a fat and rather irascible animal who had very firm and fixed ideas about hunting, retrieving and the general duties of a spaniel. Hunt he would not, that was a mug's game in his opinion, far too energetic for a dog of his age and, in any case, he strongly objected to burrs and brambles in his ears and coat.

Retrieving was a different matter since it offered interesting gastronomic opportunities. Jock would investigate and pick up anything, or almost anything, so long as it appeared to be potentially edible; the problem was what he did with the object afterwards. First I had tried him with dead sparrows; these he had picked up with no hesitation, crunched twice and swallowed with obvious relish. Next, I had thrown a starling for him. He had ambled sedately up to the dead bird, sniffed it doubtfully, picked it up gingerly – and had then immediately spat it out, turning his face towards me with his nose wrinkled and his lips curled and showing yellow fangs in a vivid expression of revulsion and disgust.

The final test had been with a woodpigeon. This had met with Jock's full approval. Picking up the bird with an uncharacteristic display of speed and energy, he had galloped with it to the end of the garden; there, in the shade of a rosebush, slowly and methodically and with the dedication of a gourmet, he had eaten the entire pigeon, head, feet, feathers and all. Attempts to dissuade him had been met with a menacing growl, and sadly and reluctantly I had come to a conclusion which Jock had known all along – that he was a house dog so set in his ways that he would never make a gundog.

Then Lady Luck took a hand. 'Would we give a home to an eleven-month old, pure bred Irish setter dog whose sorrowful owners had suddenly been posted to the Far East?' I was elated, and 'Rufus' proved to be a particularly handsome Irish setter, a big-boned, happy and affectionate dog, as willing and eager to please and to learn as Jock was not. I had bought Richard Sharpe's classic book, '*Dog Training by Amateurs*', and I had read it from cover to cover. While training Rufus I followed it religiously page by page. At the end I had a very steady and well-trained gundog, and a setter which – contrary to traditional practice – was also a surprisingly good retriever.

The winter that followed started as a mild one, but in January there came a severe cold snap. The canal was frozen over and the marsh was a sea of sparkling white. More out of curiosity than hope, I took Rufus to hunt through the brittle rushes, which crackled as I pushed steadily through them with my .410 over my arm. Suddenly Rufus froze a few yards in front of me, his body rigid in a classic setter pose. Puzzled, I walked slowly towards him and then – without warning – it happened.

The matted, frost laden rushes at my feet seemed to explode in a shower of icy particles and something – a dark object – rocketed skywards. Instinctively I flung up the little .410 and fired. The rocketing object folded in mid-air and with a graceful parabola fell, with a muffled thud, in a dense clump of tall reeds.

For a moment I just stood and stared with my mouth open, then I recovered. "Rufus, go fetch" I said excitedly. The big dog, who had been waiting, quivering with eagerness, plunged swiftly into the dense patch of tall reeds. Minutes later he was bounding towards me, carrying something in his mouth; halting at my feet, he delivered the bird gently into my waiting hand. Holding it by the neck I turned the bird slowly over, hardly believing my eyes; the vivid colouring and the tightly curled tail feathers were unmistakeable, even to a novice. I had shot my very first wild duck and a fine drake mallard at that – *and* with what my game keeper friend had jestingly referred to as 'a pop-gun!'

I glanced down at Rufus; if ever there was a broad grin on a dog's face there was one on his. Suddenly I was filled with elation. I had shot a real wild duck; I had shot it flying; and it had been found and retrieved perfectly by a dog which I had trained myself. My chest swelled; I was a real wildfowler at last! Slinging the duck from a thong on my belt, I turned for home. "To heel, Rufus," I said, shouldering my little gun with a swagger. "Ian's not going to believe this!" But I had maligned my elder brother. For me my mallard drake was certainly a 'Glorious First', but with the help of my brother my first true foray after wildfowl – another 'Glorious First' – was yet to come.

*   *   *

Having shot my first wild duck, my chest swelled; I truly was a real wild-fowler at last – or was I? I had read and re-read avidly the works of James Wentworth Day and of Colonel Peter Hawker. I could quote them almost by heart and to me true fowling belonged to the salt marshes and the mud flats of the coast; those regions were really wild and above all, free. Sadly I realised that my true ambition was still to be achieved.

Everyone had been surprised at my shooting of a wild duck with my little .410, not least the old drake mallard who had been the victim of the drama. However, my elder brother Ian, seven years older than me, a good horseman and a keen rider but something of a dilettante as far as shooting was concerned, became inspired. "I've been talking with John Barlow in the office," he said airily, a few days later. "He suggests that we should go wildfowling with his friend George Cooper next week-end. Would you like to come along?" I didn't have to answer; the look on my face was enough!

The following Friday evening we drove up to John Barlow's flat in London in my brother's old Riley. In the back were our guns, thigh boots, sleeping bags, food and my Irish setter, Rufus, whom I had trained with meticulous care and who was a really good retriever. Ian had wanted to bring along our rheumaticky old cocker spaniel, Jock, also, but I had persuaded him not to. "He'll only eat the birds," I had said, remembering my efforts to train him. "And anyway the cold will kill him." Reluctantly, Ian had agreed.

John Barlow was a bachelor and his large and comfortable flat smelt of a mixture of tweed, leather and gun oil, with faint background aromas of whisky, pipe tobacco and a hint of cigar smoke. He himself was a big, burly, cheerful young man who fitted well into his surroundings. "We'll be heading for this area," he said, spreading a large-scale map of the Medway estuary on his dining table, his forefinger pointing at a patchwork maze of saltmarsh and mud flats on the north shore of the estuary, an area marked as 'Stoke Saltings.' "We'll leave tomorrow morning and meet George Cooper at the railway halt at Middle Stoke. George knows the area like the back of his hand. We'll do a recce', then take the evening flight. After that we'll sleep in the cars and take the morning flight on Sunday to finish off. I hope you've got enough blankets?" he added questioningly. "It's real brass monkey weather down there now."

Curled up on John Barlow's sofa, I didn't sleep much that night, and the following evening I found myself, keyed-up and expectant, crouching on the bank of a narrow creek in the middle of the Stoke salt marshes. At last I was on my first ever real wildfowling expedition. George Cooper, a tall, angular young man who – in his long thigh boots and his balaclava and carrying a battered old magnum 12 bore – looked every inch the wildfowler to my admiring eyes, had met us at Middle Stoke as planned and had then led the way across the marsh, dropping the three of us off at various strategic points. "You ought to get a shot here," he had said, staring doubtfully at my little double-barrelled, folding .410, but cheering visibly when I had told him that I had just shot a duck with it.

As the light faded the as yet unfamiliar sounds of the saltings were music to my eager ears; the trickle of water in the gullies, the pattering of crabs on the mud banks, the screaming of redshanks, the enchanting, bubbling call of curlew, and then suddenly one of the wildest and most thrilling sounds of all to the wildfowler – the high-pitched *wee-oh* of cock wigeon. I crouched lower on my mud bank, tense with excitement; beside me and quivering with a mixture of cold and eagerness was my Irish setter, Rufus.

Something flickered past in the gathering dusk. The flat report of my little gun was answered by the scornful wail of a curlew, but the next fleeting target was not so lucky. There was a splash in the creek and Rufus soon returned carrying something and my hand confirmed my eyes as I felt the long, slim, curved bill of a curlew.

More shadows were now flashing past but at higher speed and further out on the marsh I could hear the occasional scattered shot. My three companions

*Graylag Geese Landing on the Marsh – a painting by Peter Scoll.*

appeared to be getting some shooting, but my own wild shots at the fleeting shadows seemed to be wasted on thin air. Then it happened.

I had stood up to ease my cramped legs when, with a rush of wings, a shadowy flight of duck came low over me on fixed pinions heading for the middle of my little creek. I fired instinctively and one of the shadows folded and fell with a soft thud in the *spartina* grass on the bank. Tail wagging, Rufus brought the bird to me and to my excited eyes my pocket torch revealed the chestnut head of a cock wigeon; another first!

Eventually, George Cooper led us off the marsh to the waiting cars, a brace of wigeon, a mallard and a teal swinging from his belt. Ian was happy with a teal, while I was like a dog with two tails. Only John Barlow was crestfallen – he had been in the wrong place and hadn't fired a shot – but all of us were cold and hungry. However, hot stew from John Barlow's giant vacuum flask soon warmed us up, and tired but happy I crawled into the sleeping bag in the back of our car. Cramped as I was – and not helped by Rufus's snores and painfully accurate kicking – I slept fitfully, dreaming of great clouds of wigeon and curlew screaming with laughter at my little .410.

Well before dawn we again set off across the marsh. It had been a very cold night and a thin film of ice crackled under our feet as we carefully picked our way out towards the open estuary. This time George Cooper placed me by a much larger creek from where I could clearly see the lights of Sheerness twinkling in the far distance, some six miles away to the east.

As soon as I settled in, a pair of duck swung past; just in time I saw that they were shelduck and held my fire. A flight of curlew kept well out, laughing at me as they towered. Then, in the still dim light, a large, dark shape suddenly appeared straight ahead; its size and wingspan were unmistakeable to my excited young eyes – a goose, *a real wild goose.*

Cursing the puniness of my little shotgun, I swung my .410 well ahead of the speeding shadow and fired. There was a rattle of No. 5 shot on rigid pinions, the big bird staggered, and then – to my astonished and disbelieving eyes – it started to plane down on fixed wings in a long, slow glide, disappearing over the glistening mud into the gloom. But, straining my ears, in the far distance I clearly heard a faint, muffled splash.

Tense with excitement I turned to Rufus who was quivering with eagerness. "Go fetch," I said. The big dog was off in a flash, disappearing across the mud in great, squelching bounds. Some time later Rufus reappeared, plowthering through the mud with a large bird in his jaws; as he got closer I saw that the mud-covered dog had become a setter as black as the bird he was carrying. When I took the bird from him, Rufus was certainly not reluctant to let it go, and holding it at arms length, I stared at it in growing disbelief and disgust; it stank of stale fish and its beak was the wrong shape – it was an old and scabby cormorant!

Swallowing my disappointment, I hurled the foul smelling bird far out into the creek. Then a sudden thought cheered me. Hadn't Colonel Peter Hawker written that some of the old time fowlers had relished cormorant as a delicacy and that in old wildfowling parlance shooting a cormorant was referred to as 'lowering a parson'? Well, I had now experienced my first real wildfowling expedition, and since it had ended with my 'lowering a parson', I felt that I really was a true wildfowler at last! With a happy smile I picked up my still empty game bag, and with my mud-black setter at my heels, I set off in search of George Cooper and a possible last shot at a curlew.

# Chapter IV

# The Making of a Rifleman

In 1935, the year of the Silver Jubilee of King George V and Queen Mary, shortly before my sixteenth birthday, my father took me to see the Indian Army contingent encamped at Hampton Court for the Jubilee celebrations; it was then that I made what was arguably the single most important decision in my life – I was going to join the army. I don't mean the British Army, which was outside my scheme of things and which, in any case, I could not afford; nor the Salvation Army, that fine body of practising Good Samaritans which solicitous friends have long averred would have been the saving of my sinful soul; but the *Indian* Army and, influenced by the example of my favourite uncle (about whom I have written at length in Chapter II) and having now also seen, for myself, the supremely smart and alert little Gurkha riflemen on parade, the 3rd Q.A.O. Gurkha Rifles at that.

My parents, who for several years had become increasingly worried about my future, were both relieved and delighted when I told them of my decision; they fondly imagined that I had now seen the light, turned over a new leaf, and was dutifully following family tradition. In their eyes, what possible niche could there have been, in this hard world, for a boy whose sole

*For the greater part of his military career, the author served in his family regiment, the 3rd Queen Alexandra's Own, Gurkha Rifles*

interests hitherto appeared to have been field sports and natural history, and who seemed to want nothing more in life than to be out with his rod or his gun and his dog.

It would have been unkind and pointless to have shattered my parents' fond illusions. Otherwise, I could have confessed to them that my decision was based on purely mercenary and pragmatic considerations; that I had very little real interest in soldiering as such, but that the Indian Army seemed to me to be the only feasible solution to my problem, which was how to earn a reasonably comfortable living in a way which would keep me mainly out of doors, rather than in an office – the very idea of which made me feel like a trapped animal – and at the same time hopefully allow me endless opportunities for shooting and fishing. I could also have pointed out that it was well known that, in the Indian Army, an otherwise impecunious subaltern could both live on his pay and enjoy a wide variety of field sports. The very idea that anyone could possibly be thoughtless enough to disrupt my carefully laid plans, by foolishly starting anything so time wasting and dangerous as a major shooting war, never even crossed my youthful mind!

There was, of course, one serious snag to my decision. Previously I had been a complete maverick at school, a near drop-out, and to implement my decision meant that I would have to change my former rebellious attitude to all school activities and both work and play extremely hard, not only to gain entry into Sandhurst at all, but also to obtain some sort of scholarship to make this financially possible. Among other things I had to join the O.T.C. (The Officers' Training Corps, the forerunner of the present C.C.F) from which I had hitherto shied. Fortunately for me, the R.S.M. of the Berkhamsted O.T.C., a battle scarred old warrior by the name of F.E. Bunker, had served in my paternal grandfather's old regiment, the K.R.R.C. (60th Rifles); regimental loyalties paid off and with the help and encouragement of R.S.M. Bunker, as a comparatively elderly recruit to the O.T.C., I rapidly graduated from .22 to .303 full bore rifle shooting in the Berkhamsted School Shooting VIII; there, with the single stripe of a Lance Corporal on my arm, I found my true forte – that, as befitted an aspiring Rifleman, I was a natural rifle shot! I tell the tale now because it is a gift which, in a very few years, was going to stand me in good stead in the jungles, the hills and the bushland of India, Burma and Africa.

Berkhamsted School Shooting VIII enjoyed the use of a long rifle range at

*The Berkhamsted School's Shooting Team in 1937.*
*The author is fourth from the left in the rear rank*

Piccott's End near Hemel Hempstead and not far from my home. There we practiced and shot postal competitions, using the old tried and tested service rifle and cartridge combination the .303 Short Magazine Lee-Enfield with Mark VII Ammunition. But our Mecca was Bisley Camp, the meeting place for top marksmen from all over the world, and to there we went on pilgrimage at least twice a year; in June for the Sussex County Rifle Association meeting, when we shot for the Cusack-Smith Challenge Bowl, and in July for the Imperial Bisley meeting when we shot for the Ashburton Challenge Shield for which the Cusack-Smith was regarded as a rehearsal. Despite sportsmanlike efforts, Berkhamsted had never done very well at Bisley, but in June 1937, the year after I joined the O.T.C., at the 'Coronation Meeting' of the Sussex County R.A., with a promising new team the School's prospects looked a little brighter than hitherto.

June 12th, 1937, was a clear, sunny day on the Bisley ranges, but there was a tricky gusting cross-wind which needed careful watching. There were 32 school O.T.C. teams competing for the Cusack-Smith, a competition which required each member of a team of eight to fire a sighter and seven shots at both 200 yards and 500 yards, the maximum possible score per person being 35 points and for the team 280 points at each range. By the end of the 200 yard shot Berkhamsted had scored a creditable 241 points, to which I had contributed a score of 32, so the team was then at least in the running.

At the 500 yard firing point tension rapidly began to mount as the gusty wind played havoc with competitor after competitor. Each team shot in pairs and of the Berkhamsted team I was in the last pair with a boy called Sykes; when he and I mounted the firing point I learnt, to my alarm not only that the two of us were one of the few remaining pairs to shoot in the match, but also that the Berkhamsted team was already among the leaders. Worse was to come! Firing second to Sykes, I had fired six shots out of my seven, scoring 27 points out of 30, when I discovered, to my horror, that my seventh and last shot was also going to be the very last shot to be fired in the entire competition – and on it depended the fate of the Berkhamsted team! We were then running neck and neck in the lead with King's College School, Wimbledon; no other school was now in the race. If my last shot was a magpie or worse, we would drop to second place; if it was an inner the result would be a draw; for Berkhamsted to win I had to score a bull; it was a real photo-finish!

As I brought my rifle up to the aim for my last shot the atmosphere on the firing point was electric and it needed a conscious effort to control my nerves. Hitting the very centre of the target at 500 yards and in a strong but fluctuating cross-wind, using a standard service rifle with open sights, is by no means easy at the best of times, let alone when the marksman knows that everything depends on his shot ... The target shimmered and danced in front of my eyes, then steadied. With the butt firmly in my shoulder and cuddling the stock tightly against my cheek, I squeezed the trigger as slowly and as gently as I knew how. Suddenly the rifle bucked in my hands; with relief I opened the bolt and laid the weapon down; I had done all I could, now it was up to the markers. Shading my eyes I stared at the butts; R.S.M. Bunker was muttering something behind me; the waiting seemed interminable.

At last the marker frame began slowly to rise, like a genie, from the distant butts, hesitated, then stopped half way with only its top two squares exposed; to my relief, they were empty. I must have scored either an inner or the all important bull, but which? The tension on the firing point was electric. My

## The **MILD** cigarette would have saved him . . .

The man who _coughed_ at Bisley

*Cartoon from* The Daily Mirror, *June 12th, 1937*

mouth was dry and my heart was thumping in my chest as I held my breath. Suddenly, the frame shot up to its full height, revealing its bottom two squares; the left hand square was empty but the right one was filled with a white marker card. I let out a long, pent-up sigh of relief. I had scored a bull and for the first time ever, and by the narrowest possible margin of one point, Berkhamsted School Shooting VIII had won the Cusack-Smith Challenge Bowl!

King's College School, Wimbledon, was second in the match with a score of 486, but no other school team was even in the running at the end, the next nearest team score being a full ten points lower. It amused to me to think that my own team had been so far ahead of the field that, even if my last shot had missed the target altogether, Berkhamsted would still have been placed second. In fact, the whole event reminded me strongly of the pitfalls, the uncertainties and the excitement of the Grand National! The following day the competition was highlighted in the national press. '*PUBLIC SCHOOLS AT BISLEY*', announced the headlines in the *Daily Telegraph*, '*BERKHAMSTED WINS*

*The Cusack-Smith Challenge Trophy*

*THE CUSACK-SMITH.*' For me it was indeed a 'Glorious First' and a fitting stepping stone on my way to my chosen career.

If Bisley was for me the scene of a true 'Glorious First', then the School's range at Piccott's End was the scene of my fall from grace. Later in the year, after mounting the 200 yard firing point at Piccott's End, I noticed something moving in the bushes on the bank by the butts. I was the first person to shoot that day and, as I came up into the aim, to my astonishment I suddenly spotted an old cock pheasant creeping through the bushes to the right of the targets. No one else appeared to have noticed it and almost instinctively – and certainly without thinking of the consequences – I took a snap shot. There was a spurt of dust from the bank, the pheasant disappeared, and the butt markers signalled a miss! To R.S.M. Bunker's caustic reprimand I replied (may the Lord forgive me) that my elbow had slipped, but to my profound relief neither he nor anyone else seemed aware of what had really happened.

When the shoot was over, the coach returned us to the School where I collected my bicycle. By that time – for financial reasons – I had become a day boarder, and on my way home I took a long detour via the Piccott's End range. I searched the area of the butts and there, under the bushes, I found the old cock pheasant; the high velocity, solid, .303 bullet had drilled a neat hole through his breast; my snap shot had been a compete fluke. Ironically, it was the first pheasant I had ever shot but scarcely a 'Glorious First'. I had infringed about every shooting law in the book, not least the unwritten one which ordains that one must shoot one's game bird quarry in flight! The only thing to be said in my favour is that my shot, against a high bank, had been a safe one.

Hurriedly stuffing the pheasant into my saddlebag, I cycled home, arriving very late. At my story my father roared with laughter but my mother was horrified, refusing to accept my sinful offering. So, on the Sunday, a friend and I plucked and spit-roasted the old bird over a camp fire. But the old cock pheasant had the last laugh, he was a veteran of many seasons, with spurs like golf tees, and in the end the only one who appreciated a share of the meal was my Irish setter, Rufus.

All that happened nearly 70 years ago, and now that I have at last confessed to my transgressions, I trust that my sins will be forgiven!

# Chapter V

# The Way of a Transgressor

*The Way of a Transgressor ... and another man's geese*

I first saw the big gun standing in the shop window of Messrs Gale, the gunmakers in Barnstaple. Backed by a row of elegant, best quality, 12-bore sporting guns, the old, single barrelled 4-bore, with its massive proportions, stood out like a shire horse in a racing stable! I had read much about these big wildfowling guns, but never before had I seen a 4-bore, let alone fired or even handled one, but I was late and after lingering briefly to stare in awe, reluctantly I hurried on.

That sighting was in the summer of 1936, when I was on one of my frequent visits to my favourite uncle who had retired to live in Northam, near Westward Ho! In those days that part of North Devon was a near paradise for any lad with a sense of adventure, a spark of initiative, and a love of field sports and the countryside. Trout and sea fishing were there for the taking; pre-myxamatosis rabbits swarmed everywhere; the trawler skippers out of Bideford were happy to allow a keen lad on board for a trip or two; for those in the know, the drifter to Lundy Island often beckoned; and in the autumn and winter my thoughts and energies turned to wildfowling.

In the September of that year, on returning from camping on Lundy Island with my friend Dick Lawson, I noticed that the 4-bore had vanished from Gale's window. I had wanted to examine the old gun, but I was disappointed to learn that it had been sold to a local wildfowler. However, almost exactly one year later, when I again called in at Gale's for cartridges, there – standing in the gun rack at the back of the shop – was the old 4-bore. Soon I was cradling it in my hands, all 14lbs of it, admiring its gleaming brown, 36 inch, damascus barrel – engraved with the maker's name, T. Bland – its mighty hammer and its massive under-lever. There was a hole in its stock for a breeching rope for its occasional use as a punt gun, and with its breech opening and closing with a heavy, metallic clang, and its great, black powder cartridges like small shells, it reminded me more of a gun turret on a battleship than a normal shoulder gun.

My questions revealed that, from the moment he bought it, the previous owner had been so scared of the 4-bore that, when he had fired his first shot with the big gun, he had made the cardinal error of leaning up against a gate post to help absorb the recoil. When his head had stopped reeling and he had picked himself up from the ground, he had discovered that his collarbone was broken. The next day he had taken the 4-bore back to Gale's and traded it in for a 12-bore magnum!

"Could I hire it?" I asked, still lovingly clasping the big gun. The proprietor stared at me doubtfully – until I mentioned my uncle's name. "Ah, the Colonel," he said, his face brightening, and a deal was rapidly clinched. Ten minutes later, Dick Lawson and I left the shop, carrying between us the great gun and a bag full of massive red and green cartridges each loaded with nearly four ounces of No.1 or BB shot.

Dick and I had long planned a wildfowling expedition to a new area of saltmarsh on the north bank of the Taw estuary. We had not been there before, but from the Ordnance Survey map it looked both promising and easily accessible from the Barnstaple to Ilfracombe road, and it seemed a likely place to try out the

*Splash with the Big Gun*

4-bore for the first time. So, a few days later, dressed in thigh waders and waterproofs, and complete with guns, rations and Dick's big Springer spaniel, 'Splash', we set off by bus. We were objects of interest and some hilarity to the other passengers, but we reached our dropping off point with our resolve unshaken and the conductor bid us a cheery farewell with 'Rather you than me, lads!'

From the moment we stepped onto it the marsh looked good. In the distance, over the estuary, there was continuous movement; small parties of duck and waders lifting and flying in all directions. On the marsh itself there were several cow byres, which suited our plans admirably. Our intention was to take the evening flight below the high tide mark, bivouac for the rest of the night, take the morning flight, and then return home. The weather looked mild and all looked well.

Of the actual shoot, although it was the first time I had ever used a gun bigger than a 12-bore, there is not much to tell. At the evening flight, Dick bagged a brace of mallard and, in the gathering dusk, I fired the 4-bore for the first time in a flock shot at wigeon. The old gun went off with a mighty 'WHOOMPH', a blinding flash, and a great cloud of white smoke. To my surprise and relief the recoil was more like the mighty push of some giant hand than the shattering kick of the proverbial mule, and when I looked through the drifting smoke there were four wigeon floating paddles up.

That night we ate and slept in a cow byre and the morning flight was almost a carbon copy of the evening before, leaving us with three more wigeon, another mallard, and a teal which had given 'Splash' a lot of trouble by diving repeatedly. Eventually, as mid-day approached, we packed up, left the foreshore and headed back across the marsh toward the main road. And then it happened.

'STOP!' roared a stentorian voice behind us. Surprised, we turned to see, advancing rapidly towards us, a large, tweed-clad and obviously hostile figure, brandishing a stick and accompanied by an outsize and even more belligerent looking black Labrador. Out of curiosity we stopped and waited, and as the figure got closer there was no mistaking the threatening aura of an experienced and very angry gamekeeper.

"And wot d'yew think yew might be doin' yurr?" queried the figure menacingly, in a rich Devonian burr, halting a few feet from us, blackthorn at the ready. "Good morning," we replied politely, which seemed the sensible thing to do. "We've been shooting along the foreshore, below the high tide mark." The keeper snorted. "Ahr, av'ee now! Don'ee know the squire owns all the foreshore rights along yurr? Yew'll come to the 'all wi' me." Whereupon he waved his stick threateningly towards a large house nestling in a small clump of distant trees and motioned us to precede him. After a moment's hesitation we decided it would be wisest to comply and we walked without talking, the silence broken only by the keeper's heavy breathing, the clumping of our waders, and deep rumblings from the big Labrador whenever 'Splash' strayed from our heels.

The big, oak door of the Hall was opened by an immaculate butler, an elderly man who stared at us with an expression which changed rapidly from amazement through disbelief to disgust. Standing in front of him, with the gamekeeper fuming in the background, he saw a wet, dirty and shivering spaniel and two muddy and dishevelled youths of some 18 years, festooned with dead birds and – after a night in a cow byre – looking and smelling like scarecrows. "*Yes?*" he enquired haughtily; but even as he spoke a pungent odour of black, estuarine mud, liberally mixed with fresh cow dung, billowed into the doorway. The butler recoiled and retreated coughing. "Stay here," he spluttered, hurriedly closing the door firmly in our faces.

After a few moments we heard raised voices and then the door was flung open again by a large, middle-aged man in riding kit. "What's all this about, Coombes?" he demanded belligerently. Taking his cue the keeper stepped forward to denounce us, after which our explanation and humble apology, accompanied by the offer of our duck, merely fuelled the flames. We soon discovered that the squire was both a J.P. and in good voice; he gave us a dressing down which I have never forgotten and after ten minutes, and watched regretfully by the keeper, we shuffled humbly away with the squire's parting words ringing in our ears – "Now, get off my land and take your damned birds and that cannon with you. If I ever catch you on my land with a gun again, I'll have you gaoled." When we had reached the main road and were waiting for our bus, Dick Lawson turned to me and said thoughtfully – "You know, I think he meant it."

There was an unexpected sequel to this sorry saga. Towards the end of the same year I received the good news not only that I had passed well into Sandhurst, but also that I had been awarded a King's India Cadetship which made it financially possible for me to go there. Like my parents, my favourite uncle was delighted and invited me to stay for a few days to celebrate. As usual, he met me at Bideford station in his old Armstrong Siddely, and on the drive to Northam he said – "I've been invited to quite a good shoot tomorrow; pheasants and some duck flight ponds. I told my host that you were coming down, before going to Sandhurst, and that you are a keen shot, and he said – 'Bring him too.' How do you feel about that?" H grinned; the delighted expression on my face was answer enough.

The next day we drove off early and after a few miles I began to feel uneasy. More and more familiar landmarks caught my eye and when at last my uncle turned the car into the drive of a big house nestling in a small clump of trees, I shrunk into my seat, pulled my cap down low over my eyes, and prayed for strength and guidance.

"So, this is your nephew who is going to Sandhurst," boomed the large, middle-aged man who was our host, in a voice that I would have recognised anywhere. "Congratulations, my boy. Glad to have you with us."… "Should be plenty of duck today, Colonel," he added, turning to my uncle. "Coombes has got the better of those damned poachers from Barnstaple this year. Caught two of them in September, walking across the marsh from the fore-shore in broad daylight, as bold as brass, carrying a punt gun. Damned nerve. Youngsters, mark you and quite polite. Gave them a talking to. Don't know what parents are doing nowadays." "Disgraceful," commented my uncle, giving me a sly look, while I mumbled something polite and kept my head well down.

It *was* a good shoot and there *were* plenty of duck, but when he was placing the guns and picking up, the keeper kept staring at me with a puzzled look. At the lunch break, weary of the suspense, I decided to pluck up courage and reveal my identity to my host. "Do you remember, Sir," I said hesitantly, taking off my cap and laying my gun down in a safe place, "I was one of the poachers your keeper caught in September. You told me that if you ever found me on your land again, carrying a gun, you'd have me gaoled!" For a long tense moment my host stared at me open-mouthed, then recognition dawned and with a roar of laughter he slapped me on the back. "I'll dine out on this one, my boy," he chortled. "But we mustn't tell Coombes, he'd have apoplexy!"

My host had underestimated his keeper. When I received a brace of birds and slipped him the customary tip, the keeper looked at me with a twinkle in his eye. "Yew be usin' quite a dif'runt gun today, Surr, I zee," he said with a straight face. All I could muster in reply was a wan smile!

\* \* \*

During my 'teens I did a lot of wildfowling on the saltmarshes and mudflats in the estuaries of the Medway in Kent, and of the Taw and the Torridge in North Devon. No foray ever produced more than a few birds but, by the end of December, 1937, I had shot virtually all the species of wildfowl which were then on the 'fowler's recognised quarry list, including brent geese on the shores of Whitstable Bay. There was one outstanding omission; I had yet to see, let alone shoot, the wildfowler's ultimate prize – a grey goose.

In January 1938, I became a cadet in No. 5 Company of the Royal Military College, Sandhurst, and for the first two months my feet scarcely touched the ground. It was like being tossed into the middle of a cross between a cement mixer, a cocktail shaker and a whirlpool, and there was no time to think about anything beyond basic survival. Eventually I surfaced, fitter and more alert than I had ever been; and looking around me I realised that the army had long ago mastered the art of cutting people down to size and paring the corners off square pegs until they fitted snugly into a wide variety of round holes. There were surprisingly few rejects!

There was now time to think and to play as well as to work, and my thoughts again turned to wildfowling; but, as I was a member (and finally Captain) of the R.M.C. Shooting VIII, all my spare time in the summer and autumn was taken up with competition shooting, with a variety of weapons, at Bisley. However, the pending Christmas leave offered a fine chance to organise a really serious wildfowling expedition, a trip which, because of my aim to join the Indian Army, clearly called for careful planning since it could well prove to by my last wildfowling foray in the British Isles for a very long time.

As autumn approached, my friend and fellow cadet, Adrian King, and I got out our Ordnance Survey maps and, after much thought and discussion, we made two main decisions – that our chief quarry should be grey geese and that our operational area would therefore be the Solway Firth. Having settled that, we then got down to administrative planning, including such vital matters as weapons and transport, the latter problem being solved by my benevolent parents generously (and trustingly) agreeing to lend us the family Morris Minor, which was quite adequate for our needs.

Adrian had long awaited an excuse to purchase a true 'fowler's gun and he settled for a 12-bore, 3 inch magnum, a sound and honest boxlock ejector, with 32 inch barrels, made by Messrs Lewis of Birmingham. I myself was happy to place my trust in my tried and tested B.S.A, a double-barrelled, hammerless, non-ejector, 2½-inch case 12-bore with 28 inch barrels. Costing new all of 12 guineas (the ejector model cost 3 guineas more!), my parents had given me the gun on my 16th birthday when I had announced my intention to try for the Indian Army; it had already given me sterling service and was to continue to do so until its untimely end in Burma, some three years later. Using Eley 'Maximum' cartridges, with 1¼ ozs of shot, I had found it a handy and effective gun for wildfowling and – most important – I could hit things with it! It had even won me a simple silver cup for clay pigeon shooting at Bisley, and I was confident that, with 1¼ ozs of BB in each barrel, I could deal with any goose which came within reasonable range.

In mid-December, our little car, bulging with 'fowling gear and clattering like a tinker's van, rattled stubbornly up the Great Northern Road. After a night's bivouac in Dumfries, Adrian and I headed southwards to have a pre-liminary look at the mouth of the Nith. Topping a rise, our delighted eyes were greeted with a sight that would have thrilled the heart of any wildfowler; it was a glorious day, bright sunshine and freezing hard; below us stretched vast acres of frozen saltmarsh, sparkling with ice and dotted with small parties of resting duck. There was no need to seek any further, and by mid-morning we had established ourselves for a week's stay in the cottage of a friendly fisherman in Glancaple.

Over the next few days we rapidly got on terms with the local duck – wigeon, teal, pochard and pintail – but the geese eluded us; all we ever managed to see of them were wavering smudges in the sky, disappearing shorewards around a distant headland. Finally, with only two days left, Adrian and I had an urgent conference. Out came our Ordnance Survey maps and a mid-day recce confirmed a country road leading past a remote farmhouse, a point from where a public footpath led to the stretch of distant foreshore over which the geese appeared to by flighting.

That night, as we drove to the lonely farm, the moon was so bright that we scarcely needed even our side-lights. We parked the car on the grass verge and set off along the foot-path to the foreshore. Two hours still remained before dawn and the expected arrival of the geese, and the moon was still high in the sky. The foot-path followed the lee of a high hedge and we had not gone more than two hundred yards, chatting quietly, when – from the field beyond the hedge – there was a sudden clamour, a cacophony of sound like a hound kennels at feeding time. With our ignorance of the habits of grey geese, we had not realised that on bright moonlight nights they often fly inland to feed at night!

In a flash we were crouching in the shadow of the hedge, our guns, whipped swiftly out of their slips, ready and loaded with BB; our Sandhurst training had not been wasted! Yelping and baying like a pack of foxhounds in full cry, a wavering skein of geese came sweeping straight over us, scarce 30 yards up, clearly silhouetted against a drifting patch of fleecy cloud. Four shots rang out and, as the skein scattered yelping wildly, four heavy thumps sounded in quick succession as four very dead geese hit the ground.

For a moment, Adrian and I stared at each other in the bright moonlight. Then, suddenly, the enormity of what we had done dawned on us. Reacting automatically and without evil intent we had shot four geese on private land! We hesitated no longer. Each of us seizing the necks of a brace of fat greylags, we ran back to the car. As we drove away, breathing sighs of guilty relief, lights were beginning to appear in the farmhouse.

The following day was our last and we split up for a winder over the saltmarshes near Glencaple. Towards mid-day, using my binoculars, I was surprised to see a pair of geese apparently feeding busily in the middle of the marsh, entirely on their own. No other geese were anywhere in sight. It was a long and difficult stalk but there were a few shallow gullies and it was worth trying. Using every scrap of fieldcraft I knew, I worked my way slowly but steadily along the gullies towards the geese until, covered with mud, I thought I must be somewhere near them. At last, easing my head gently over the edge of a bank, I was astonished to see the two geese only 25 yards away. The surprise was mutual. For a split second we stared at each other, then the geese leapt and I sprang to my feet. Five minutes later I had clambered out of the slippery gully and was picking up a brace of pinkfeet. It had been another satisfying right and left.

The next day we said a regretful farewell to Glancaple and set off on our long journey south. It was freezing hard and on the roads there were frequent patches of black ice. On a hill near Carlisle the car in front of us braked suddenly and as I stamped on my own brakes we hit a patch of black ice. Our little Morris Minor glissaded forwards and I watched helplessly as the rear of the car in front rushed towards us. There was a rending crash; all four doors of our little car sprang open; and in a moment the road was littered with dead geese, duck and curlew. The scene looked like a poulterer's shop!

We were towed into Carlisle and the train journey that followed was a long, slow nightmare, barring one fact – it is surprising how quickly a 3rd class railway compartment will empty when two muddy wildfowlers, carrying guns and sacks full of dead birds, make a polite but smelly entry!

# Chapter VI

# The Tale of the Dulikhet Panther

Seven thousand feet up in the cool, pine-scented hills of Kumaon, that scenically beautiful region of the lower Himalayas made famous by the late Jim Corbett in his spine-tingling books, *'The Man-eaters of Kumaon'* and *'The Man-eating Leopard of Rudraprayag',* lies the pretty little hill station of Dulikhet, the scene of my first encounter with a marauding leopard.

In August 1939, Dulikhet was also a small cantonment, then garrisoned by 'B' Company of the 2nd Battalion, the Royal Berkshire Regiment. While this detachment was relaxing and enjoying itself in the cool, sybaritic comfort of the little hill station, far below in the arid plains of the United Provinces, in the torrid heat of the sprawling, historic city of Lucknow – with its blood-stained memories of the Indian Mutiny – the bulk of the Battalion sweltered, sweated and swore its way through the last period of the hot weather.

In the halcyon days of the Raj, British officers selected for the Indian Army – for which there was keen competition – were first required to serve, for up to a year, attached to a British regiment stationed in India. The object of this attachment was to enable these young officers to learn something of the country, its people, and the Urdu language (the *lingua franca* of the army) before being placed in command of Indian or Gurkha troops. Fortunately for me, on my arrival in India in August, 1939, it was to 'B' Company of the Royal Berkshires, stationed in the idyllic surroundings of Dulikhet, that I was ordered to report for duty; for me it was the start of the penultimate stage of that long and involved process – commencing with the entry into the Royal Military College, Sandhurst – through which every young man had to pass before he would be accepted into the commissioned ranks of a regiment of the Indian Army.

It had been in the autumn of 1937, that, to almost everyone's surprise, I had managed to pass the entrance exam into Sandhurst with, what my parents later proudly proclaimed as, 'flying colours' – I was 8th out of an accepted entry of 236! Furthermore, after a searching interview at the India Office in London (influenced I am sure, by my father's fine record as a Senior Commissioned in the Imperial Indian Police) I had been awarded a 'King's India Cadetship', which had taken care of all my Sandhurst fees and expenses.

Although I say it myself, I had also managed to do rather well during my 18 months' training at Sandhurst, ending up in the most senior cadet rank of 'Under Officer', of which rank there were a total of 24 at any one time, in a total cadet force of 700 cadets.

As, in addition, I had ended up with a 'Shooting Blue' and the Captaincy of the R.M.C. 'Shooting VIII', by the end if June 1939, I had been officially regarded as having passed out of Sandhurst well enough not merely to be commissioned as a Second Lieutenant in His Majesty's Land Forces, but also to be accepted for appointment to the limited entry into the Indian Army. I had then immediately become a member of that nebulous group of fledgling officers known as the U.L.I.A. (Unattached List Indian Army).

After kitting out for life in the East and fond farewells to relations and friends, early in August 1939, this fresh batch of raw U.L.I.A subalterns had sailed for India on the troopship 'Somersetshire'. By that time the dark, threatening clouds of war had already begun to gather rapidly over eastern Europe, but I must confess that, throughout our voyage, the thoughts of myself and of my friend, Paul Coventry, had mainly been focussed elsewhere, our minds being filled with visions of exciting prospects of boundless *shikar* (field sports) ahead.

As our ship had steamed through the Mediterranean, down the Red Sea, and across the Indian Ocean, at regular intervals Paul and I had anxiously checked, cleaned and oiled our respective armouries to protect our weapons against the ravages of the humid heat. My own armoury then consisted of my faithful B.S.A 12-bore, an old but very accurate .275 (7 x 57) Waffenfabrik Mauser magazine rifle, and a treasured .455 Smith and Wesson revolver. Both the latter weapons I had bought second hand from Messrs Fultons of Bisley for the princely sums of £2.10s and £1.15s respectively. Fultons' salesman had been a confirmed devotee of Kipling. "Just the weapon for stopping them savage, charging Pay-thans, Sir," he had said with obvious relish, handing me the Smith and Wesson after I had told him that I expected to serve on the North West Frontier. One look at the .455 cartridge was enough to convince me of the soundness of his opinion!

Finally our journey to and across India had ended, and Paul and I, both wearing our enormous regulation pith helmets and our wide khaki shorts from which protruded our long, pink-kneed legs – the whole outfit giving us the appearance of a pair of animated mushrooms – had arrived in Dulikhet and reported for duty to 'B' Company of the Royal Berkshire Regiment. The date was August 27th 1939 – my 20th birthday!

The Adjutant of the Royal Berkshires, a very senior captain who was temporarily in Dulikhet with the detachment, greeted us with noticeable lack of enthusiasm. This was understandable, for to him subalterns of the U.L.I.A were alien birds of passage, often troublesome individuals with strange ideas about India and little interest in his own regiment. However, he was helpful enough when we asked him about opportunities for *shikar*. He said that he had heard rumours of panther (as the leopard was known in India) in the district and that only the previous week a cocker spaniel belonging to one of the sergeants had mysteriously disappeared; one evening at dusk there had been a rustle in the bushes, a strangled yelp, then silence. The dog had not been seen since. He then turned to his bearer and told him to bring the local shikari (hunter), one Mohammed Shafi, to see us in our peaceful bungalow on the pine-covered hillside.

That evening, as we sat on our verandah enjoying a sundowner, we heard a sound resembling the sawing of wood coming from the valley below. "That woodcutter's working late," I remarked idly, but our bearer's hands shook until the glasses on his tray rattled and there was a look of alarm in his eyes. "Baghera (panther), Sahib," he whispered and disappeared hurriedly into the bungalow.

In those days I had started to keep a detailed shooting diary, and from this point on I could do no better than repeat what I wrote, at the time, in that now battered old book:

'On September 3rd, we heard that war had been declared. The news was brought to us by Piari Lal, the Mess cook, who had heard it in Dulikhet bazaar. The official news came from Lucknow some hours later! An order was immediately issued forbidding us to leave the cantonment area – damned silly! However, our *shikari* brought *khabbar* (news) of a pair of panther which had been taking goats and dogs from Dulikhet bazaar. Luckily the bazaar lies within the cantonment boundaries, so I immediately routed out the local magistrate and got the necessary permission to shoot in cantonments. That same night I got the *shikari* to fix up a *machan* (high-seat) in a small, bushy tree on the hillside, some 400 yards below the bazaar. The *machan* was made of an old *charpoy* (rough string bed) and though only five feet from the ground it was very well camouflaged.

The *shikari* tethered a goat on the hillside below the tree, and I climbed into the *machan* at about 6.30 pm, with my shotgun loaded with an contractile bullet in the right barrel and SSG in the left. Paul was unable to accompany me as he was on duty as Orderly Officer. I waited until nearly midnight but nothing came, and as it then started to pour with rain I whistled up the *shikari* with his lantern and trudged back to my bungalow.

Next morning the *shikari* rushed into our bungalow to say that, in the early hours of the morning, a panther had killed the goat and also a pi-dog close by, but had not eaten either of them. That night both Paul and I crammed ourselves into the small *machan*, with our shot-guns loaded with contractile bullets and SSG as before. We were in the *machan* by 6 pm and made loop-holes so that Paul was watching the dead dog, while I was watching the dead goat which was on the other side of the tree. Having no means of fixing our large electric torch to either of our guns, we had painted white stripes down their middle ribs and arranged that if the panther came to Paul's kill, I would shine the torch for him to shoot, and vice versa.

We sat very quietly, listening to some monkeys chattering in the trees below us and the sound of wailing music coming from the bazaar above. I was very sleepy after my previous night's vigil and soon began dozing off. Suddenly, at about 6.45 pm, just as dusk was falling, Paul nudged me; turning slowly sideways, I saw a panther standing over the dead dog, glancing from side to side with the tip of its tail twitching. Paul quietly cocked his old hammergun and raised it to his shoulder; at the same time I shone the torch full on the panther; as I did so, Paul's gun went off with a roar and the panther disappeared.

"Did you hit it?" I shouted very excited. "I don't know," Paul replied irritably. "It moved as I fired. You shouldn't have shone the torch; it wasn't needed and it scared the beast. What a *bloody* nuisance!" It was true that there had still been plenty of light to shoot by, but I had merely

*The 'machan' (tree hide)*
*from which the panther was shot at night*

*The stock-raiding panther shot by the author, at night,*
*from a 'machan' (a hide in a tree)*

carried out our prearranged plan. However, I realised how sick Paul must have been feeling at missing a panther only 20 feet away. The beast had glanced up when I shone the torch, but I think the miss was due to excitement.

As it was rapidly getting dark, we shone the torch around in the faint hope of seeing a possibly wounded panther, or signs of it, at the same time turning the air blue with our language at having missed such an opportunity. Then the torch bulb failed and the air was rent asunder by a volley of really pungent and colourful oaths as suddenly we were plunged into the deep gloom of approaching night.

We were left with a tiny sixpenny torch as our sole source of light, and we were in the process of trying to change the bulbs between the torches, still talking loudly, when – suddenly – out of the corner of my eye I spotted, slipping through the bushes a few yards away, the shadowy form of a panther. In a flash the torchlight was out and we sat like statues, scarcely breathing.

After what seemed like years, but could not have been more than ten minutes, I again saw a shadowy form creeping, foot by foot, towards the dead goat, which it was now too dark to see. I eased my gun up, but waited with my heart beating like a sledgehammer. At last the beast – whatever it was – was standing over the kill and started to drag it away. This was the moment. I nudged Paul and he shone the tiny torch; it was of little more use than a candle, but at least it showed me my foresight and a vague yellow shape, which had halted with the goat at its feet. I aimed carefully at where I thought that the shoulder of the yellow form must be and squeezed the trigger. The contractile cartridge went off with the usual tremendous 'WHOOF' and for a moment or two we could see nothing. Then there was a rattling growl, and straining our eyes in the dim torchlight we could just see a shadowy shape lying on the ground. I fired the SSG cartridge at it to make sure and there was silence.

Wildly excited, we waited for ten minutes and then, calling up the *shikari* with his lantern we climbed down from the tree and approached the still body with guns at the ready; but the panther was quite dead.

The marauder proved to be a fine female panther with a perfect coat, nicely marked, and exactly seven feet in length from tip of nose to tip of tail. The bullet had hit her slap in the right shoulder and the second shot (SSG) had not been required. However, the coat was not damaged by the shot, although in her death throws the panther had bitten deeply into her right forepaw.

We slung the panther on a pole and then started a triumphal procession through the bazaar, gathering followers at every corner and even stealing the disciples of a Hindu religious procession! We halted at house after house, chairs being brought out for us to sit on, and while the *shikari* – who had an unexpectedly fertile imagination – explained to the village elders how the Sahib had slain 'the ravening beast that ate their goats, their dogs, and sometimes even their *bachas* (babies)', the women and children came out with bulging, wondering eyes and stroked the yellow fur.

The panther was finally laid out ceremoniously on the Mess verandah. Much liquor then flowed in an atmosphere of surprise, congratulations and admiration, heavily laced with envy, for not many people have the luck to slay a panther during their first ten days in India – and a stock

*Panther Skinner at work*

raider at that! But to this day I cannot understand why the panther ever returned at all after being fired at, let alone so soon, although they can be bold beasts. Possible it was a different panther, but even then it must have heard the first shot. Regretfully, I shall never know the answer."

So ends the account in my old shooting diary. For me it had been a thrilling experience; a sobering lesson in how a strikingly handsome predator, such as a leopard, can easily become a dangerous menace; and finally, truly a 'Glorious First!'

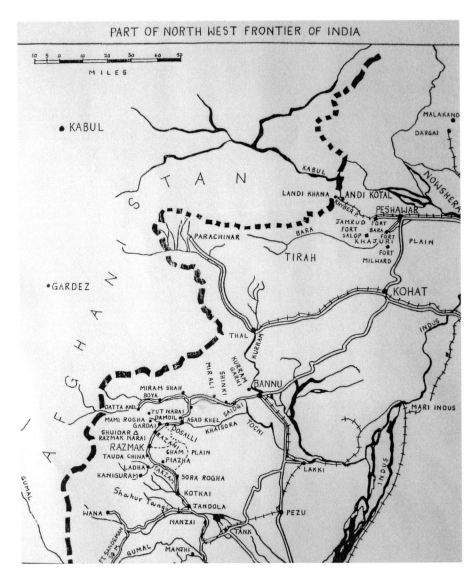

*Part of North West Frontier of India*

# Chapter VII

# The Final Test

A week after my encounter with a panther at Dulikhet in the Himalayan foothills, in September 1939, I received a letter for which I had been anxiously waiting. The letter was from the Adjutant of the 1st Battalion of the 3rd (Queen Alexandra's Own) Gurkha Rifles, in nearby Almora. Kindly and informal, not only did his letter put most of my doubts and fears to rest, but also it offered me an exciting chance to experience, for the first time, the renowned sporting qualities of *Caccabis chukur*, the chukor partridge, that handsome game bird the size of a grouse, which is found in fast flying coveys throughout the lower Himalayas and in the barren hills along India's North West Frontier.

I read,

Dear Kinloch,

Thank you for reporting your arrival with the Royal Berkshire Regiment in Dulikhet. We had already heard from our retired officer who interviewed you at Sandhurst, that you are keen to join this Regiment, so it is helpful to know that you are now so conveniently close.

The Colonel has asked me to invite you to visit us here in Almora, as our guest, the week-end after next; this will enable you to meet our officers and men and to see how we live and work. Most of the officers are going on a chukor shoot on the Saturday; if you would care to join them, bring your *bhistra* (bedding roll) with you. We look forward to meeting you … etc etc.

Friendly and welcoming as the letter was, it left me under no delusions that the whole purpose of the invitation was other than to enable the Regiment thoroughly to inspect me, and to assess whether or not I was suitable, in their eyes, for admission to the select membership of the 3rd Q.A.O. Gurkha Rifles – and certainly not vice versa! However, the letter had dispelled any doubts which I might previously have held about the Regiment's degree of interest in *shikar*, and I felt that at least my own obvious keenness on field sports could be a strong point in my favour, no matter how poor a showing I might make in other respects! One thing was certain, there would be no second chance.

At the time of which I write, the Gurkha Brigade of the India Army consisted on ten Gurkha Rifle regiments, each one of them having its own individual Home Station (or Regimental Centre) scattered at suitable points along the length of the foothills of the mighty Himalayan Range. But in one respect the 3rd Gurkha Rifles was unique – it was the only Gurkha regiment to have *two* Home Stations, that of its 1st Battalion being in Almora, in Kumaon, only then miles south-east of Dulikhet across the hilltops, but more than double that distance by road. The historic reasons for this difference from the other Gurkha regiments are too long to be recorded here. Suffice it to say that, for various family reasons, my own choice of regiment was the 3rd Gurkha Rifles, with a preference for the 1st Battalion; so Dulikhet was the ideal place for me to complete my required period of attachment to a British regiment.

For weeks prior to my all important visit to Almora, every evening, as the last rays of the setting sun had touched the distant Himalayan snow peaks – Trisul, Nanda Kot and Nanda Devi – turning their towering snow caps from pearly white to rose pink, I had listened, deeply stirred, to the haunting notes

*The Himalayan Snow Peaks taken for Dulikhet*

*Smiling Ghurka Soldiers*

of that most poignant of all bugle calls *The Last Post*, played by a bugler of the 3rd Gurkha Rifles as the Quarter Guard in Almora lowered the flag at sunset. Faint but clear, the call had reached my eager ears in Dulikhet, for despite the distance the still air of the mountains had been no barrier to the pure tones of the silver bugle.

I can remember arriving at the Adjutant's office in Almora on the Friday evening, but as to the details of leaving Dulikhet and of the journey itself, my mind is now a complete blank. Tension can do strange things; all I know is that I didn't walk there! I was met by a subaltern in uniform, wearing a wide-brimmed Gurkha hat at a rakish angle and a cheerful grin. "My name's Chris Pulley," he said. "I'm Orderly Officer this week-end and the Adjutant instructed me to look after you. Been a bit of a hiatus here this week. The Colonel's been shot off to the Middle East; something to do with the war. The Second-in-Command, Major Foster, is acting in his place. You'll meet him in the Mess this evening."

"The Adjutant's gone ahead with the shooting party;" he went on, "they're camping in the *dak* bungalow at Lamgara; you'll join them to-morrow; it's several hours march so (with a grin) we've laid on a charger with a *sais* (groom) in case you need it. There'll be a mule for your *bhistra*, and Rajbir here," he added, turning to a Gurkha rifleman who sprang to attention and saluted smartly, "will act as your orderly. You're staying in my bungalow tonight, so come in and have a wash and brush up; then I'll take you down to the V.C.O's (Viceroy's Commissioned Officers) Mess to meet the Gurkha Officers." What he really meant was that the V.C.Os (the subedars and jemadars who were the backbone of all Indian Army regiments) would be the first to interview me – albeit covertly and courteously – and their considered

*Orderlies of the 3rd Gurkha Rifles crossing the Kosi River 1942*

judgement would be passed on to the Commanding Officer by the Subedar Major, who was the Colonel's right hand man and advisor on all matters relating to Gurkhas.

The V.C.Os Mess was like a quietly buzzing bee-hive, full of cigarette smoke, cheerful Mongolian faces and the strong smell of '*Rosa*' rum which came from the brimming jugs carried by several energetic orderlies. As we entered, the subedars and jemadars scrambled to attention until Chris Pulley introduced me and bade them relax. Sitting between two grizzled and bemedalled subedars, I tried to make intelligent conversation in my halting Urdu. I was helped by the fact that the Battalion had comparatively recently returned from two years very active service on the North West Frontier, so I was able to keep the discourse flowing with questions about the notorious Faqir of Ipi and his rapacious followers. My undoing was the rum-bearing Gurkha orderly who hovered solicitously behind my right shoulder. Whenever I turned from addressing my neighbour on my left, I found that my half-empty tumbler of neat rum had mysteriously refilled itself to the brim. It was my first experience of drinking rum and I was amazed how innocuous it was – until Chris Pulley said our formal farewells and the cold night air of the Kumaon Hills at 5,500 feet hit me like a pole-axe.

With the hills spinning around me, I somehow reached the Officer's Mess. Dinner was a nightmare. Sitting next to the acting C.O., I don't think I spoke an intelligent word throughout the meal, nor ate more than the odd mouthful of food, while from the walls around me, the stuffed heads of ibex, markhor, ovis ammon and red bear stared down at me in haughty disdain through their glazed eyes. Later I was told that my face had been a sickly green, but Major Foster had merely smiled indulgently; to him it was a familiar and oft-repeated scenario when new officers arrived, and when I excused myself to retire to bed, he bade me an amused but sympathetic farewell.

In the bungalow I managed to reach the *gussalkhana* (primitive bathroom) where the walls seemed to collapse on top of me and I knew no more until the grey light of dawn. I awoke to find myself lying fully clothed on the concrete floor, freezing cold and with my head feeling as if it had been split open with a battleaxe. I just had time to strip and clamber under the blankets in the bedroom, when Chris Pulley's bearer appeared with a steaming pot of tea. Gulping this down, followed by a long, hot soak in a tin hip-bath, restored me to a state of near normality – apart from my head – and I joined my waiting animal convoy almost on time.

With Rajbir carrying my shotgun and leading the way, and with my *sais* and horse, plus another Gurkha rifleman leading a mule with my kit, both following me, we marched steadily northwards through the mountains, with occasional glimpses of the Kosi River glistening far below. As midday approached I had a raging thirst and my water bottle was empty, but my sanity was saved by a goat-herd; who was sitting beside the track with a blackened iron bowl full of goats' milk warming over a wood fire. Smoky in flavour and full of bits of floating charcoal as it was, I gulped the lot. With a smile he refused payment, but as we left I dropped a few coins beside him and marched on with a new spring in my step.

Eventually we caught up with the shooting party, who were having *tiffin* (lunch) in a sheltered spot on the mountain side, and I met the Adjutant, Robert O'Lone, and several other officers, all of them amused, sympathetic, but not surprised at the familiar story of my downfall. That afternoon the shoot started again, with two sections of Gurkha riflemen acting as beaters on each side of selected valleys, while the guns lined out along the valley bottoms.

Some of the hillsides, particularly along the valley of the Kosi River, which we crossed and re-crossed many times, were heavily terraced and cultivated and these proved to be fine holding ground for chukor, my first sighting of which I shall never forget.

There was a shout from a Gurkha, high up on a hillside, as a covey of some eight chukor exploded from the rocks in front of him and – diving and curling like the fastest of driven grouse – swept down and across the valley, straight over my head. My two wild and bewildered shots were met with a derisory chuckle. I turned ruefully to my neighbour. "Not easy, are they," said Gavin Seagrim sympathetically. "It takes time to get the knack."

Take time it did, but by the end of that day I was beginning to connect. My first success gave me the confidence I needed. A single chukor came off the clifftops and flew straight down the valley through a barrage of ineffective ack-ack fire from the other guns. By the time it reached me the chukor was very high and travelling fast, but I flung up my gun and swung desperately. To my surprise the bird folded like a book and fell, in a fountain of spray and to wild cheers from the Gurkhas, slap in the middle of the shallow Kosi River. Grinning widely, Rajbir retrieved it in a series of splashing leaps. For me that was the start and, after a good night's rest at Lamgara, I slowly began to average 1 in 3. It was hard exercise and exciting shooting enlivened by the keenness and enthusiasm of the Gurkhas.

By the end of the two-day shoot we had a bag of 64 chukor to a party of keen but not very expert guns, and I had learnt one interesting fact about the Gurkhas. During one drive the line of Gurkhas on the hillside suddenly broke ranks and bounded wildly down and around the rocks, yelling and shouting and hurling stones at something which dodged in front of them. I discovered later that it was a hare and that, for some strange reason, the sight of a hare is one of the few things which seems capable of disrupting the iron discipline for which the Gurkha soldier is justly famous!

On the Sunday evening I returned to Dulikhet, tired but exhilarated after a 'Glorious First.' A few days later I received a letter from the Adjutant. 'The Battalion will shortly be moving down to Lucknow for cold-weather training.' He wrote. 'And the Colonel has asked me to tell you that we shall look forward to welcoming you into the Regiment immediately after Christmas. I hope your head is better!'

With a sigh of relief I put the letter down. It had been a long haul since I

*Regimental crests of the regiments comprising the Brigade of Gurkhas up to 1947*

had decided, in the summer of 1935, that if I wanted a career which would offer me the best opportunities for shooting and fishing – and at the same time enjoy a very active and worthwhile job – then I had to join a regiment of the Indian Army. Not just *any* regiment, mark you, but a *Gurkha Rifle* regiment and, hopefully, the 3rd, Q.A.O. Gurkha Rifles, the regiment in which my favourite uncle, Lt-Colonel George Kendall Channer, D.S.O., had served with such distinction. Now, at last, my dream had come true!

Until I went to Sandhurst, in January 1938, I had not realised the strength of the competition for vacancies in the ten Gurkha Rifle regiments of the Indian Army. It then dawned on me that I would be wise to have a second string to my

*A portrait of my maternal grandfather,*
*General G.N. Channer, V.C., C.B.*
*late of the 1st King George V's own Gurkha Rifles)*
*hangs in the 'V.C. and G.C. Gallery' of the Gurkha Museum in Winchester*

bow, in case the 3rd Gurkha Rifles, for some reason or another, could not, or even (a horrible thought!) *would* not, accept me. I therefore decided to name, as an alternative choice, the 1st, King George V's Own, Gurkha Rifles, the only other Gurkha Rifle regiment with which I had a family connection; in this case in the shape of my maternal grandfather, General George Nicholas Channer, V.C., C.B.

I never actually knew my maternal grandfather, for I was a late arrival, my mother being nearly forty when I was born, while my grandfather, after a spectacularly meteoric career to full General, died at the early age of 62 – 14 years before I was born. However, as soon as I was old enough to appreciate it, I learnt all about the daring and dramatic actions for which he was awarded the Victoria Cross.

This momentous event took place in December, 1875, when my grandfather's battalion of the 1st Gurkha Rifles was operating against well-armed rebel forced in the dense hill jungles of Malaya. Full details of this dramatic action, and of my grandfather's brilliant career, are given in a book entitled *The story of Gurkha V.C.s.* published by the Gurkha Museum in Winchester, courtesy of whom I am repeating them here: – 'For conspicuous act of bravery on December 20th 1875, at the Bukit Pass and stockades in Negri Sembilan, Malay Peninsula, Captain Channer was awarded the Victoria Cross and promoted to Brevet Major.

The citation in the *London Gazette* of April 14th 1876 stated:

For having, with the greatest gallantry, been the first to jump into the Enemy's Stockade, to which he had been dispatched with a small party of the 1st Gurkha Rifles, on the afternoon of the December 20th 1875, by the Officer commanding the Malacca Column, to procure intelligence as to its strength, position, etc, Captain Channer got completely in rear of the Enemy's position, and finding himself so close that he could hear the voices of the men inside, who were cooking at the time, and keeping no look-out, he beckoned to his men, and the whole party stole quietly forward to within a few paces of the Stockade. On jumping in, he shot the first man dead with his revolver, and his party came up, and entered the Stockade, which was of a most formidable nature, surrounded by a bamboo palisade; about seven yards within was a log-house, loop-holed, with two narrow entrances, and trees laid latitudinally, to the thickness of two feet.

The Officer commanding reports that if Captain Channer by his foresight, coolness, and intrepidity, had not taken this Stockade, a great loss of life must have occurred, as from the fact of his being unable to bring guns to bear on it, from the steepness of the hill, and the density of the jungle, it must have been taken at the point of the bayonet.

Major Channer was Mentioned in Despatches and promoted to Brevet Lieutenant Colonel during the Afghan War 1878–80. He was appointed CB and again Mentioned in Despatches whilst commanding the 1st Brigade on the Second Black Mountain Expedition in 1888. He was promoted Major General in 1890, Lieutenant General in 1893, and General in 1899. He died at Westward Ho, Devon, on December 13th 1905, aged 62.'

Among its many dramatic exhibits, the Gurkha Museum has a colourful diorama depicting the action at the Stockade in the Bukit Pass, for which my grandfather was awarded his Victoria Cross. There is also a large portrait of my grandfather in the Museum's gallery of V.C. and G.C. winners; it is a typically Victoria portrait and makes my grandfather appear stern, humourless and rather lugubrious, whereas, as far as I know, he had none of these negative attributes! However, I have often thought that the strain of his meteoric career could well have been a major contributory factor to his early death.

Certainly, my grandfather's military career was so impressive that to me, a very young and impressionable subaltern, it was almost intimidating. In fact, while I was at Sandhurst, I had often had the uneasy thought that a posting to the 1st Gurkha Rifles, might well result in that regiment expecting me to live up to my grandfather's awe-inspiring reputation. It had therefore been with a sense of great relief, that I had learnt that my first U.L.I.A. posting was to be to a company of the Royal Berkshire Regiment, on detachment in the tiny Himalayan hill station of Dulikhet. Since Dulikhet lies virtually in the shadow of Almora, the home hill station of my favourite uncle's old regiment, the 3rd Queen Alexandra's Own, Gurkha Rifles, I had then decided that fate must *surely* be on my side!

# Chapter VIII

# A Christmas Camp in India

Throughout the years of the British Raj, the great Indian sub-continent remained a near Utopia for the true fieldsportsman. For the horseman the plains abounded with quarry for hounds or the spear; the game-filled jungles offered all the thrills and excitement which could fairly be craved by the keenest devotee of the pursuit of dangerous game; the mountains and valleys of the mighty Himalayan Range held unique trophies of superb quality, trophies which provided an irresistible challenge to the dedicated hill stalker; many of the rivers swarmed with fish of a size, power and fighting spirit that tested the skill of the ablest angler; and for the shotgunner, almost everywhere there were game birds which, in terms of variety and species, if not in numbers also, were unrivalled by any other region of the world. There was something for everyone and all of it virtually free for the taking, subject to universally respected game laws and a strict code of sporting ethics – while one of the highlights of the Indian fieldsports year was the traditional Christmas camp.

In India the Christmas week was at the height of the cold weather, a time of clear, bright sunny days followed by crisp, cold nights, and the traditional Christmas camps could vary from the spartan to the luxurious; from two or three simple tents nesting quietly in some shady and secluded grove, to a sprawl of spacious marquees clustered around a large inspection bungalow in a select forest block, the whole swarming with horses, dogs, Indian servants and a pad elephant or two, for all the world like a scene from the Crusades – except perhaps for the elephants!

It was to the prospect of my first Christmas camp (one of the humbler sort!) and also – as a keen wildfowler – to the allied prospect of experiencing India's fabled duck shooting, that I was eagerly looking forward when, early in October 1939, my friend Paul Coventry and I arrived in Lucknow, in the United Provinces of Agra and Oudh, to rejoin the main body of the 2nd Battalion of the Royal Berkshire Regiment in cantonments. In Europe this was the period of the 'phoney' war with little more than verbal abuse being fired by the main contestants; the disasters in Norway and Crete, the start of the campaigns in Africa, and even the shock of Dunkirk were yet to come. In India the only real war appeared to be the perennial guerilla campaigns which, at regular intervals, simmered and erupted on the North West Frontier, and life in Lucknow was still following the long established peacetime pattern.

For the six weeks prior to our return to Lucknow, Paul and I (both newly joined subalterns of the Unattached List, Indian Army) had been on detachment, with 'B' Company of the Regiment, enjoying the cool, pine-scented air and sybaritic foothills of the Himalayas. During that time I had been fortunate enough to outwit a stock-raiding panther and enjoy the thrills of shooting chukor almost in the shadow of the mighty Himalayan snow peaks of Trisul, Nanda Devi and Nanda Kot, which tower up to an awe-inspiring height of over 25,000 feet. Now I had almost literally come down to earth with a bump, for the ancient and turbulent city of Lucknow, with its blood-stained history of the Indian Mutiny, lies in the hot, arid, low-lying plains which stretch for hundreds of miles on either side of the course of India's holiest river, the Ganges.

The wide valley of the Ganges and its many tributaries is a buzzing hive of intensive peasant cultivation. This vast region is a patchwork quilt of irrigated paddy fields and small, mud-walled villages, the whole dotted with occasional

*Himalayan Village*

*Author playing in snow*

groves of carefully tended trees and – of vital importance to both villager and wildfowler – numerous *tanks* (dams), *jheels* (shallow, reed-fringed lakes) and peripheral marshland. To these bountiful feeding and resting grounds every year there came countless numbers of duck of over twenty different species, together with swarms of snipe and numerous geese, all from their breeding grounds in Kashmir, Central Asia and beyond.

The first arrivals heralded the end of the dreaded hot weather of the India

*A simple tented camp by the "Temple" Jhil near Lucknow.*

plains, with its torments of oven-like, airless nights and prickly heat and its plagues of ever hungry mosquitos and sandflies. The teal and garganey and the snipe came first, joining the resident population of spot-billed duck, whistling and cotton teals, and the semi-migratory comb duck. They were followed, as the weeks passed, by great flocks of gadwall, mallard, wigeon, pintail and red-crested pochard, with smaller numbers of shoveller, common pochard, tufted duck, marbled teal, and occasional rarities all sandwiched in between. The build-up was progressive and by the end of November most of the larger *jheels* and *dams* were black with wildfowl, but the old hands, the experienced *shikaris*, carefully conserved the best *jheels* for the traditional Christmas shoot.

Including Paul and myself, there were six impecunious young U.L.I.A. subalterns attached to the Royal Berkshires in October 1939, and we lived together like a litter of boisterous puppies – in a large, rambling cantonment bungalow, surrounded by our dogs and borrowed horses. Few of the Berkshires' own officers (three of whom bore the surnames 'Sweet', 'Salt' and

'Savery'!) shared our youthful enthusiasm for fieldsports, but this had its advantages as well as its disadvantages. It meant less pressure on the best shooting areas, but it also aggravated our main problem – lack of transport. One of the exceptions among the Berkshires' officers was John Hill, a kindred spirit and a valued friend and ally, but one who was tied by many regimental commitments. Twenty-five years later, after retiring from the army, *Colonel* John Hill (as he then was) became a director of first, Webley and Scott and then W. and C. Scott (Gunmakers) Ltd, and Chairman of both The Gun Trade Association and the Shooting Sports Trust; but in 1939, John Hill was a cheerful, able, but lowly lieutenant, as short of cash as the rest of us!

Our eventual saviour was a Sapper major in R.E.M.E. who had a large, open, American touring car into which he could cram, at a pinch, five passengers in addition to himself; he also had several small, light metal punts which were easily transportable and thus ideal for use on the *jheels*. Major James was a bachelor and a very keen shot who was delighted to discover several officers as keen as himself to make up shooting parties, even though they were all half his own age! With the Major, from mid-October to mid-December, we made regular forays after duck and snipe in various marshes and *jheels* around Lucknow, sometimes being joined by officers and men of the 1/3rd Q.A.O. Gurkha Rifles (my regiment to be) who had arrived in Lucknow before moving up to the North West Frontier. The best place we discovered during our week-end wanderings we called the 'Temple Jheel', and after a good reconnaissance shoot we decided to try to 'keep it on ice' as the site for our planned Christmas camp.

It was very early in the morning of Christmas Eve when five of us left Lucknow in Major James's car; it was so early, in fact, that the moon was still high in the sky, casting an eerie light across the nearby countryside. Over the long, straight road, which was raised several feet above the surrounding paddy fields, there hung a pall of dust from the grinding wheels of a long line of bullock carts, nose to tail, each cart drawn by a pair of doe-eyed oxen plodding slowly and patiently along while the driver slept soundly on the creaking shafts. To pass them at all on the narrow, dusty road, and at night, was hazardous, and with awful visions of being late for our carefully planned morning flight on the 'Temple Jheel', we shouted and cursed despairingly to clear the road. But our luck held. With a last frantic blast on the horn we passed the sleepy, open-mouthed driver at the head of the column and, as the blackness of the eastern

*The author with a brace of Shotbill*
*during a duck shoot on Christmas Day, 1940*

sky began to turn to a pearly grey, we pulled up under a small grove of big mango trees scarcely fifty yards from the western shore of the 'Temple Jheel.'

Everything was ready for us; tents pitched; punts at the water's edge; the bearded *shikari* (hunter guide) waiting expectantly by a flickering camp fire with a small group of shivering villagers who, with the prospect of fat, Christmas *baksheesh* (tips) dancing before their eyes, had eagerly volunteered to act as beaters and retrievers. Major James was an old campaigner and a good organiser.

Paul and the Major drew the long straw for the two punts, so the other two guns moved off to hide in the reeds. I had elected to remain ashore as I had my dog with me and this was to be his debut, his first full scale shoot. 'Wok' (short for the 'Jabberwock' of literary fame) was a busy talkative young golden cocker spaniel. I had obtained him as a pup, as soon as I arrived in India, from the famous gundog kennels of the Maharajah of Patiala. Now, at ten months, after careful training he was showing signs of being a useful little gundog and I was keen to give him a try.

The 'Temple Jheel' was a shallow, roughly oval-shaped lake of some 150 acres, lying in a wide, grassy plain dotted with trees and distant grazing cattle.

The lake was fringed with long grass and reeds which, in places, spread far out into the lake itself. At the northern end, where the *jheel* narrowed, the reeds grew thicker and there was a thin belt of shady acacias backed by gently rising ground, while here and there in the shallow water there were unexpected outcrops of rock. At the southern end there was a small village of mud-walled, thatch-roofed huts and a white-washed Hindu temple, whence the *jheel* took its name.

After a short search I found a half-submerged rock close by a clump of reeds at the northern end of the *jheel*. The rock was right in the open, but since duck decoys in Britain have always used a dog of Wok's colour to attract waterfowl, I decided to leave him sitting on the rock while I waded out to hide in the nearby reeds, accompanied by my other retriever, one of the villagers.

The sun was topping the horizon when, as arranged, the first shot was fired by the Major; it was followed by a prolonged roar of wings as hundreds of duck lifted from the open water in a dense, black cloud and then began to circle the *jheel* in small groups and at varying heights and speeds according to species. I crouched lower in the reeds, thigh deep in water, my faithful B.S.A 12 bore in my hands, my cartridges worn in a belt slung across my

*Paul Coventry (left) and Major James afloat on the 'Temple Jheel' during a duck shoot on Christmas Day, 1940*

*'Wok' waiting to retrieve from the 'Temple Jheel'*

chest like a Mexican bandit, fervently hoping that my khaki drill trousers – securely fastened at the ankles – would defeat any hungry leech.

Within minutes a pair of duck appeared over the reeds, travelling wide and fast. Seeing Wok they flared, only to reform and dive down for a closer look, giving me a very satisfactory right and left; it was a good start to the day, which boosted my confidence. They were spot-bill, the colour of a mallard duck but the size of a well-fed drake; perhaps a little large for an early retrieve by a young cocker spaniel, so I let the villager collect these, which he did with a broad grin and great, splashing bounds.

From then on the duck came thick and fast. Teal and garganey, followed by mallard and gadwall, shoveller and wigeon, pochard and tufted, and then another right and left, this time at pintail. For nearly an hour, helped by the villagers beating the reeds, the action was virtually continuous and my barrels grew almost too hot to hold; then suddenly it faded; the duck had departed for the safety of normally less favoured neighbouring *jheels* and it was time to pick-up.

I sent the villager back to the camp for more cartridges and then gave Wok a chance to prove his mettle. He had already showed his staunchness under fire, sitting on his exposed rock, quivering with excitement but not moving, while duck splashed into the water all around him. Now, plunging and swimming eagerly among the reeds, he proved to be an able little retriever. Some of the duck which had fallen far out in the open water defeated him, but that was my fault not his; he could not scent or see those birds and his hand-signal training still had far to go, so I waded out and collected them myself.

Scarcely half an hour later there was a sudden tearing sound high in the sky, followed by a sizzling rush of wings, a hiss and a splash as a flight of teal landed abruptly among the reeds, only to rocket skywards again at the sight of my crouching figure. The duck were back again from the surrounding *jheels*, but this time they were more wary, flying higher and in smaller parties. For the next hour or so the shooting went on steadily but at a more leisured pace. Finally, as midday approached, the firing ceased; the duck had finally departed for safer haunts. The only sound now was the distant slapping of wet cloth on stone as the village women did their daily laundry on the far shore. It was time for a final pick-up.

It took me a good half hour to collect my birds and my final count was 8

*Bruce G. Kinloch with 'Wok' (swimming)*
*shooting duck at Christmas on the 'Temple Jheel'*

teal, 5 garganey, 4 mallard, 4 shoveller, 3 gadwall, 2 pintail, 2 pochard, 2 spot-bill, one tufted and one wigeon, a total of 32 head. Not only was it the best bag of duck I have ever made in terms of sheer numbers, but also in the fascinating variety of species. When we had the final count in camp the total bag for the five guns was 83 teal and duck, 8 snipe, one comb duck, one pigeon – and one fox, which had been shot by an irate gun when it emerged from a belt of reeds with his only mallard clamped firmly in its jaws! On all counts it had been a glorious first Indian Christmas shoot which left me with vivid memories to recollect and savour.

I arrived back in Lucknow later on Boxing Day, to find an urgent message waiting for me; it was from Robert O'Lone, then Adjutant of the 1st Battalion of the 3rd Gurkha Rifles, and his note said:

The Battalion has just received orders to report, immediately, to the 3rd India Brigade, near Bannu, for operations in Waziristan.

Robert's note continued:

Apparently, a Pathan named Mehr Dil, one of the lieutenants of the notorious Faqir of Ipi[1], has been causing a lot of trouble in that part of Waziristan, where he is leading a big lashkar[2] of mixed Wazirs and Mahsuds, and 3rd Brigade have been instructed to sort him out.

The Battalion will be entraining on the Frontier Mail, the day after tomorrow, so please get yourself organised for a long spell on the Frontier. Report to Battalion H.Q. as soon as you can.

With mounting excitement, I put the note down and sat back, memories of my favourite uncle's vivid tales of active service with his Gurkhas, on the North West Frontier, filling my brain. Now it was to be my turn – but much sooner than I had expected!

---

[1]  Some say that the Faqir of Ipi was Waziristan's Osama Bin Laden of his day.

[2]  Guerilla force.

# Chapter IX

# Frontier Flash-back

From where I am sitting, relaxed and comfortable in our new Moorish style home high in the Andalucian coastal hills of the Sierra Cabrera, I can look out of two windows. From the window in front of me I gaze down on the deep azure blue of the Mediterranean, the wide expanse of its calm, blue waters gleaming invitingly in the warm sunshine and dotted with small white specks which are Spanish fishing boats from the little fishing harbour of Garrucha, a few miles up the coast.

If I swing round through ninety degrees however, I can see through another window and the contrast is striking. From this window I have to lean back and look up to see the jagged ridge-tops of the barren, rocky, sun-scorched hills which tower above our dwelling. They are so close that, even with the naked eye, I can see every gully, cave and crevice; and these barren hills remind me *so* strongly of the North West Frontier of India, that – with the flick of an eyelid – my thoughts flash back just over forty three years to

*Shell Bursting during the attack on the summit of Ahmedzai Saliant*

*A Pathan Sniper*

February, 1940, and the 'Battle of the Gumatti Tangi' in North Waziristan, which was watched (believe it or not!) by people sitting in deck chairs on the roof of Bannu Club, drinking pink gins and exchanging binoculars, tactical advice and reminiscences of other frontier campaigns.

So powerful is the resemblance that, with no effort at all, I can virtually 'see' – yet again – the small, stocky figures of my Gurkha riflemen climbing, ant-like, slowly but steadily up the rocky, precipitous slopes, while the hills around them echo and re-echo with the irregular but menacing and potentially deadly rifle-fire of well hidden Pathan snipers, the 'TOK D-O-O-O-NG, TOK D-O-O-O-NG' of the snipers' rifle shots mixing with the echoing roar of the shells of the 3.7 inch mountain guns (mule-borne, Kipling's 'screw guns'!) bursting on the ridge-tops in plumes of grey-black smoke; and all the time the deep rattle of long, steady bursts of heavy machine-gun fire – the covering fire of the Vickers guns – and the short, sharp, staccato bursts of light machine-guns as the Gurkhas flushed the wild Wazirs and Mahsuds from their ambush points among the rocks.

Occasionally, there would be savage cries and the flash of kukris and Pathan knives in the sunlight as the Gurkhas closed in for the kill – quick, efficient, but inevitably bloody.

The enemy, at the time, was a Pathan by the name of Mehr Dil – one of the most active Lieutenants of the notorious Fakir of Ipi, who had been stirring up trouble against the British along the Frontier for a number of years – and his 'Lashkar' (guerrilla army) of a thousand or so well-armed and fanatical Wazirs and Mahsuds – with a renegade Afghan 'doctor' whome we later identified among the dead!

Meh Dil had established his operational base in the barren, rugged hills of the Ahmedzai Salient in North Waziristan, cunningly sited astride the deep gorge of the Grumatti Tangi, close to the border with British India. From there Mehr Dil and his 'lashkar' had been raiding down into the plains, until eventually they cut the metre-gauge railway line between Mari-Indus and Bannu – which was just *too* much for the sorely-tried patience of the British frontier authorities, for this was the main supply-line for many of the British military garrisons, stationed in lonely outposts among the rugged hills, and charged with the difficult task of controlling the wild Pathans in their tribal territory and keeping the King Emperor's peace along the length and breadth of the North West Frontier.

*A Gurkha position*

*3rd Queen Alexandra's Own Gurkha Rifles on the North West Frontier in the 1930s.*

By kind permission of the Gurkha Museum, Winchester.

*Gurkha Outpost on road above Bannu*

So, a punitive expedition was launched (the troops involved including my battalion, the 1st Battalion of the 3rd, Queen Alexandra's Own, Gurkha Rifles) to teach Mehr Dil a sharp lesson and drive him and his rapacious guerilla army from their fortress stronghold in the towering hills of the Gumatti Tangi – a site deliberately and audaciously chosen (with typical Mehr Dil bravado!) because it virtually overlooked the administrative and military base of Bannu, one of the gateways to the tantalising riches of the plains of India – fat, wealthy babus with their hordes of rupees and bejewelled, nubile women.

At the time, I had a marvellous Commanding Officer, the late Lt-Colonel McKay-Forbes, who had an infectious sense of humour and was a very keen and very good game-bird shot. He had issued a battalion standing order that if *anyone* came upon a covey of chukor or sisi (a small, *very* fast flying hill partridge) *anywhere* and at *any* time, an immediate signal should be sent to Battalion H.Q. where he kept his shotgun on one of the mules of the Intelligence Section. I myself was then a very newly joined subaltern, but an equally keen game shot, and I kept *my* shotgun on one of my Company H.Q.

mules (sadly, the Japs got that treasured gun in the Sittang River Battle in Burma, two years later!).

At the height of the Gumatti Tangi battle, my Gurkha orderly and I put up a small covey of chukor from the slopes of a ridge which we were clearing, but they only flew a short distance round the shoulder of the ridge and settled among the rocks. Obeying orders to the letter, I instructed my Gurkha signaller to send an appropriate message, in morse (by flat), to Battalion H.Q. in the valley below; and within a few minutes, I saw the tall figure of McKay-Forbes, followed closely by his stock Gurkha orderly carrying his Colonel's shotgun, strolling calmly up the hill towards me.

"Get your gun and we'll walk 'em up, Bruce", the Colonel said, when he reached me! I obeyed with alacrity, and as the thunder of battle raged amongst the hills around us, we fanned out and walked-up the covey as if we had been on a Scottish grouse moor in August! The covey eventually got up with a whirr and swung away down the hillside. McKay-Forbes dropped two birds stone dead with a clean right and left, while I myself – affected by the excitement and the tension – missed clean with both barrels!

As the flat echoes of our shotgun blasts died away, drowned by the main thunder of battle, I heard a faint and distant cheer. Looking up to the highest ridge, I saw the small figure of a lone Gurkha rifleman standing on top of a strong stone sanghar; in one hand he held a gleaming kukri, with the other he was triumphantly waving a strange flag bearing the Moslem symbol of a sickle moon – it was the banner of Mehr Dil; barring necessary mopping-up, the 'Battle of the Gumatti Tangi' was over!

This morning I walked a few hundred yards up onto a ridge overlooking the site where our house has been built. Below me, my Springer Spaniel, 'Dee', working the hillside, put up a covey of eight 'chukor' (Spanish version!) which shirred away round the shoulder of the hill. Immediately my mind went into reverse for forty odd years – and there I was, back in Waziristan, trying to choose the best positions for my piquets and straining to see how high my Gurkha rifle sections would reach before being shot at by the watching Pathan.

With a conscious effort I turned round and looked down on the blue of the Mediterranean. Some of the little sardine boats were hurrying back to port after their long night's fishing, the foaming white of their wakes sparking in the early morning sun. Slowly my mind came back to the present – and reality!

*Mehr Dil's Banner*

I wrote the above brief account of the battle for the Gumatti Tangi, the entrance to the Ahmedzai Saliet, shortly after Elizabeth, my wife, and I had moved to Spain in April, 1983. We were then living in a ranch-style house, built to our own design, which nestled in the hills between the small, white, hilltop township of Mojacar and the fishing village of Garrucha, which lies far below on the Andalucian coast of Spain.

This story, first published in *'Shooting Times and Country Magazine'* in February, 1984, is an account of my own first experience, as a very young subaltern, of warfare on India's turbulent North West Frontier. It was also my first experience of being on the receiving end of a great deal of uncomfortably accurate sniper fire!

As a staunch devotee of the works of Rudyard Kipling, I had rather expected this, for I had long been aware of the reputation of the Pathan tribesmen as being supremely accurate marksmen. Since all of them are almost literally born with a rifle in their hands, they could hardly be expected to be much else! Kipling brings these facts to light in his famous poem *'Arithmetic on the Frontier'*, in one verse of which he wrote:

'A scrimmage in a Border station –
a canter down some dark defile –
two thousand pounds of education
drops to a ten rupee *jezail*[1]
the Crammer's boast, the Squadron's pride,
shot like a rabbit in a ride!

I find the above verse particularly poignant because, on September 29th, 1879, during the 2nd Afghan War, one of my great uncles, Major Francis Garden Kinloch of the Gordon Highlanders, but then attached to the 5th Bengal Cavalry, was killed in just such an action at Thal, on the Kurram River, on India' North West Frontier, close to the Afghan border.

It so happened that, early in May, 1940, during the closing stages of the Gumatti Tangi battle, having led a fighting patrol up the Kurram River, I found myself close to Thal. As soon as I reached this part of the Upper Kurram valley, a region of steep, rocky hills, and deep, scrub covered valleys, it dawned on me how easy it would have been for the wild Pathan tribesmen of this area, to ambush my uncle and his troop of cavalry *sowars.*[2] It was a sobering thought.

I found no sign of hostile action during my fighting patrol and, shortly after I had reported back to my Battalion, it was officially announced by the Army Commander, General Sir John Coleridge, that, as Intelligence reports confirmed that all remnants of Mehr Dil's forces had finally disappeared from the region, the Ahmedzai Salient operation – an always difficult and sometimes hazardous mission – was now considered to have been successfully concluded, for which he had to both congratulate and also thank all the forces involved.

The Force Commander, Brigadier Barstow, then said, in his farewell message, that he hoped that whenever he raised his standard again, the 3rd Gurkha Rifles would be his main support! After receiving this flattering accolade, my Battalion was ordered to move to Razani, a tented perimeter camp some 15 miles east of the military base of Razmak, where, during the long years of their rule in India, the British had maintained a permanent strike force, ready

---

[1]   A long-barrelled musket once used by Pathans and Afghans.

[2]   A trooper of the India Cavalry, from the Persian 'sawar', a horseman.

and prepared for rapid deployment in the event of any serious hostile action by the turbulent Pathan tribes of South Waziristan.

Our main role of Razani, a duty which we shared with the 1st Battalion of the Worcestershire Regiment, was defined as 'Road Protection'. This, in turn, involved the establishing, twice a week, of a protective screen of troopers in the hills above a long stretch of the motor road linking Razmak with Bannu, its supply base at railhead, some 50 miles to the north east. These occasions were referred to as 'Road Open' days, when convoys of lorries carrying supplies and troops, in both directions between Bannu and Razmak, could do so in comparative safety, free from the otherwise inevitable ambush by the ever watchful and trigger-happy Pathan tribesmen of North Waziristan. For them, the ambushing of any government forces was as much a national sport as football is to the British!

Some additional protection for convoys on 'Road Open' days was provided (in theory at least!) by permanent picquets, manned by *Khassadars,*[3] strategically placed at various commanding points above the motor roads concerned. The only real danger in relying too much on this particular system of protection was that, just occasionally, a 'target' would appear that the ever-itching trigger fingers of the watching *Khassadars* would find it impossible to resist! We experienced just that sort of occasional shortly after my Battalion moved to Razani.

At the centre of Razani camp, there was a small parade ground which doubled as a site for both a basketball pitch and also, from time to time, the screen for a temporary outdoor cinema, the latter operating mainly when British troops were stationed at the camp. A few days after our own arrival, the 'powers that be' decided to show a very dramatic 'Wild West' style film depicting the famous American film actor, Douglas Fairbanks, in mortal combat with hundreds of North American Indians of the Sioux tribe. Suddenly, at a critical point in the film, when Douglas was about to be felled by a Sioux warrior wielding a tomahawk, there was a rapid series of ear split-ting, high pitched 'cracks' as the screen was riddled by a volley of rifle shots!

Instantly, every light in the camp was dowsed and the 'Stand To' sounded while the hillsides above the camp were anxiously searched with binoculars

---

[3]  Armed tribal levies loosely controlled by British Political Officers.

for any signs of movement in the moonlight – but to no avail. However, one of the *Khassadar* picquets had already aroused our suspicions and we warned our sentries to be fully on the alert, in case there was to be a surprise attack, similar to the one that Mehr Dil's mixed force of Wazirs and Mahsuds, had made on my Battalion at Kurram Garhi, near Bannu, just before the start of the Ahmedzai Salient operations, earlier in the year.

Nothing further happened that night, but when the Political Officer responsible for the region visited Razani a couple of days later, we told him all about the incident and of our suspicions that a particular group of *Khassadars* could well have been the culprits. The Political officer took our report very seriously, promising a full investigation followed by appropriate action to deal with this most serious problem.

The Political Officer was as good as his word; he had an astute mind and a fertile imagination which led him not only to discover the truth but also to solve the problem in a simple but most effective way. Two weeks after the first sniping incident, our cinema screen at Razani was again the night time target of a volley of rifle fire, this time however there was no possible doubt as to where the shots were coming from. Our shrewd Political Officer, when replacing the diminished stock of ammunition held at the *Khassadar* post immediately above Razani, had left them with several packets of 'tracer' cartridges. So, half a dozen arcs of light leading from the cinema screen to the *Khassadar* post left no one in any doubt as to where the shots were coming from!

We heard later, that the *Khassadars* concerned, who were both heavily fined and summarily dismissed, had complained bitterly that the way in which they had been discovered was quite contrary to their concept of the ethics of Frontier warfare!

During the long years of the British Raj, law and order and the 'King's Peace', along the length and breadth of India's frequently turbulent North West Frontier, was initially maintained with the help of lightly armed and very mobile militia units of the Frontier Corps, named as 'Scouts'. Thus, for South Waziristan's Mahsud country, there were the South Waziristan Scouts, which became the Tochi Scouts, based on Miranshah in the Tochi Valley, for North Waziristan's Wazir region.

Further north again, the various 'Scouts' units became first the 'Zhob Militia', then the 'Chitral Scouts' and, finally, right up north on India's border with the Sinkiang Province of China, there were the 'Gilgit Scouts'.

But, of all of these various 'Scouts' units, I myself only became personally involved with the Tochi Scouts, when, at the beginning of August, 1940, I was ordered to take my Gurkha rifle company to assume control of the 'Beau Geste' style Tochi Scout fort of Dosalli, on the Bannu to Razmak road, ten miles north east of Razani.

The officers of the various 'Scouts' units of the Frontier Corps were each and all of them volunteers, seconded, for various tours of duty, from their parent regiments in the regular India Army. This system, which certainly produced a keen, efficient and dedicated Frontier officer corps, also resulted, from time to time, in some unexpected anomalies. This was because the Frontier 'Scouts', unlike the India Army, were classified as 'Civil Armed Forces'. So, when I reported for duty with my rifle company, at Dosalli Fort, I was not surprised to find myself (then a very young and inexperienced lieutenant), talking to a Tochi Scouts captain, who was much senior to me both in age and length of service – yet it was I who, *theoretically*, was now in command of Dosalli Fort!

During the month that I was in Dosalli, the Fort was occupied, in addition to my company of Gurkhas, by a company of Tochi Scouts of the Tori Khel Wazir tribe (commanded by the captain whom I have just mentioned), plus a troop of armoured cars from the Scinde Horse, commanded by a very recently commissioned 2nd Lieutenant. Over that month there were eight 'Road Open Days' all of which passed without any serious incident, but for me, personally, one of these 'Road Open Days' happened to be particularly notable, since it was on August 27th, 1940, my 21st birthday!

Far away from both kith and kin and even old friends, I had planned to celebrate this notable event in the fleshpots of Srinagar, in nearby Kashmir, the traditional playground for officers serving on the North West Frontier. In fact, I had already applied for the necessary ten days leave, which only started and also ended when crossing the River Indus. In the event, there had been a frontier 'scare' and the only missive I received on my 21st birthday, was a helio message, flashed over the hills from my Battalion in Razani, which read 'For Kinloch in Dosalli STOP Many happy returns! STOP Regret all leave stopped! STOP.' So, in the event, I celebrated my 21st birthday, in the company of the Tochi Scout Captain and the Scinde Horse subaltern, over a bottle of Johnny Walker whisky, in the monastic seclusion of a Tochi Scout fort on India's North West Frontier!

*The author riding in a drag hunt*

The unusual and somewhat unfortunate series of circumstances, which finally led to the celebrating of my 21st birthday taking place at a Tochi Scout Fort in North Waziristan, inevitably feature prominently in my memory of the North West Frontier. However, prior place in my 'memory bank' of the Frontier, must undoubtedly go to a most dramatic event which happened at the garrison post of Wana, in South Waziristan, just over a month later.

In September, 1940, my Battalion was ordered to move from Rozani to Wana, which, being virtually a carbon copy of Razmak in North Waziristan, was a military base housing a permanent strike force, which was always ready for rapid deployment in the event of hostile action by the Mahsuds, the dominant tribe of South Waziristan.

When my Battalion arrived in Wana from Razani, in North Waziristan, South Waziristan was still in the midst of an exceptionally long period of comparative peace, tranquillity and freedom from any form of tribal unrest or insurrection. So much so, that the troops forming the garrison in Wana at that time, which included a number of Frontier veterans, had been lulled into a false sense of comparative security. Despite their past experience, these troops had forgotten the first and most important rule of frontier warfare – never to be seen to be in the habit of doing anything, in the same manner, and at the same time, on any particular day of the week. In order words, never to be observed to be operating to any fixed pattern.

Wana, in 1940, boasted a flourishing drag hunt, organised and run, very efficiently, by the officers of a Mountain Gun battery. This hunt, which, like the rest of the Wana garrison, had been lulled into a false sense of security had, for some time, been operating to a fixed programme, moving out of the perimeter camp on the same day of the week, at about the same time of day and frequently out of the same gate. Then, on one particular day, shortly after my own Battalion arrived in Wana, nemesis struck!

A few hundred yards from the perimeter camp the hunt was ambushed by a gang of Mahsud tribesmen. Their first volley killed two horses, the riders being thrown but luckily not injured. Immediately and as we watched, fascinated, before our eyes four of the other riders staged a spectacular rescue; two of them galloped up to each of the fallen riders, scooped up the dazed men by their arms and then, with the dismounted riders dangling between them, galloped back to the safety of the camp under the covering fire of the perimeter machine guns. By a miracle no other horse or rider was injured!

*That* is a scene I shall *never* forget!

# Chapter X

# To the High Himalayas

The morning of September 12th, 1940, found me in Kashmir, perched uncomfortably on a wooden bench seat in an old and rickety Indian bus, rattling slowly southwards down the road that leads from Srinagar to Jammu. To the east and north the sky was filled with the towering massif of the mighty Himalayan Range, while to the west and south of the road sprawled the impressive ridges and crags of the Pir Panjal, some of its jagged peaks topping 16,000 feet.

I had three fellow passengers in the bus; there was my *Shikari* (hunter guide), a lean, bearded and dour Kashmiri of indeterminate age, with a deep cleft – like an axe blow – in his left temple, caused (so he claimed!) by a glancing blow from a bear's paw; then there was the *Shikari's* large and cheerful young assistant; finally there was a third Kashmiri, a jovial Friar Tuck of a man who doubled as camp cook and personal bearer. This was my temporary retinue supplied, at very short notice, by an agent in Srinagar from whom I had also hired the bus and the clutter of tents, cooking pots and camp gear which filled the back of it. It was the start of my first ever hunt for *Ursus torquatus*, the Himalayan black bear – or for any species of Himalayan big game for that matter.

If it was to stand any reasonable chance of success, a hunting trip in the Himalayas, in those days, normally called for adequate time preceeded by careful thought and meticulous planning weeks if not months in advance. In contrast, the launching of my own first hunting trip in the Himalayas could hardly have been more rushed and muddled and the events leading up to it less propitious, for … but let me start at the beginning!

January 1st 1940, my Batallion, the 1/3rd Q.A.O. Gurkha Rifles, had moved to the North West Frontier for the Ahmedzai Salient operations in North Waziristan. From then on the Batallion had been continuously engaged in active operations in that turbulent region, and as a keen but raw and very young subaltern of not quite twenty-one years, I myself had revelled in my first experience of soldiering on the Frontier. But, after seven months of active campaigning in the exacting conditions, harsh climate and savage terrain of Waziristan, even my youthful appetite for the excitements of border skirmishing had become a little jaded and my thoughts had begun to turn to the well known pleasures of the fleshpots of Kashmir, the Frontier's traditional playground. So, near the end of August when I was on a month's detachment with the Tochi Scouts, I had applied for ten days local leave, my object being a delayed celebration of my 21st birthday which I had spent in the monastic seclusion of Dosalli, a Beau Geste style Tochi Scout fort deep in Tribal Territory. For once – and strange for me – all thoughts of shooting and fishing had receeded to the back of my mind!

Scarcely had my leave been approved when it had been cancelled, the reason given being a security alert somewhere in Waziristan. However, within a fortnight the threat had receeded, my leave had been restored, and I had arrived in Srinagar expecting to meet a friend from the 16th Punjab Regiment; instead there was a telegram from my friend saying his leave had been cancelled. That had been my second hiccup and, after only two days on a houseboat on Nagin Bagh, I had reluctantly concluded that I had not been long enough on the frontier properly to appreciate the traditional pleasures of Srinagar. But, since leave from the Frontier commenced and ended on crossing the Indus River, the boundary of the North West Frontier Province, it had meant that I still had six clear days to enjoy in Kashmir, so I had decided to get out and see what the country was like and (yes!) try to get some shooting.

In Srinagar agents and outfitters were two-a-penny; most were sharp, some were charletans, a few were good. 'Try Bahar Shah and Son at the third bridge,' I had been advised and I had not regretted doing so. The firm had greeted me with cheerful and efficient courtesy, and in no time at all they had fixed up an excellent *bandobast* (arrangement) for a hunt for Himalayan black bear. There had been only one major problem – I had brought no rifle with me!

"We can lend you this one, *Sahib*", Bahar Shah had said, offering me a .315 (8mm x 56) Mannlicher-Schonauer carbine and a packet of cartridges. I had examined them both doubtfully; the carbine's barrel showed patches of rust and it looked old and tired, the cartridges even more so. On a nearby range three hangfires and a misfire had then confirmed my worst suspicions and I had been thankful that my target had not been a large and angry bear. Finally and with a flourish Bahar Shah had produced a very nice, long barrelled .280 Ross – which some trusting officer had left in his safekeeping! And so, on the morning of the fourth day of my leave, I had set off in my hired bus, full of high hopes, heading for Qazigund, some 60 miles south of Srinagar, an area which my *Shikari* had sworn to be a favourite haunt of the Himalayan black bear.

Sadly for our treasured childhood fantasies, the popular image of all bears as amiable, ambling animals, with endearing human traits, harmless, innocent creatures gentle by nature and simple of mind – an image fostered from the nursery by the vintage cult of the teddy bear and its numerous progeny such as Winnie-the-Pooh and Paddington Bear – is no more than an anthropo-morphic myth. In fact, and in its homeland in particular, the Himalayan black bear for one has an evil reputation for being of uncertain temper, savage when roused, quick to attack, immensely powerful and quite unpredictable, a beast which will not hesitate to kill or inflict terrible injuries on any luckless peasant who may stumble upon it unawares. Not for nothing has the bear long been the recognised symbol of Soviet Russia!

To add to its unpopularity, the Himalayan black bear, in the areas in which it occurs, is a serious and ever present threat to both crops and domestic stock;

*Shikari (Hunter)*

it is an omnivorous feeder with catholic tastes ranging from wild roots, berries and honey, to cultivated maize, fruit and nuts, from grubs and rodents in the forest, to domestic goats, sheep and even cattle and ponies. Savage and strong, sharp of sight and keen of hearing and with remarkable powers of scent, swift of foot and an excellent swimmer, all in all the Himalayan black bear is a formidable adversary and many a Kashmiri hillman who has been lucky enough to survive an encounter with *Ursus torquatus*, carries to his grave the marks of the bear's terrible claws – a crippled shoulder or a face disfigured for life. It is small wonder that the peasants of the hill villages regard the black bear not merely as an unwelcome pest, but as a dangerous menace to be eliminated whenever and wherever possible. As we approached Qazigund, with its mainly terraced maize fields, I began to see for myself unmistakable signs that the black bear's evil reputation was well deserved.

A few miles from our destination, an old fakir in long white robes and with a flowing henna beard stepped into the road and waved to us to stop. Courteously he requested a lift and my *Shikari* helped him aboard. "Where is the *Sahib* going?" he asked. My *Shikari* told him, adding that I was looking for black bear. "Will the *Sahib* get any bear?" my *Shikari* concluded, having implicit faith in the all-seeing eye of the holy man. The latter did not immediately reply, but spread some pebbles on the bench seat beside him and studied them intently. Just before we reached Qazigund the old man signalled us to stop; climbing down from the bus he *salaamed* politely and turning to my *Shikari* he said gravely – "The *Sahib* will shoot two bears on his third day." Then, with a final courteous *salaam*, he walked slowly away.

That evening we made camp in the shade of some walnut trees close to a small stream and my *Shikari* went off to do a reconnaissance and gather information from the local villagers. Long after dark he returned with the news that several bears had been raiding the maize fields near the village for the past week. The bears were very bold, the villagers had reported, and feeding at night the greedy animals had eaten or damaged much of the crop. We would go out at dawn, my *Shikari* said, and intercept the bears as they left the maize fields to return to lie up and rest in the wooded ravines during the hours of daylight.

The next day we sallied forth at dawn and searched miles of maize fields, and again at dusk until the moon rose, but we neither saw nor heard a sign of a bear. The following day the pattern was the same and that evening in

*The big bear had a really massive head*

*The Big Black Bear surrounded by the beaters*

camp we held a council of war. The *Shikari* opined that the bears, having gorged themselves for days on ripening maize, had – temporarily at least – retired to the hills and found food to their liking in the bush-filled ravines. Since I then had only one spare day left (my third and last in the Qazigund camp) the *Shikari* recommended that the next day we should resort to driving the neighbouring hillsides and ravines. I was in no position either to disagree or argue, so, very early the following morning, the *Shikari* assembled a dozen villagers armed with knives, axes and staves, and we moved off into the nearby hills.

The first beat was a noisy one, with shouts, whistles and the rattling of sticks; the villagers knew what could happen if they surprised a drowsy bear and they were taking no chances. The hillside was cut by a deep ravine; I was on one side of it, the beaters on the other. I was thinking of the warning that a hunter should never get below a bear, when suddenly a black shape appeared bounding through the bushes on the opposite slope. For a brief moment the bear halted in a clearing, the white crescent on its chest gleaming like an aiming mark as it sniffed the air, but at the sound of my shot it rolled out of sight with a deep growl. I had scarcely had time to reload when there was a crashing in the bushes on the slope above and the bear bounded into view again only a few paces from me. I just had time to leap aside and fire blindly into its shoulder as the angry animal tore past me to disappear into the dense bush beyond, leaving me not a little shaken!

The *Shikari* took some time to organise the second beat, for before that could start we had tried to track the bear I had hit. To begin with there had been a few widely scattered drops of blood, but these had soon petered out in the dense bush and reluctantly we had been forced to give up. The second beat, when it started, was quieter and for nearly an hour I saw nothing. Then, suddenly and without warning, on the hillside only fifty yards below me appeared an enormous bear. It seemed to materialise from nowhere, but in a flash the 140 grain, copper pointed bullet from the .280 Ross, travelling at 2,900 feet a second, was on its way. I literally saw the fur fly as the bullet caught the beast behind the shoulder; slowly the bear's legs crumpled beneath it and it never moved again.

The bear turned out to be a very old and very large male, 6 feet 8 inches from nose to rump and with a really massive head. The villagers gathered round examining the animal closely and chattering excitedly. The old bear was well known, they said, and they rejoiced because he had been a cattle killer who had also mauled three men, one of them fatally.

In no time at all the big bear had been skinned and by early afternoon we were back in camp; there I found that my hired bus had already arrived and was waiting to transport me and my entourage back to Srinagar. The *Shikar* had insisted on sending his assistant to find and skin the other bear, guided by villagers who knew some caves much favoured by these animals. Unlike me, the *Shikari* had implicit faith in the holy man's predictions; he was quite convinced that my first bear was dead and he had instructed his assistant to bring the skin to Srinagar by the next bus or lorry which passed Qazigund.

The following afternoon, before laving Kashmir, I called at Bahar Shah's premises to settle my account, return the rifle, and arrange for the curing and forwarding of the skin of the big bear. To my surprise, awaiting me was my *Shikari's* assistant. With a grin he picked up a heavy sack and emptied its contents at my feet; it was the glossy, black pelt of my first bear!

Before I left Bahar Shah's office I had one final surprise. On his desk I had noticed a small but ornate tray of a strange and irregular shape and made of papier maché (a craft for which Kashmir has long been famous) it was coated with gold leaf and decorated with the heads of Himalayan big game; the pictures of ibex, markhor, barasingh, wild sheep and bear looked strangely familiar. "My father told me that he had made two of these trays to the order of an *Officer Sahib*," observed Bahar Shah, himself an elderly man, in response to my query. "He said that the *Sahib* took one tray but never came back for the other," Bahar Shah went on, reaching for an old and dusty ledger. "That was over sixty years ago, *Sahib*," the old man continued, opening the ledger and turning it towards me, his gnarled fore-finger pointing at a carefully penned name. 'A.A.A. Kinloch', I read; without knowing it I had crossed my grandfather's old trail, for the pictures on the tray were from his famous book '*Large Game Shooting in Thibet, the Himalayas, Northern and Central India*'!

When I left Kashmir the bizarre tray went with me, a treasured reminder of my grandfather's colourful travels and my own first ever hunt for big game in the Himalayas.

# Chapter XI

# Tiger, Tiger

*Tyger! Tyger! burning bright,*
*In the forests of the night,*
*What immortal hand or eye*
*Could frame thy fearful symmetry?*

So wrote the poet William Blake nearly two hundred years ago, vivid words which reflect the deep feelings of awe and admiration, and frequently of fear, which that magnificent animal the tiger has aroused in the human breast since time immemorial, emotions which are felt most strongly amongst those simple peasant folk whose lot it is to lead their daily lives in close proximity to and often in deadly fear of the tiger.

But what do we know of this great cat to which, in 1758, the amazing scientist, Linnaeus gave the scientific name of *Felis tigris*, only to have it changed to *Panthera tigris* two centuries later when the world's taxonomists indulged in a veritable orgy of re-classification! According to that great zoologist R. Lydekker, writing at the beginning of the last century, the geographical range of the tiger extends from the Caucasus through Northern Persia (now Iran), India, Assam, Burma, and the Malay Peninsular to the Malay Islands, China, Manchuria and Korea. Surprisingly, the tiger has never occurred in Ceylon, the assumption being that – in terms of evolutionary time – the tiger is a comparatively recent immigrant from the north or east into the Indian sub-continent; there it is found from Cape Comorin in the south to the Himalayas in the north, where it often reaches heights of 7,000 feet or more above sea level.

In my book it is the elephant which should be dubbed 'King of the Beasts', and not the lion, but it is also my contention that even the title of 'Crown Prince' should be awarded not to the lion but to the tiger. To my mind the lion, in his legendary regal role, is no more than a poseur, an idle lay-about who leaves it to his numerous wives and acolytes to supply food for the royal banquet table, while he, as often as not, whiles away the hours lounging in the shade of some spreading thorn tree, eating, sleeping and looking bored. Not so the tiger who is himself a beast of restless action; a mighty hunter, stronger and more handsome than the lion, he hunts alone or with his tigress – for him only one consort at a time – and when he hunts the jungle trembles and is still. No, when it comes to a choice as to which is the more deserving of an accolade of royalty, to my way of thinking there is no contest between the tiger and the lion. Even the elephant, which in Africa treats the lion with contempt, in Asia faces the tiger not with deference but with caution and respect.

Nowadays, to mention shooting a tiger in India is guaranteed to produce instant reactions of horror and condemnation expressed at maximum decibels by usually well-meaning but frequently ill-informed members of the cuddly bunny brigade to them, judging and pontificating from the comfort and security of their urban or suburban homes, far removed from the harsh realities at the scene of action, deliberately to kill a tiger is a crime second only to infanticide. But then they have never had to watch in horror while, in front of their very eyes, a cattle-killer takes their only cow, or crouch helpless night after night in a fragile hut, shivering with terror as from the outer darkness the heavy breathing of a man-eater sounds through the flimsy walls.

Major-General James Elliott, in his fine book '*Field Sports in India*', writes '… a cattle killer … can so easily become a man-eater. He can cause complete communities to desert their villages and move away. In the mid 1860s, the heyday of the years of plenty, tigers in Bengal along were killing over 2,000 people a year and there were neighbourhoods where it was a question of whether tiger or man would prevail: and sometimes the tiger won.' Even in 1947, the year of India independence, there were still an estimated 70,000 tigers in India, necessitating regular control of their numbers, but twenty-five years later their numbers had dwindled to a mere 2,000 through excessive hunting and poaching, and destruction of their habitat. However, at the time of which I write tigers were still common and often a problem in the India sub-continent.

Between 1939 and 1947, I had a number of encounters with tigers. In one instance, during a jungle fowl beat in the Deccan, a large tiger came out of the jungle scares ten paces from me. I was only armed with a shotgun loaded with No 6s, so I stood still and held my breath, eventually letting it go with a deep, pent-up sigh of relief when the tiger, after studying me with a long and scornful look, gave a contemptuous flick of its tail and strolled slowly away. On another occasion, when I was out with a fighting patrol in the Chin Hills on the Burma border and bivouacked for the night in wet, leech-ridden hill jungle at 7,000 feet, I awoke to find the deep pug marks of a tiger which had circled my sleeping form! But my first encounter with a tiger took place in December 1940, at which time my batallion was based in Wana, South Waziristan, on India's turbulent North West Frontier.

It all started with a letter from my cousin, David Davis, then Chief Conservator of Forests of the United Provinces and a keen and experienced *shikari* (hunter). 'I have reserved a very good forest block near Pilibhit for our Christmas camp,' he wrote. 'Do join us if you can get some leave, and bring a friend with you if you would like to. There are plenty of jungle fowl and peafowl, and there is a good chance of a tiger as a pair of them in the block have started killing cattle. In fact, last week the tigress killed and partially ate a cattle herder and thus have got to be dealt with. So, if you have a suitable rifle bring it, as well as your shotgun.'

When I applied for ten days leave, the officers' mess of the 3rd Gurkha Rifles buzzed with envious comment. The Christmas camps of senior Forest Officers were famous for their efficiency, comfort and lavish hospitality; there were nearly always several trained elephants in attendance and the sport was invariably of the highest order, so invitations were much sought after. Very young subalterns are normally seen but not heard in any regiment, so I was pleasantly surprised suddenly to find myself unusually popular. I was showered with friendly offers of drinks and advice and I had some difficulty in selecting an appropriate hunting companion, but my real problem was a suitable rifle. Eventually, Major Bradford, the Second-in-Command (a kindly man and a gallant solder who was killed in the Battle of the Sittang River in Burma just over a year later) came to my rescue; he offered me his very nice Rigby .350 Magnum magazine rifle which, with a soft-nosed 225 grain bullet at a muzzle velocity of 2625 feet per second, was a suitable weapon for tiger, if not an ideal one.

After a long journey from the Frontier, first by motor convoy and then by rail, my friend and brother officer Austin Price and I arrived at Pilibhit, in the far north of the United Provinces, two days before Christmas. David Davis's

*As dawn breaks the hunt begins*

camp, only some thirty miles from the foothills of the Himalayas, exceeded my expectations; set in a wide expanse of beautiful sal forest, much of it like open parkland dotted with herds of chital (or spotted deer), the camp consisted of a number of large tents and marquees clustered about a forest inspection bungalow like chicks around a mother hen; and when we first saw it, on the evening of our arrival, there were three pad elephants being given a drink from a water pump and India servants were hurrying purposefully in every direction. The guests, in addition to members of the family, were a cheerful and interesting mixture of military and civilians, and prospects for a convivial Christmas looked bright!

Immaculately clad in well pressed Khaki bush jacket and shorts, a habitual pipe clenched firmly between his teeth, David Davis himself had met us a Pilibhit railway station. His tall, lean figure towering over my stocky little Gurkha orderly, Rifleman Dilbahadur Thapa, David had greeted us warmly before leading the way to his battered old Chevrolet; and as the miles had sped by on the long, dusty drive to the camp, David had told us more about the tigers mentioned in his letter.

The tigers had last killed a cow the previous week, in a village near the

*Off after tiger!*
*left to right: the author's Gurkha orderly, Austin Price, the author and the mahout*

northern end of the forest block, David had said, swerving past a lurching bullock cart; he had therefore tied-up baits in that part of the jungle, which he was now keeping free from disturbance by confining the Christmas bird shoots to the southern section of the block, a good three miles from the baits and conveniently close to the camp around the forest bungalow. The baits, of which there were three, were young buffaloes purchased from the villagers; these were firmly tethered at strategic points in the jungle – such as known nullah crossings and junctions of well used forest tracks – and visited, fed and watered every morning and evening. To date, David had concluded, none of the baits had been touched and there had been no further signs of the tigers, but this was not particularly surprising, he had added, as there was plenty of natural prey in the block.

*The author (then just 20) on his first man-eater hunt!*

Over the next two days we enjoyed some excellent bird shooting. Driven jungle fowl are as testing as any pheasant, while a peacock, hurtling over the treetops with the wind in his tail, looks like a heavy jet bomber with its after-burners on, and it's almost as hard to bring down! In between times we went *ghooming* (roaming) in the beautiful sal forest, on the backs of the pad elephants, the latter's high vantage point and virtually silent tread being the ideal way to approach wild game, either to hunt or to view. One of the elephants was a skilful retriever and, by the edge of a small swamp, partridges and snipe which we shot from her back were picked up from the rushes by her searching trunk and handed up gently to her mahout! But news of tiger continued to be lacking.

Christmas Day was celebrated in traditional fashion, with roast peafowl providing an excellent substitute for turkey, and there was the usual Boxing Day bird shoot. That night everyone slept soundly – except me! I went to bed thinking about the tigers and shortly after midnight I awoke with a start. Something, some sound, had roused me. I sat up in my camp bed and looked out between the flaps of my tent. It was a bright moonlight night and the usual jungle noises were strangely still; it seemed as if everything in the forest was holding its breath and listening. Then I head it, the far distant moan of a tiger … the sound was sad but spine-chilling and full of menace. With a thrill of excitement, I leant across and shook Austin Price, who was in the other camp bed, and the two of us listened in rapt silence as the moans were repeated at internals, eventually dying away in the distance. Setting our alarm clock, we resolved to be up before dawn and ride on one of the elephants to inspect the baits ourselves. Then we both lapsed back into fitful sleep.

The first pale streaks in the eastern sky found us perched high aloft on the swaying bulk of Ranee, the staunchest of the elephants when it came to tiger, striding along a forest path at a mile-eating place, heading for the first of the buffalo baits. As we neared the final nullah crossing we slowed and approached cautiously, only to find the buffalo sleepily chewing the cud. The second bait was the same, but as we closed on the third buffalo the first rays of the morning sun were beginning to gild the treetops and in the dust of the jungle track we saw the clear pug marks of a tiger.

The mahout gave us a warning glance and eased the elephant slowly for-ward until we could see where the bait had been strongly tethered. The buf-falo had gone, and there were signs of a heavy body having been dragged through the long grass which bordered the track and on into a patch of thick

*Shot between the eyes,*
*the man-eating tigress dropped in her tracks*

jungle. Austin and I had a hurried, whispered conference. Should we go straight back to camp, leaving the tiger undisturbed, and ask David to arrange a beat (as we ought to have done) or should we follow the trail of the drag to see if we could find further signs of the tiger? With the impatience and rashness of youth, coupled with lack of experience, curiosity prevailed; throwing caution to the winds we decided to take the latter course!

The mahout looked surprised but did not hesitate; he eased Ranee forward again along the trail of the drag, but within twenty paces she halted, blowing softly through her trunk. There in front of us, on a patch of flattened grass in a small clearing in the bushes, lay what was left of the buffalo; its rear portion was almost entirely eaten but its head and forequarters remained virtually untouched. Even as we looked, from the nearby jungle came a stead 'Tok – tok – tok – tok – tok', the warning call of an alert peacock, while the elephant suddenly started tapping the ground with the tip of her trunk, making a strangely metallic 'Tonk – tonk – tonk', a signal which alerted the

130

mahout on the instant; turning his head slowly towards us – 'Bagh!' (Tiger!) he whispered.

I noticed that Dilbahadur had stiffened and was staring fixedly at a small gap in the bushes scarcely fifteen paces from us. Following his gaze for a moment I could see nothing, then suddenly the play of light and shadow took shape – it was the face of a tiger, staring straight at me! My reaction was automatic. Slowly and gently I raised the .350 Rigby; as the butt touched my shoulder the sights were on target, my finger tightened on the trigger and the jungle echoed to the 'CRASH' of the heavy rifle, the sound weaves rolling across the treetops to the accompaniment of raucous screams from frightened peafowl and the startled cries of a troop of langur monkeys. I looked at the bushes again; the face had disappeared and nothing moved.

I turned to Austin "We'd better wait five minutes and then take a look in those bushes," I said; he nodded excitedly. The time dragged interminably but at last I nudged the mahout and the elephant moved forward yet again, cautiously, foot by foot, while I held my rifle at the ready. All of a sudden, as if parting a curtain, the elephant swept the bushes aside with her trunk and there lay the tiger – stone dead; my bullet had taken it almost straight between the eyes!

Chattering like magpies a passing group of excited forest workers gave us a willing hand, and an hour later, with the handsomely striped body of the cattle-killer lashed on the elephant's back, we strode proudly into camp before the astonished eyes of late-rising guests. And when the tape measure had been used, we discovered that the cattle-killer was a fine tigress, 8 feet 9 inches between pegs, and with a perfect winter coat. I eventually had her head mounted on a shield by Van Ingen, the famous taxidermist in Mysore, and in later years, when I looked at this striking trophy, I often used to reflect how fortunate I had been for, within my first sixteen months in India, and still in my twenty-first year, I had bagged a stock-raiding panther, a rogue bear, and a cattle-killing tigress; beginner's luck indeed!

# Chapter XII

# The Mule Saga

Having seen the Bn off, Alan Macrae and I were left to hold the fort; Alan to see to the mules and myself to recuperate and do the odd job. Bill Milne of the 1/4 G.R. also stayed behind to deal with the animals of his Bn, and between us and our respective girlfriends, we made the most of our spare moments during those four days grace and even managed another crack at the lock duck.

But all good things come to an end and after loading the mules with much profanity, followed by a final evening and tearful farewells at the club, our 'donkey' train steamed out soon after 1.00 am on January 30th.

Besides the three of us there was Oxlade of the 2/5 R.G.R. who had just recently joined his Bn, and Williams, a field cashier whose only order was to head for Burma at a moment's notice, and who, despite his name, might well have been an advertisement for 'Cherry Blossom' boot polish. Oxlade, we rapidly discovered was a 'line-shooter' Grade 1; he had been in China in some kind of customs job and as such posed as a Japanese expert. Thirsting for knowledge of the 'children of the Rising Sun', we at first listened enthralled, but this soon changed to scepticism and complete disbelief as his stories of Chinese and Japanese 'dope' smugglers changed from the improbable to the impossible.

After travelling along the very beautiful eastern coast of India through Madras and Orissa and by the shores of Lake Chilka some 30 miles long, I determined that if ever I got the chance I would visit the place again, especially Valtair.

We arrived in the dock area of Calcutta soon after dawn on February 1st and after hunting around for some considerable time we eventually unearthed some officers of the 'Movement Control' (so-called) staff. This title, I feel, is a misnomer and should be changed, for of the many members of this honoured sect that I have met, few have produced much 'movement' and seldom has there been any vestige of 'control'!

A 'glorious personage', with a lovely clean armband, eventually informed us that there was a ship in and that it was to carry mules, and, "Oh yes, it must be yours". However there were other animals to go on as well, belonging to A.T. Coys, Field Ambulances etc, and so there would not be enough room for all the men or any of the line gear and extra baggage, and only two officers could go on her.

We had nearly 600 horses and mules to go aboard and were allowed about one man per 6 animals. But the 'glorious personage' assured us it would be alright as all the spare men and kit would sail in another ship in the same convoy, with the three spare officers, and they would load tomorrow morning. In the meantime these lucky officers could go into Calcutta and stay at the Grand Hotel. The remainder however were to load immediately as the ship was to pull out into the river at midnight and wait for the convoy there. Bill Milne and I said we would sail in the first ship, as Oxlade had a wife, and Alan Macrae a number of girlfriends in Calcutta.

Then started a long day of toil, sweat and profanity – dragging mules up a gangway and hurling them down a chute into the hold or between decks. Kicking, braying, biting, the recalcitrant ones were often hurled bodily over the top by a bunch of enraged Gurkhas, to cascade down the chute into the bowels of the ship.

Eventually the job was done, the men herded aboard, and our kit, which some satellites of the Movement Control staff had sent, in a sudden surge of unaccustomed energy to the wrong dock, rescued. Macrae, Oxlade and party had disappeared to happier realms long since, and the story of their trials and tribulations is a tale in itself. At last a remarkably good meal, and we gird our loins to sail; but what is this? A lorry roars up and stops alongside, and a corporal runs up the gangway. "Ere y'are sir, two Lewis guns and twenty thousand rounds of ammo' for anti-aircraft protection". Grand, we think and "Thanks very much, you were just in time" we say, and retire to bed content. We sailed at midnight, but next day, when we prepared to mount the guns for battle, came the sequel. Up came our Naik, one of the few men who had served long enough to know about Lewis Guns, and said "We can't fire those guns". "Why not?" we say. "They came straight from Ordinance and haven't got any bolts in them!" Sure enough there in the box, so beautifully sealed, was a slip of paper with the words 'For bolts see package no! ...'

And so we sailed with a full armament of thirty odd rifles and three revolvers plus two U.S. Lewis guns to protect us from the horrors of sea and air!

As we sailed we had opened our sealed orders and found what we expected.

'Destination, Rangoon-Burma' but when we got out into the Hoogli there was no waiting for any convoy, we just steamed on, unarmed and unescorted with the news of Jap submarines sinking ship after ship in the Bay of Bengal, ringing in our ears.

The 'S.S. *Manon*', as she was called, was an old tub of the B.I. line and an extremely dirty old tub, with a chequered career. She had been built for the Germans before the last Great War, in the course of which we had captured her and handed her over to the Italians. We had again captured her, from the Italians this time in Mombassa, in this 'World War Two'. She was then condemned and of course, as a result, put on the Indian Run after carefully changing her name! She was without doubt one of the dirtiest ships I have ever seen and the dirtiest I have sailed in, a mass of coal dust, grime and rust and she had been carrying mules for several trips without a chance of cleaning up, so the total sum was 'pretty ripe'.

It was impossible to keep clean for more than five minutes at a time and Bill and I had a minute cabin, not much bigger than a wardrobe, with steel walls, next door to the engine room. This caused it to vibrate like a tuning fork and at night with the door closed and the skylight and portholes blacked out, the temperature was something terrific and completely unbearable, so that sunset was 'lights-out' for us, as far as our cabin was concerned.

The best part of the old '*Manon*' was her ship's officers, and the food, which, cooked by a Chinaman, was really good, and plenty of it. Most of the officers had been torpedoed or mined in other ships and seemed 'all set' to 'catch it' again. The first officer came into breakfast daily with a long face and longer list of ships sunk in the Bay all round us! The chief engineer was a very ancient Scot who had retired and then returned to do his bit again in the merchant service at the beginning of the war. He had a complete contempt for the black out and at night a 'neon-beam' streamed from his cabin door – partially screened by a ragged black curtain. His 'Second' was also a Scot, of about twice life-size, an enormous man with fiery red hair and a voice that sounded as if he was afflicted with a permanent sore throat. He kept us enthralled with stories of being dive-bombed and machine-gunned in the Mediterranean and off Crete and Tobruk, and his 'embroidery' of them was a work of art.

We spent a lot of time in the cabins of the two 'sparks' – good fellows – they were not allowed to transmit for fear of radio-location, but received many interesting and at times disturbing messages; this or that ship sunk or damaged!

The men were enthralled by the sea, it was dead calm the whole way and so no-one was sick. We churned on at our steady four knots through a sea like a mill-pond, and after sunset a brilliant moon turned night into day, mirrored in a sea of molten glass, broken only by the flaming phosphorescence of our bow wave. One night we were leaning over the rail, when the flashing phosphorescent trail of a torpedo shot towards the bow. We watched fascinated as the white fiery streak approached and then – turned – a porpoise? The men never tired of watching these and when the flying-fish appeared, they danced with delight, and their expressions of wonderment were exhausted.

The few ships we saw were scanned anxiously, with all the field – glasses and telescopes on board, until they were out of sight, for this lonely little tramp, unarmed and unescorted, creeping unobtrusively through an oily-calm sea, even at night silhouetted sharply against a brilliant moon, was a 'sitting bird' for any submarine or surface raider.

Then on the third day out, the tired old engines 'gave up the ghost' and we lay becalmed, a submarine's dream, while for two hours not even the blistering profanity of the Clyde side could get us going. However this 'gentle' coaxing had its effect, and the old ship eventually shook herself and staggered on.

On the evening of the fifth day a man of war of some sort appeared over the horizon and we eyed her with some trepidation, for she appeared to be enormous. However a welcome anti-climax occurred for she turned out to be a small R.I.N. sloop come out from Rangoon to meet us and escort us in. The shock had been too much for the old *Manon* however, and her engines missed a stroke and expired again, and she lay wallowing while the sloop steamed fussily round us, with a bearded and irate officer roaring through a megaphone. After another couple of hours she rallied again and we resumed our stately progress.

As dawn broke on the sixth day, we found ourselves rapidly approaching the mouth of the Rangoon river and three or four other ships had appeared on the horizon. As we steamed down the river we got our first glimpse of Burma, paddy-fields and story-book houses, and the sun glinting on the golden domes of countless Pagodas, each one larger than the last until we came in sight of the famous Shweydagon pagoda itself, its massive dome of pure gold-leaf towering over the houses of Rangoon. The whole effect was rather spoilt by the air-raid alarm and we chugged on with our anti-aircraft protection of a dozen riflemen clustered round the funnels! While we approached and docked we saw our first signs of war, buildings burnt and shattered by air-bombing, but it was the heart of the city that had caught it most.

We moved down the gangway to be met by more 'G.C.B.S's' of the Movement Control Sect who informed us that all the dock labour had run away and we were to unload the ship ourselves but we were to be 'helped' by a Madrassi labour unit, who would also help us to lead the mules to the station some five miles out; for some reason the nearest station could not be used.

Beckdall of the 2/5 R.G.R. and Hawkins of the 1/4 G.R. met us on the dock. They had been left behind in Rangoon with the first reinforcements but there was no-one from the 1/3rd. They were full of stories of the air-raids and of the fighting on the Salween River. There was very heavy fighting going on, they told us, and our Brigade had just been moved up towards the front after sitting in Mingladon for several days, but they didn't know exactly where they were.

The Madrassis had started off well by leading one of the horses over a 15ft drop from the gangway on to the dock and there were a number of groups of mules leading Madrassis round the docks at the double; however, neither the horse nor the Madrassis seemed to be hurt, so I decided I had better go ahead to the station and get the two special mule trains ready. Having bid farewell to the Ship's officers with the usual admonitions of 'Give those little yellow b-s hell!' I jumped into a lorry with a few men and sallied forth through the city past houses shattered and pock-marked by bomb splinters and machine-gun bullets. Expressions of gratified approval came from the men as we passed many attractive little Burmese girls, not at all unlike their own Gurkha women. We also saw, for the first time, some of the A.V.G. (American Volunteer Group) pilots nipping through the streets in their 'Jeeps' bristling with pistols and tommy-guns.

At the station I found that the whole of the railway system was being run by a skeleton staff, mainly Anglo-Burmans, stout-hearted fellows who had stayed behind when the general 'marathon' started after the first heavy raid on Rangoon.

Two special trains were shown to me, due to leave that night so I got busy marking out the carriages, greatly heartened by seeing a Jap plane falling like a 'winged' duck out of the sky. When the job was done, I put out the 'boys' on the various entrances to the station to direct the Madrassis and then waited. After hanging around for a bit a dust cloud appeared on the horizon and I was soon greeted with the interesting spectacle of a large edition of the 'Grand National'; seventy-odd mules and horses flat out across country, led by a fine chestnut gelding, through gardens and rubber plantations, taking fences and ditches in their stride. It was an eye-opener, some of those 'donkeys' were shifting enough to make the steeplechasers back home sit up and look at their odds. After the first big bunch had come up 'the home straight', odd 'also rans' started rolling in, followed a long time afterwards by our 'Hired helps', the Madrassis, limping and hobbling along in twos and threes like a herd of refugees, most of them carrying their boots in their hands and about one in fifty leading a mule. Then started an animal hunt of the first magnitude. Bill rolled up and with the men, we stalked and caught (or failed to catch) and swore and sweated, far into the night. Those mules had lower taste than we thought, and apart from gardens and rubber plantations, we routed them out of grain-shops, grog-shops and brothels in all the foulest corners of the bazaar. Eventually there was a milling mass of animals in the station sidings, wandering about in the blackness of the night, occasionally scattering wildly as an engine roared through them with headlights blazing. All this time the raids had been going on, and the night was filled with the hum of aero-engines, the rapid barking of the Bofors guns, and the occasional 'crump' of bursting bombs, while the tracer-shells of the Bofors made pleasing patterns across the sky.

Amid this chaos we again loaded, sweated and swore, until by 2 am one train was full. Bill and I decided to go ahead with this and get things organised at the other end, as we expected chaos there as well. So we took our boys and left the R.I.A.S.C. personnel to bring along the second train. It took us some time to get out of that station, for the engine-crew were not as stout-hearted as the rest of the railway staff, and the progress of the train was interrupted by a series of air-alerts, during which the engine crew slammed on their brakes and dived for the nearest slit-trench.

Eventually at 4 am we made our jerky way out, and dirty and tired we rolled over on the seats and went to sleep.

Soon after dawn we were rudely awakened as the train screeched to a halt, and looking, bleary-eyed out of the window we were greeted with the sight of one of our mules galloping over the paddy-fields, having, by some gymnastic feat, jumped clean out of its truck. After the brute had been caught we had to back up for three quarters of a mile into a wayside station to reload it again.

The train chugged on and soon after midday crossed the bridge over the Sittang River, little did we think at the time how vital this same bridge was to become for us before so very long.

A short time later we steamed into Kyaikto and were told by a wandering staff officer that we had to unload our mules there, although our orders in Rangoon had been to proceed to the next station. Eventually a slightly more exalted staff officer strolled up and told us our mules were to be marched to an area seven miles away and in the opposite direction to our Bde; guides were to be provided, A.T. Coy personnel to help unload and some lorries to take our kit and rations. But that was as far as it went, no help or lorries arrived, so we unloaded the train ourselves and being lucky enough to meet Flack of the 1/4 G.R., I went off in his truck to our Bde to get help and lorries and saw the Bn again, remarkably cheerful considering the extent to which they had been mucked about. Hubbard was doing Adjutant as poor old Bishop had landed in hospital in Rangoon after parting company with his motor-bike at high speed.

Some guides from the Burma Rifles appeared at the station in the evening and we sent off our miles in three separate parties all our activities being carefully watched by a yellow-robed Pongyi, we were suspicious but had not learnt the true calibre of these gentlemen at that time. Bill and I went ahead with the lorries and rations and though we waited and waited, only one party of mules turned up. We searched high and low but finally had to give it up and slept like logs till dawn, when we drove back twelve miles to our Bde area and found the mules had turned up there. Evidently the guides had decided to remove themselves and the men took the mules to the only camp they knew, leaving us with mules in two camps twelve miles apart and kit and rations in only one! To add to the confusion the second mule train rolled up in the morning complete with our Transport Havildar, who, being dead drunk in Rangoon had been left behind. I had found him by the railway line fast asleep and failed to wake him, though I shook him, dragged him, slapped him, poured cold water on him, and finally three times picked him up bodily and flung him on the ground, to no avail, for one could hear the country-spirit sloshing up against his back teeth.

Then started three days chaos with the help of Division H.Q. – order – counter-order, disorder. We were told to march the animals to one camp, then back to the other, backwards and forwards, up and down, the numbers

dwindling each time as mule after mule galloped off into the rubber plantations, until eventually this oscillation ceased, and all those who wanted or were
told to have mules, had mules, and the odd horse or two, of some colour,
shape and size, and we, giving thanks for our deliverance, rejoined our Bns,
– but not before an irate signal-officer roared up; his line to Bde H.Q. had
gone dead, investigation disclosed that our little Gurkhas, rising to the occasion
and using their initiative, had cut down the wire to tie up the stray 'donkeys'.

I feel that I just cannot conclude this chapter without paying a sincere
tribute to the mule. Tough, resilient, adaptable and courageous as they are,
without our mules we could never have operated – and survived – as a fighting
unit, in often trackless country, varying from barren, rugged mountains such
as the North West Frontier, to dense, tropical jungle, such as in parts of
Burma and Malaya. They carried everything for us from mountain guns to
medical supplies, from heavy machine guns to rations, from mortars to wireless
sets, from ammunition stocks to a few creature comforts. In fact, anything
and everything, in conditions ranging from bitter cold to steaming heat, and
usually with little or no complaint.

I have the greatest fondness and respect for the mule – after all I have little
option, since the mule is my wife's family crest! – but the mule can also be
temperamental and stubborn to the point of bloody-mindedness, and at such
times one's loyalty to this mixed-up beast is severely strained. Such were my
feelings on many occasions during that eventful mule journey from
Secunderabad, in southern India, to the jungles of south eastern Burma.

# Chapter XIII

# The Elusive Sambar

Of the numerous species and sub-species of deer which occur on the Indian sub-continent, *Cervus unicolor*, or the sambar – sometimes spelt 'sambur' or 'sambhur' – a big deer with large ears, a thick bushy tail and coarse hair of uniform dark brown forming a heavy mane on throat and neck, is by far the largest. In fact, a full grown sambar stag, a heavily built animal often standing close on five foot (or nearly 15 hands) at the shoulder, can weigh anything up to 700lbs – more than twice the weight of a really heavy Highland red deer stag.

As a trophy the sambar's horns – each of which consists of brow-tine followed by a main beam ending in a simple fork – are noteworthy for their massiveness rather than for their length; the longest pair on record are from a sambar shot many years ago by the Nawab of Bhopal; they measured just over 50 inches on the curve, but nowadays anything over 40 inches is considered good, with the average mature head measuring nearer 30 than 40 inches.

The sambar is a forest-dwelling animal with a preference for rocky, forest-clad hills; largely nocturnal in its feeding, and moving around singly or in small groups rather than in large herds, it is a favourite prey of the tiger, and because of its acute senses of smell and hearing, together with the nature of its habitat, it presents a real challenge to the hunter. There are a few regions where the sambar can be 'stalked' – as the term is understood in Scotland – and there only in the early mornings and late evenings when the sambar may be found grazing in the open grassy areas on the edges of the hill forests into which they retire during the hours of daylight. Otherwise, still-hunting or driving are the only ways of getting on terms with the sambar, an elusive and worthy quarry whose range extends from India and Sri Lanka (Ceylon) eastwards through Burma to Malaya and beyond.

My own first ever encounter with a sambar took place in southeastern Burma, on February 21st 1942, in circumstances that I am never likely to forget! On December 7th 1941, in an act of unrivalled treachery, Japan had,

*Badge of the 3rd Gurkha Rifles*

without warning, attacked Pearl Harbour and invaded Malaya and the Philippines. At a stroke the whole world war scene had changed and within weeks the tough, well trained and fanatical troops of the Japanese Imperial Army had swept through Malaya until, by late January 1942, two of its crack, full strength divisions had entered south eastern Burma, there to be faced by one grossly under strength and ill-equipped British formation, 17th India Division, later to become famous as the 'Black Gate'. It was into this chaotic scenario that, at the end of January 1942, the 48th Gurkha Brigade, comprising 1/4th, 2/5th and 1/3rd Gurkha Rifles (my own battalion), all trained and equipped for operations in the Western Desert, had been rushed from India to be flung into the breach in a despairing attempt to help stem the yellow tidal wave of Japanese military might.

Within two weeks of landing in Rangoon, the three Gurkha battalions of 48 Brigade, along with the other and already weakened units of 17 Division, had found themselves locked in bitter fighting with the Japanese 55th Division along the line of the Bilin River, while the Japanese 33rd Division, helped and guided by Burmese traitors, was sweeping fast through the jungles on the northern flank heading like long dogs for the half-mile wide Sittang River. And so, on February 21st, had begun a race for the undefended Sittang Bridge, the very gateway to Rangoon and the heart of southern Burma, a race along a jungle track winding its way through tinder-dry teak forest, a track inches deep in grey, choking dust that filled the eyes, the ears and the throats

*P40 "Tomahawk" flown by American Volunteer group in Burma in 1943*

of the weary, plodding troops. And then at ten o'clock in the morning had come the air attacks!

First came the Japanese bombers, the red roundels on their wings shining mockingly in the sun as they droned lazily overhead to drop clusters of fragmentation bombs with deadly precision on the weary marching column, scattering men and animals into the surrounding jungle. Next came the

*Dry Jungle Burning*

Japanese fighters, the 'Zeros', fast and accurate, followed by a brief lull; and then, all of a sudden, the sky was filled with familiar aircraft, 'Blenheims', 'Hurricanes' and 'Buffaloes', accompanied by the multi-gunned P40 'Tomahawks' of the A.V.G. (American Volunteer Group), Chennault's famed 'Flying Tigers', with the fearsome symbol of a tiger shark's bared teeth painted vividly on their engine cowlings. As the R.A.F's distinctive roundels gleamed in the sunlight, hoarse cheers of relief arose from the tired troops, but their relief was short lived; a moment later one by one the planes banked, the bombs began to fall again, the fighters swooped low along the column with machine-guns blazing, and the cheers choked in dust-filled throats as horrified soldiers dived for any possible cover. It was a sight I shall never forget.

The dry jungle was burning from the bombing and strafing and I found myself crouching, dazed and bewildered, behind the smouldering bole of a small teak tree, with my Gurkha orderly beside me, while the fighters dived again and again with guns blazing and the cries of wounded men, the screams of injured mules, and the crackle of burning vehicles came through the drifting smoke; it was like a scene from 'Dante's Inferno'. Six days previously Singapore had fallen and to us the obvious answer was that the treacherous Japanese were using captured British planes against us so, seething with anger, we fired and loaded and fired again, automatically swinging through as if our targets were wind-blown duck. Little did we then know that an Intelligence Officer in Rangoon had given the wrong bomb-line, a grievous error, which finally led to the disaster of the Sittang.

Suddenly, through the smoke and flames came a galloping figure. For a moment I though it was one of our mules stampeding and then, as it bounded past me, so close that I could have touched it, I saw that it was a massive stag, horns laid back, its mouth agape, and its eyes wide with terror; it was a sambar, the first I had ever seen. Excitedly I turned to my orderly, but Rifleman Dilbahadur Thapa, my cheerful companion on many a hunt, lay ominously still ... Three momentous days later, with a shattered bridge and a thousand yards of swirling, moonlit water behind me, I waded wearily ashore on the west bank of the Sittang River.

Two and a half long years, hundreds of weary foot-slogging miles, and

*In December 1944, the author was appointed Second-in-Command of 4/9th Gurkha Rifles, in General Wingate's 'Special Force' named the 'Chindits'*

*The famous insignia of General Wingate's airborn 'Special Force'*
*known as the 'Chindits'*

many a bloody jungle battle were to pass before I next encountered a sambar stag. In the jungles of the Pegu Yomas and the upper Chindwin, and in remote forested corners of the Naga and Chin Hills, from time to time I found sambar tracks, and on several occasions, on moonlit jungle nights, I heard the strangely metallic trumpeting call of a sambar stag, a sound referred to by hunters as 'belling', but although during this time on several occasions I caught glimpses of sambar hinds, it was not until late in 1944, that I again came face to face with a sambar stag; the circumstances of this second encounter were almost as bizarre as those of my first.

By the cold weather of 1944, the tide of war in Burma had finally and remorselessly turned against the Japanese and I found myself posted as Second-in-Command (and a Column Commander) of 4/9th Gurkha Rifles, a battalion of 111 Brigade of Special Force (alias 'Chindits') then training in the jungles of Central India for the invasion of Malaya. Our jungle camps and training arcas were sited north of the Narbada River, in rolling country dotted with low, rocky hills and covered with sal and dwarf teak, the whole being rich in game including tiger, panther, sloth bear, wild pig and sambar. But as a specially equipped, glider-borne unit, destined to spearhead an invasion of being crash-landed in the Malayan jungle (a prospect that I found less than appealing and tried not to think about!), our training was intensive and tempting as it was we had no time to spare for hunting. However, on our long forced marches I was often able to supplement our hard rations by shooting green pigeon, or a jungle fowl or two, with the American .30 calibre M.1 carbine with which I had been issued; a very accurate little semi-automatic rifle, with a 15 round magazine, weighing a mere 5½ lb and firing a 108 grain bullet at a muzzle velocity of just under 2,000 feet per second, the carbine made up in handiness what it lacked in killing power!

For several weeks all went well until, one day, on a particularly arduous cross-country forced march, I became doubled-up with stomach cramp, a recurrence of the effect of the stresses and strains of prolonged jungle warfare. In agony and scarcely able to move I hobbled to the battalion's Medical Officer, a cheerful and earnest but very recently qualified young Indian. "Sir, this is no problem", he beamed, opening his pack and taking out a small black bottle. Pouring a generous potion into a medicine glass, he handed it to me. "What is it?" I asked. "Sir, this is atropine", he said confidently. "Excellent for troubles of the stomach". I looked at the glass doubtfully. What I knew of atropine was that oculists used it as eye-drops to dilate the pupils of their patients' eyes. Furthermore, I remembered that atropine is derived from the poisonous plant *Atropha belladonna*, better known as 'Deadly nightshade', and I had never heard of atropine being taken internally. Then another spasm of cramp doubled me up and grabbing the glass I swallowed the dose at a gulp.

A quarter of an hour later my legs gave way under me, then my arms lost all power and finally my tongue seized up; I could not speak, I was paralysed! A very worried doctor had me hoisted on to the back of a pony and lashed into the saddle, and by the time we reached our bivouac I was semi-conscious. That night, as I lay, wrapped in blankets, beside our campfire, I experienced what I imagine a 'trip' under the influence of LSD could be like. For a long time I saw devils and demons dancing, grinning and mocking me from the flickering flames; again it was like a scene from 'Dante's Inferno' and I thought that at last I had ended in Hell! Then came merciful oblivion.

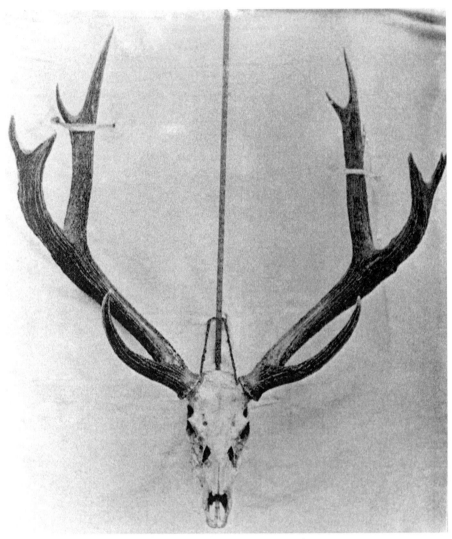

*Skull and Horns of Indian Sambar with abnormal antlers.*
*From a specimen in the possession of Mr Bertram Carey*

The next morning I awoke partially recovered but still not fully able to control my legs. So again I was hoisted on to the back of a pony and, with my .30 carbine slung across my back and my new Gurkha orderly leading me, I was sent off, across country, to the base hospital. We followed jungle paths and game trails until, near midday, as we entered a grassy clearing, it happened

– out of the long grass, not twenty paces from me, like a genie from a magic lamp, there rose a massive sambar stag; his mighty antlers could not have measured less than 40 inches, and as he stood there motionless, staring at me fixedly with his head raised imperiously, he was a living sculpture of Landseer's famous 'Monarch of the Glen'. What a trophy!

Quietly I unslung my .30 carbine, raised it slowly to my shoulder and centred the foresight on his massive neck; at that range I could hardly miss, even from the back of a pony, while I knew that for a well placed neck shot even the light, low velocity .30 calibre bullet would be adequate. Then something stayed my hand. We were miles from anywhere and I was going into hospital so there was no way that my orderly and I could recover the head or the meat of an animal the size of a horse, nor could I get anyone else to do it. For a moment I hesitated, then – "BANG" – I shouted. "You're mine!" At the sound of my voice, with one bound the stag vanished as suddenly as he had appeared, only the bent and waving grass stems showing that something had just been standing there.

That night, as I lay in my hospital bed, I could imagine – as I do now – the massive horns of that sambar stag hanging on the opposite wall, and I was glad that I had not shot him; it would have been too easy, so then, as now, I was content to count him as a very special 'First'!

*ORIGINAL COPY OF A SECRET CIPHER MESSAGE ISSUED AFTER THE*
*"SITTANG RIVER BATTLE", IN WHICH THE 1/3 Q.A.O. GURKHA RIFLES*
*RECEIVED AN OFFICIAL "SHABASH".*

BG S    To See Feb 25/2 (2046/6)

SECRET CIPHER.    MOST IMMEDIATE.

108

TO:-   17 DIV, 1 BURDIV   Pass to 6 Army TRELLIS & ZIGZAG
     PORT BLAIR     CENTRAL AREA    U.B.A.

From: BURMARMY

ORIGINATORS NO. 0 873            DATED 24/2

SITREP EXXT 1700 HRS 24/2 (.)

RANGOON (.) Have taken over RANGOON where there is now no
    police fire services hospitals ambulances conservancy
    or labour (.) Disappearance of Police has released all
    convicts from jail who are now engaged in looting and
    arson (.) Will probably take over PEGU-PROME-BASSEIN
    districts from Civil tomorrow (.) Railways have ceased
    working but are taking over from PROME and TOUNGOO
    forthwith and hope to get skeleton service going (.)
    Telephones still working (.) Military are manning power
    and water supply (.) Tactical responsibility or few
    British Troops available prevent any extensive use to
    bolster up civil administration but situation is in hand.

AIR (.) No raids reported today (.)

NORTHERN FRONT (.) MANDALAY and PYINMANA raided 20 Feb (.) At
    latter 70 killed and 140 injured and Ry Stn damaged (.)
    13 Inf Bde now concentrated on TOUNGOO approach and
    Chinese 6th Army movement into SOUTHERN SHAN STATES
    continues (.)

SOUTHERN FRONT (.) FIRST (.) Continuation account in my C 851 of
    withdrawal 17 Div across SITTANG (.) Withdrawal
    continued during 23 Feb and by 2045 hrs several parties
    16 and 46 Bdes had managed to get across river from
    various points (.) Brig JONES and EKIN swam the river
    and Div Comd was hoping to sort out more personnel than
    previously anticipated (.) Full story of action not yet
    available but several units in particular 1/3 G.R. who
    had C.O. and Adjt killed fought very gallantly and enemy
    undoubtedly had severe casualties in bitter hand to hand
    fighting (.) Full details including casualties both
    sides have been called for (.) Reports just received
    from visiting staff officers indicates following
    personnel already rejoined 17 Div (.) Almost all
    personnel from Div Arty plus four Mtn Guns and all A.A.
    guns and A Tk guns (.) R.E. all complete (.) Inf KOYLI
    200 D.W.R. 300 1/9 Jats 550 1/7 Gurkha 300 Baluch 700
    Dogras 30 3/7 Gurkha 150 1/3 Gurkha 100 1/4 G.R. complete
    2/5 G.R. 200 4 F.F.R. complete less casualties (.)
    Burma Rifles practically nil (.) Signalling equipment
    practically non existent within Div and
    other equipment lost owing obstruction SITTANG River
    which precluded salvage of very heavy equipment (.)
    Reports from other units and from other sources indicate
    enemy suffered heavy casualties in very bitter fighting
    in areas of which forward brigades fought their way
    through enveloping enemy dets towards SITTANG (.)
    All concerned report magnificent fight put up by Gurkha
    Bns of 46 and 48 Bdes (.)
    SECOND (.) Following on conference reported my 0 837 23
    BURMARMY issued operation order p.m. same day (.)
    Intention to deny line of PEGU River to enemy as long as
    possible with a view to receiving reinforcements and
    organizing arrangements for demolition RANGOON area IF
    repeat IF latter necessary (.)

*Copy of very important Secret Cypher Message sent during the Battle*

# Chapter XIV

# The Battle for the Sittang River Bridge

*Burma – February 1942*

## BACKGROUND

'More than perhaps any campaign in the Second World War, save the Russians' defence of Stalingrad, the Burma campaign has the elements of a great Homeric saga. It took place in a fantastic terrain, isolated by great mountains and jungles from any other theatre. It went on unbroken for three years and eight months. It covered vast areas. It sucked into its maelstrom nearly 2,000,000 men. It encompassed great disasters and ended in great triumphs. It produced prodigies of heroism, patience, resolution and endurance. It brought about great suffering, but fascinated and enthralled those taking part in it, both victors and losers. It was like no war that had ever been in the history of conflict.'

Arthur Swainson in Purnell's
*'Illustrated History of the Second World War'*

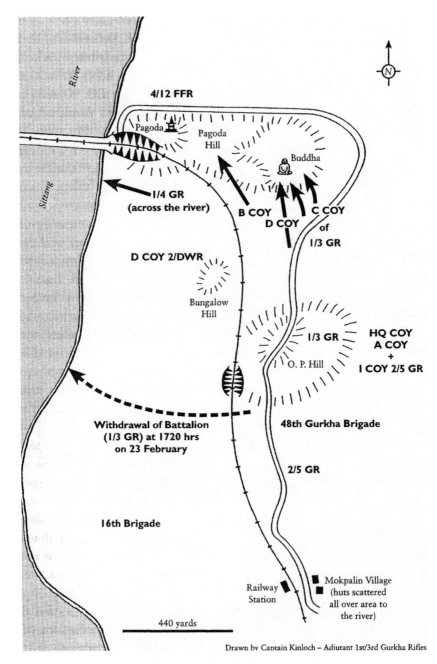

*Map of the Battle for the Sittang Bridge*
*February 21–23 1942*

# Part 1

# Sittang – The Fog of War

## *One Soldier's View – A Very Personal Account*

by Major Bruce G Kinloch, M.C., late 1/3 Q.A.O Gurkha Rifles

I f ever a battle epitomised the phrase 'The fog of war', it was the battle for the Sittang River bridge in Burma in February 1942; it was another *'Bridge Too Far'* and a disaster since taught at the Royal Military Academy, Sandhurst, as the prime example of how not to blow a bridge.

The root cause of this tragic disaster was the almost complete failure of communications between division and brigades, between brigades and battalions, and finally between battalions and their infantry companies locked in close combat, in dense jungle, with a determined, well trained and fanatical army.

This break down in communications was due to the British forces' dependence on the wireless sets of that period of the war, sets which were unreliable and temperamental at the best of times and often useless in dense jungle, particularly in the hands of inexperienced operators. These sets were certainly not designed or built to withstand the damage caused by bolting mules stampeded by intensive and prolonged low-level air attach, the type of attack to which – as a result of a grievous error by Intelligence staff in Rangoon, who had given, to the R.A.F. the Sittang River itself as the eastern bomb-line – the weary 17th Indian Division was subjected in its race, along a dusty jungle track, to reach the Sittang River bridge before the Japanese 33rd Division. And so, on February 22nd, 1942, when the British and Japanese forces finally became locked in fierce, close quarter fighting in the dense jungle which cloaked the approaches to the Sittang River bridge – the gateway to Rangoon and the heart of southern Burma – there was hardly a single functioning wireless set in the whole Division. The fog of war was then complete.

The 17th Indian Division, committed to the defence of southern Burma and commanded by Major-General John Smyth, V.C., M.C., was finally comprised of three infantry brigades – the 16th, the 46th and the 48th – supported by Sappers and the 21st Mountain Regiment of Artillery, 48 Brigade being an all Gurkha formation consisting of the 1/3rd, the 1/4th, and the 2/5th

*An artist's impression, by David Rowlands – and later signed by survivors –*
*of the battle which took place on February 23rd, 1942*

(Royal) Gurkha Rifles. The Japanese entered southern Burma from Thailand and after savage fighting with the Japanese 55th Division, first on the Salween – where 1/7th and 3/7th Gurkha Rifles of 16 and 46 Brigades were the first Gurkha battalions to clash with the enemy – and then along the line of the Bilin River, on February 20th and 21st, 17 Division, now led by 48 (Gurkha) Brigade, carried out an exhausting forced march – under repeated, low-level air attacks – in an attempt to reach and secure the bridge over the swift flowing, thousand yard wide Sittang River before it could be reached by the crack Japanese 33rd Division – then racing through the jungles on the northern flank.

Early in the morning of February 22nd, with little rest and no food, the weary troops of 48 Brigade finally reached Mokpalin, a fishing village of scattered bamboo huts on the banks of the Sittang River. Brigade H.Q. and the 1/4th Gurkha Rifles, who were in the van, gained and crossed the bridge, but then the advance was halted by a lorry which crashed on the bridge itself, blocking it completely, and by the time that the 1/3rd and 2/5th Gurkha Rifles entered the outskirts of Mokpalin, forward elements of the Japanese 33rd Division had reached the village in strength and put down their inevitable road block between 48 Brigade H.Q., plus 1/4th Gurkha Rifles, and the rest of 17 Division. With the almost total lack of wireless communications, resulting from the previous day's air attacks, the scenario for the Sittang disaster was then complete.

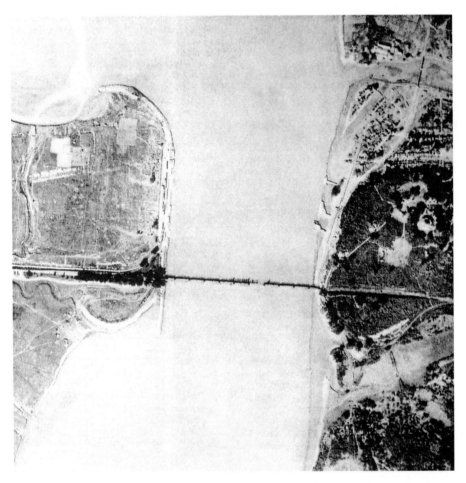

*The Life-line – The Sittang Bridge.*
*Over which the 17th Indian Division were withdrawing east toward Rangoon*

# Part 2

# The Battle for the Sittang Bridge

## Burma – February 21st to 24th, 1942

### *Some Personal Memories*

by Major B. G. Kinloch, M.C.,
then with the rank of Captain 1/3 Q.A.O Gurkha Rifles

Early in the morning of February 22nd 1942, my battalion – the 1/3rd Gurkha Rifled – approached the village of MOKPALIN in two columns, with A, B and H.Q. Coys, plus Bn H.Q., following the railway line and C and D Coys advancing along the road. When we reached the outskirts of the village we heard heavy firing ahead and we soon came under increasingly heavy small-arms fire ourselves from infiltrating Jap snipers in the surrounding jungle. We discovered that the firing ahead of us was from the 2/5th Gurkhas, who were clearing snipers from the village, and we then carried out a sweep (A and B Coys) to clear the Japs in the jungle between the railway line and the road, while our C and D Coys did the same to the east of the road.

The Battalion's R.V. was Mokpalin railway station and when the whole Battalion finally reached there at about 1100 hours, we discovered that, although our casualties in the action had been light, the acting Adjutant, Captain Hubbard, had been wounded and evacuated. In fact, since its arrival in Burma, scarcely three weeks earlier, the Battalion had been unlucky with its Adjutants; its substantive Adjutant, Captain Bishop, had been injured in a motor accident and hospitalised, and now his successor had become a casualty, so when my C.O., Lieutenant Colonel Ballinger, ordered me to take over as Adjutant, I wondered whether or not it would be a case of 'third time lucky'! This was soon to be put to the test.

The final approaches to the Sittang Bridge were dominated by a 'double' hill feature covered with dense jungle. On the Western end of this feature was a pagoda, while on the Eastern end there was a large stone Buddha – hence the names 'Pagoda Hill' and 'Buddha Hill'. After clearing Mokpalin village,

2/5th Gurkhas had attacked Buddha Hill with two companies, but with no artillery support they had suffered heavy casualties and been forced to fall back on O.P. Hill. The C.O.'s of 1/3rd and 2/5th Gurkhas then liased and planned an attack on Pagoda and Buddha Hills by 1/3rd Gurkhas supported by two Mountain Batteries.

The attack started at 1130 hours with a 25 minute concentration by the mountain guns (Kipling's famous 'screw guns'), the 19lb shells from these little 3.7 inch howitzers falling with supreme accuracy on the two hill features. Through the roar and crash of the shells and the drifting smoke came the stutter of light machine guns and the yells of our Gurkhas as – following the barrage – they found the Japs in slit trenches on the forward slopes and killed them or drove them back with bayonet and kukri. But when they reached the top of the feature they were held up by heavy automatic fire from Japs well dug in on the reverse slope.

Watching the battle from O.P. Hill was frustrating. The plan had been for B Coy to attack the Pagoda area, while C. Coy would attack the Buddha area, with D. Coy following, but once the battle was joined, we – in H.Q. – because of the dense jungle, had no means of knowing what was happening. (The first positive news we got was not until Lieutenant FAY, commanding C. Coy, who had been wounded in the arm, came in to H.Q. to have his wound dressed; but that was nearly three hours after the start of the battle, by which time disaster had struck).

By 1400 hours, with no news of the position of B. C, and D. Coys, Colonel Ballinger was very worried. At last he turned to me and said, "Bruce, I want you to find out what has happened to the forward companies". Trying not to show my inner feelings, I saluted, turned on my heel and headed for the jungle. My orderly had been killed in the previous day's air attacks, I knew that the jungle literally was swarming with Japanese, and I felt very lonely, very vulnerable and very scared – like a condemned prisoner who has just heard the judge pronounce the death sentence. A few moments later, as I was about to step into the jungle, the C.O. called me back. "On second thoughts I think I had better take a look myself, with the Battalion Recce/Group", he said. "You stay here with Major Bradford" (the C.O. .2). I then felt like the same prisoner who has been reprieved just as the hangman was adjusting the noose around his neck; but as the C.O. disappeared, accompanied by the Subedar Major and the Intelligence Section, I had a feeling of mounting concern which

*Machine-gunners of the Japanise 33rd Division firing on British troops*
*attempting to cross the Sittang River*

rapidly replaced my personal relief. Then minutes later there was a prolonged burst of light machine-gun fire in the ravine below O.P. Hill, and within five minutes the Subedar Major re-appeared from the jungle, accompanied by one five riflemen, three of them wounded, to tell the tale.

They had met a platoon of B. Coy, the Subedar Major said, held up by Jap automatic fire. The C.O. had ordered the platoon to advance with his own escort and after a short distance they had come across a party of Japs who had held up their hands in surrender. Ordering his men not to fire, the C.O. had advanced to take the Japs prisoner; as he did so the Japs had fallen on their faces and light machine-guns from behind the Japs had opened up, killing Colonel Ballinger and many of the men with him. Only the Subedar Major and a handful of men had escaped.

Half an hour later, Lieutenant Fay, followed by a runner from D. Coy, told us the situation with C. and D. Coys; how they had reached the summit of both Buddha and Pagoda Hills, where they were pinned down by heavy automatic fire; how Captain Stephens, commanding D. Coy, had been wounded in the shoulder in the first assault, but had still led a second assault on a strong Jap position – firing a light machine-gun taken from a dead gunner – only to be killed outright. But of two platoons of B Coy, under Lieutenant Macrae, which had been attacking the Pagoda area, there was still no news. With the C.O. dead and the Battalion pinned down, Major Bradford set off in a carrier to Mokpalin railway station to contact a senior officer and obtain help. There he found that the road was a shambles of jammed transport under shell fire, with vehicles in flames and the Japs continuing to attack from the South and east. Brigadier J.K. Jones (Commanding 16 Bde) had no troops to spare and ordered Major Bradford to withdraw the forward companies of 1/3rd Gurkha Rifles, concentrate on O.P. Hill and hold it at all costs.

By this time the Japs had infiltrated the ravine between O.P. Hill and Pagoda and Buddha Hills in strength and all efforts to get through to our forward companies failed, so we organised Battalion H.Q, H.Q. Coy and A Coy – plus two platoons of 2/5th Gurkhas under command – into an all-round defensive position to hold O.P. Hill. We were only just in time for, as darkness fell, the Japs launched the first of a series of attacks on O.P. Hill, attacks which continued at varying intervals throughout the night. Fortunately our position, based on a sunken road, was a strong one and our casualties (unlike the Japs) were comparatively light, although Major Bradford was wounded by a grenade which also wounded Lieutenant Fay.

Ammunition soon became a problem, but we were able to maintain the supply, during lulls in the fighting, by sorties to abandoned transport outside the perimeter. On one sortie I found a tommy-gun with a number of 50 round drum magazines (which I soon found very useful!) and during these intermittent lulls we could often hear sounds of desultory fighting from where C and D Coys were isolated on Buddha and Pagoda Hills. Altogether it was a very noisy night with heavy shelling and mortaring and streams of red tracer and very lights providing a dazzling firework display, but lying prone on the lip of the sunken road and cuddling my tommy-gun, I felt comparatively safe from anything except a direct hit! Then, at 0530 in the morning, as the first pallid hint of dawn appeared in the eastern sky, it happened – from the direction of the river, beyond Pagoda Hill, there came the reverberating roar of three enormous explosions and on the instant we realised that the bridge over the Sittang River had been blown up and our life-line cut.

As the echoes of the explosions died away they were followed by utter silence. All firing had ceased abruptly and every living thing seemed to be holding its breath. For a few moments an eerie stillness descended on the battle-field, then suddenly the Japanese, sounding like a troop of excited monkeys, broke into shrill chattering. On O.P. Hill, dog-tired with incessant fighting and lack of sleep, food and water, and believing that we had been abandoned to our fate by the other troops (we thought) had crossed the bridge and blown it behind them, we were filled with mounting anger.

When dawn broke I got into a carrier, with two volunteers, and drove down the track to reconnoitre the station area, bursting through an abandoned road block on the way. To my surprise and delight I discovered that the other troops were still there and the first officer I met was our Q.M, Lieutenant Darley. So we loaded the carrier with much needed water and ammunition and returned with it to O.P. Hill.

For a time there was a lull, then at 0730 hours to our astonished eyes some 30 Japs appeared, in close formation, marching along the railway line in the depression below us and only about 150 yards from our position; they were singing and laughing and carrying a large flag, obviously quite unaware of our presence. It was a target we could hardly miss and our light machine-guns opened on them with good effect. The survivors rolled down the railway embankment into the jungle, and although shortly afterwards a strong attack was launched on our position, it was repulsed with heavy loss to the enemy.

Soon after this attack petered out, a Jap reconnaissance plane appeared from the North, flying low over O.P. Hill. It was flying slowly and only about 100 feet above us, so low that I could distinctly see the pilot's goggled face peering down at us. Everyone who had a weapon opened fire at it and I emptied a full drum from my tommy-gun. At that range I and others could scarcely miss. In fact, the bullet strikes on the fabric could be seen distinctly, and in the area of the station the plane suddenly banked and dived into the ground, exploding in a ball of flame – as it did so a great cheer went up over the whole area, like a crowd applauding the winning goal in a football league match!

Half an hour later, Brigadier J.K. Jones arrived on O.P. Hill and gave orders for the Battalion (1/3rd Gurkhas) to hold its position on O.P. Hill, with a company of the Duke of Wellington's Regiment under command, until the following morning (a.m. February 24th); 2/5th Gurkhas were also to remain and hold the high ground to the East, the plan being that both Battalions would cover the river crossing, by night, of the wounded and the remainder of the troops of 17th Division, who by then had all come under command of Brigadier J.K. Jones. Shortly after this a few survivors from our C and D Coys came trickling in. The two companies had held out on Buddha Hill until long after their ammunition had run out. Then they had heard the bridge being blown and as they had also believed they had been abandoned, they decided to withdraw to the ravine below O.P. Hill to reform and plan, but there they came under heavy automatic fire from two sides and suffered many casualties. The rest scattered and although some eventually escaped across the river, the majority fell into Jap hands in the jungle east of Sittang village.

After the wounded, under Lieutenant Ashwell, had been evacuated to the river bank, well South of the bridge, all was quiet on O.P. Hill until shortly after midday, when British 'Blenheim' bombers came over and by mistake bombed the bridgehead and station area, straddling O.P. Hill. Then, at about 1300 hours, we heard heavy firing from the direction of Mokpalin and we prepared ourselves for an attack.

By 1630 hours, as nothing had happened, Major Bradford and I drove down in a carrier to Mokpalin to investigate.

To our surprise we found that the noise of 'heavy firing' was being caused by burning ammunition lorries and that there was no sign of any troops. We therefore assumed (rightly as it turned out) that for some reason plans had changed and that all the troops had gone without us being informed. Much later we learnt that the C.O. of 2/5th Gurkhas had sent an officer to advise 1/3rd Gurkhas of revised withdrawal plans, but the officer had been wounded and failed to reach us.

Major Bradford and I then returned to O.P. Hill where we gave orders for the mules to be unloaded and released, after which I organised the Battalion into a most unorthodox 'arrow head' formation, the head of the 'arrow' being formed of all available light machine-guns and tommy-guns, with the idea of striking due West, through the jungle, to the river and blasting our way through any opposition we might meet. As it was, we left O.P. Hill at 1720 hours and reached the river, without incident, in a small re-entrant some 800 yards below the bridge. In the re-entrant we found a large number of wounded of many different units, but no signs of other troops; the latter had obviously crossed the river – here some three quarters of a mile wide – at least two hours earlier.

Looking up-stream I stared resentfully at the broken bridge, then my interest quickened; only two spars, near the centre of the river, had been blown and the ends of these spars were resting in the water where the gap between them was tantalisingly small. An idea then began to form in my head. If the bridgehead itself could be secured, it might still be possible to get the whole battalion across the bridge under cover of darkness, but first of all I had to have a closer look.

After we had formed a defensive perimeter round the re-entrant and started the remainder of the men on building rafts, I began to walk cautiously towards the bridge. I had left my tommy-gun with Major Bradford but I had my .38 revolver and in my binocular pouch I carried two No 36 grenades with their pins flattened and ready for rapid action. I moved warily along the river bank, alert for any signs of the enemy, but everything was strangely, eerily quiet. I came across a few Indian sepoys wandering like lost sheep with vacant, glazed looks on their faces, while in the shallows by the river's edge occasional corpses rolled lazily in the ripples, but the Japanese appeared mysteriously to have vanished.

Eventually I reached the sandbagged position at the eastern end of the bridge; it was empty and from it a track led upwards through thick jungle to the Pagoda. As this feature was the key to any plan to cross the bridge and as there was still no sign of any Japanese, I decided to take a stroll up the track to see what was what. Moving quietly, carefully scanning the jungle on either side of me as I went, I walked cautiously up the steep track until – about one hundred yards above the bridge – I found myself approaching a forest giant, an unusually large tree the trunk of which forked some ten feet from the ground.

Suddenly, when I was a couple of yards from the tree, I noticed, in the shadow of the tree's fork, the outline of a head wearing a British pattern steel helmet. For a split second I was puzzled (none of our own troops should have been there), then I whipped out my revolver and challenged – and the head disappeared. With one bound I reached the tree and crouching behind its massive trunk I peered cautiously round it – to find myself looking straight into the face of a Japanese Officer! Black leather knee boots, breeches, soft khaki peaked cap and traditional Samurai sword, they were all there! I moved my head back so fast that the figure I had seen – so close that I could have touched him – was fixed in my mind like a picture taken with a high speed camera.

With one swift movement I whipped a grenade out of my binocular pouch, let the lever go, and rolled it (smoking) gently round the other side of the tree. I heard a gasp, a scuffle of feet, and a shattering explosion. Then the air seemed to come alive with the whip-like crack of flying bullets as light machine-guns opened fire from all sides. My guardian angel must have been working overtime that day, for although a heavy machine-gun from across the river also opened fire, I reached the bridgehead again without a scratch, albeit somewhat shaken and having come close to equalling the Olympic record for the 100 metre sprint!

I walked swiftly back to the Battalion with a plan forming in my head. For some reason I was sure that, at that time, there were not many Japs in the jungle above the bridge and that if we could establish a small covering force at the bridgehead, we could get the whole Battalion, plus any other remaining troops, across the bridge under cover of darkness. When I reached the Battalion I discovered that after several men had drowned, Major Bradford had stopped the rest from making flimsy rafts, but one look at the men convinced me that they were completely exhausted. There is a limit to human endurance, even in a Gurkha, and these men needed food and rest before they could be expected to do anymore. So, I approached Major Jack Robinson, Commander of 'C' Company of the 2nd Battalion, Duke of Wellington's Regiment, the Company Commander of the Duke's for the loan of two platoons, since his men, having crossed the river from the west bank only two days before, were still comparatively fresh and ready for a fight.

When we reached the bridge I ordered one platoon to take up position in and around the sandbagged position, to give covering fire if required. Then I began cautiously to scramble up the steep bank of the railway cutting south of the bridge, with the sections of the second platoon fanned out and following me. As we neared the top an eager young private – a grenade ready to throw in his right hand – pushed ahead, reaching the summit a few seconds before me. For a moment his head and shoulders were silhouetted against the skyline, then there was a whip-like crack and he turned and slid down the bank on his back, shot through the chest. As he slid past me, eyes staring, he gasped – "They're just over the top, Sir". Then his right hand opened and the grenade fell from his nerveless fingers to roll down the slope and explode among the men assembled below.

The waiting Japanese then reacted. A shower of grenades was followed by a roar of exploding mortar bombs and a hail of light machine-gun and rifle fire. The sandbagged position on the bridgehead received a direct hit from a

*A Sampan to the rescue*

mortar bomb and the men surrounding it were cut down by small arms fire, while the remaining men below me began to be picked-off one by one. The position was clearly hopeless, so we withdrew to the re-entrant as best we could.

Back with the Battalion we had a conference as night was falling and it was agreed that Darley (the Q.M.) and I, together with Mackenzie (attached to the Battalion as F.O.O. from 21st Mountain Battery) would swim the river to try and contact our troops and to organise ferry boats. So we made a small raft of bamboo supported by two pakhals, all lashed together with rifle slings. On this we piled our clothes and pistols and pushing it ahead of us we managed to cross the river, at this point, 1,000 yards wide, in just over an hour. But except for stragglers we found no sign of any troops and discovered that all the boats we had seen through our binoculars from the east hank had had their planks stoven in on the orders of the C.R.E.

Eventually, after several abortive attempts with leaking boats, we found a large sampan which was only slightly damaged and we managed to get it safely across to the east bank. From there the ferrying started with the help of

Lieutenant Headly of the Burma Rifles and continued until dawn, by which time, after five crossings with the sampan, all the wounded men – who belonged to many different units – had been landed safely on the west bank, into bullock carts commandeered from a nearby village and away inland under escort with the doctor.

The next problem was the rest of the Battalion. A conference was held with Major Bradford and it was decided that the Battalion would move to a safe harbour some two miles downstream, while Darley and I (with our boots still across the river, we were bare-footed) would cross the river once more, in daylight, to organise an expanded ferry service for the following night. This plan was set in motion and Darley and I were on the west bank of the river, searching for more sampans, when we heard firing from the opposite shore. Through our binoculars we saw Japanese troops swarming out of the jungle, followed by a brief fire-fight and then a number of Gurkhas swimming the river under fire. Some of the men were shot or drowned but eventually the survivors reached the western shore and told their sad story.

After a brief fire-fight the Battalion had been surrounded, they said, and to save what by then had become a pointless loss of life, Major Bradford had agreed to surrender; but it was not part of the soldier's code of Subedar-Major Gagan Sing Thapa, a veteran of several wars, to surrender to anyone, let alone a Japanese, so, as a Jap officer approached, the Subedar-Major drew his revolver and fired at him, and then shot himself through the heart. The Jap officer who had received Bradford's pistol, then shot the Major, whereupon a Gurkha Naik shot the Jap officer through the head. Eventually all firing ceased and the remainder of the Battalion was rounded up and marched off.

After watching this tragic sight through our binoculars, Darley and I collected together a number of stragglers and set off due west, in an organised party, to try and locate 17th Division. As we marched westwards, across open paddy country in blazing sunshine, the heat was intense and what with this and lack of food and rest for several days, we were soon almost asleep on our feet. We marched on automatically and it was past mid-day when I trod in what I thought was a thorn bush; after swimming the river my legs were bare and the prick in my ankle was painful. Then it dawned on my sleep-drugged mind that there are no thorn bushes in paddy fields and looking down I saw that coiled around my left leg was a snake with its fangs buried in my ankle!

I kicked off the snake which my Gurkhas stamped on and killed. I didn't know what it was but it looked to me like a Russel's Viper and I sat on the ground in a mounting rage. I thought of all that I and my friends had just been through and how I had believed that I was one of the lucky ones – only to be bitten by a snake when in sight of safety! We had no knife with us, not even a kukri, so Barney Darley very pluckily sucked the wound, after which we marched on, hoping for the best! My leg swelled slightly but we kept going, with occasional rests, until far into the night, when we approached the village of Waw.

Suddenly, at 2230 hours, out of the darkness came a sharp challenge. "Halt, who goes there?" To my relief the voice had the broad Scots accent of

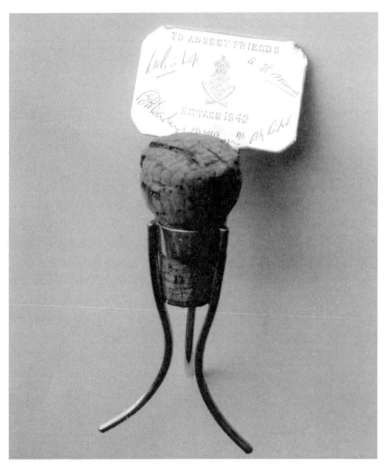

*Cork from the bottle opened in celebration of the survivors.*
*The author used it in his flask throughout the rest of the Burmah campaign*

*The author's campaign medals, including his award of an Immediate Military Cross in February 1942 for the Sittang River Battle*

a Glaswegian, and "It's only us", was all I could think of saying. "What's the password?", queried the voice suspiciously. I was weary and irritated. "I don't know any fucking password", I snapped in reply. This must have persuaded the voice that I was unlikely to be a Jap, because "Advance on and be recognised", the voice then demanded authoritatively. I was almost at the end of my tether, my leg hurt and my temper snapped at last. "For God's sake man, there's only a handful of us", I shouted and sat down. A moment later I felt a strong arm around my shoulders and a tin mug full of neat whisky thrust into my hands. "Here ye are, laddie, drink this, it'll do ye good" said a deep Scots voice. I looked up and in the moonlight I saw the friendly face of a sergeant in the Cameronians. Then I fell asleep! For me the Battle of the Sittang was over.

*The Murchison Falls, Uganda*

*Bruce Kinloch playing a hard-fighting Nile Perch in the turbulent water below the Murchison Falls*

*Game Guard with 30 lb Nile Perch at the Murchison Falls*

*The 473lb Marlin being played by the author, Maderia 1993*

*Having been brought alongside 'Margarita', the author's 475 lb Blue Marlin was first carefully measured, then tagged and finally – released.*

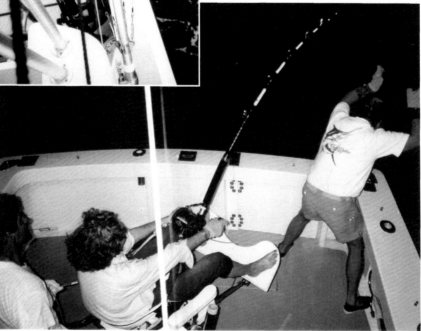

*After hours in the fighting chair, an exhausted Elizabeth watches, despairingly, as Roddy Hays attempts (yet again) to grab the leader*

*Remains of the Sittang Bridge*

*The eastern end of the Sittang railway bridge as seen in 1992*

*Bonnie Prince Charlie's diamond studded locket presented by the Prince to his ADC, Captain John Kinloch of Lord Ogilvie's Regiment (of the Jacobite Army) immediately after the disastrous battle of Culloden, in 1746*

*Jacobite silk flag carried by the 2nd Battalion of Lord Ogilvie's Regiment at the Battle of Culloden, 1746*
*Courtesy of Dundee Art Galleries and Museums*

## JACOBITE FLAG

This silk Colour was carried by the 2nd Battalion of Lord Ogilvie's Regiment, consisting of Angus and Dundee men, which rallied to the standard of Prince Charles Edward Stuart under the command of Sir James Kinloch. It bears the old Scottish motto 'Nemo Me Impune Lacesset' (No One Shall Provoke Me With Impunity) above saltire cross and thistle.

The 2nd Battalion and its flag took part in various campaigns including Culloden in 1746, when, after the defeat of the Jacobite army, it retreated southwards to Glenclova and was disbanded. The Colour was then hidden in Logie House near Kirriemuir, the Kinloch family home, and not rediscovered until 1920 when the contents of the property were sold.

# Chapter XV

# Suicide Mission

*The best laid plans o' mice and men, gang aft a'gley*

ROBBIE BURNS

A fter the first Burma campaign, what was left of the battle scarred 1st Battalion of the 3rd, Q.A.O., Gurkha Rifles, was reformed and retrained in Kohima, where it became part of the 17th Division's 63 Brigade, which, by yearly 1943, became actively operational in the Tuitum-Tiddim-Fort White area of the Chin Hills front. In consequence, following some four months of almost continuous minor patrol operations in that sector, 1/3 GR was holding positions strung out in a long, broken line in the steep hill country south of Fort White. That is the scenario, the basic background to the following true-life story!

By October 1943, the 1st Battalion had, for a long time, been holding various forward positions in the Chin Hills, south of Tiddim, during which period the Battalion had been patrolling very actively, hitting the Japs hard, time and again, with ambushes, night raids and its ever active, two-man 'tiger patrols'. But, or so it appeared to us at the time, the Staff at G.H.Q., way back in India, were not satisfied with our efforts; basking in the sybaritic comforts of New Delhi, far removed from the sound – let alone the dangers – of shot and shell, they became increasingly bellicose with every pink gin! Finally, like the Roman crowds of old at the Coliseum, their blood was up and they demanded more action – a 'spectacular' for the press and public – an action to take place on the Chin Hills front. And so the fateful instruction passed swiftly down from G.H.Q., India, to IV Corps, to 17th Division, to 63 Brigade, to 1/3 Gurkha Rifles, finally ending up in the surprised lap of Bruce Kinloch, then commanding 'D' Company of 1/3 GR!

At the time, my rifle company was well dug-in in scattered positions, at a height of some 6,000 feet, nearly four miles southeast of Fort White and at

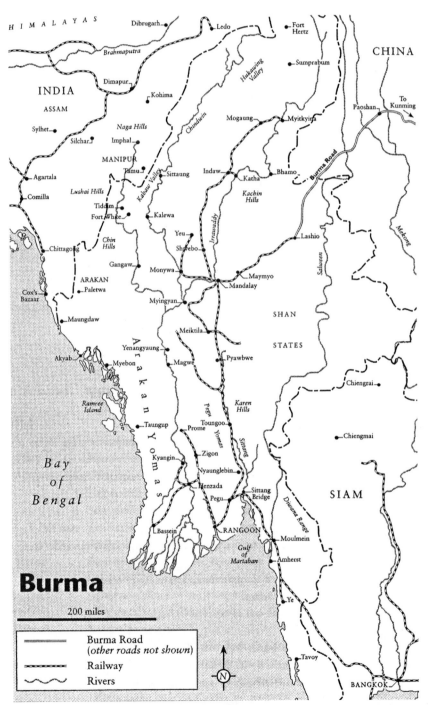

*Map of Burma*

the western end of the Ngalzang ridge, a rocky, knife-edged feature covered with dense jungle. Near the eastern end of this same ridge, and about two miles from my Company H.Q., my own patrols had just discovered a very strong Jap position, very well dug-in and – as we discovered later to our cost – fortified with deep bunkers also. The capture of this position, without a force of overwhelming strength, seemed to me to be well nigh impossible, and even then its capture would have offered no strategic gain. In a normal advance, this Jap stronghold would have been bypassed, encircled and dealt with at leisure by a process of attrition. Yet, as I discovered when my C.O. called me to Battalion H.Q. to give me my orders, this was the very Jap position that 1/3 GR had been ordered to attack!

Our C.O., at this time, was the third incumbent since Colonel George Ballinger was killed, in the Sittang River battle, in February 1942. The casualty rate among British Officers during the campaigns in Malaya and Burma had been disproportionately high, and by early 1943, G.H.Q. was beginning to scrape the barrel in their search for officers considered senior enough to command a battalion. In consequence, our new Colonel – who joined the 1/3rd when we first moved to the Chin Hills early in march – arrived with two major handicaps, the first and foremost being a total lack of any battle experience; this was a serious drawback for any officer called upon to command an already battle-seasoned battalion, several of whose British Officers and a high proportion of whose V.C.O's, N.C.O's and men had fought throughout the first campaign of the jungle-war in Burma.

Furthermore, our new C.O. hailed from an alien regiment, almost a crime in the jealously parochial eyes of a Gurkha battalion! However, although that C.O. was taken ill and finally evacuated on December 12th – being then replaced by a much liked and greatly respected officer of our own regiment – before that date and during the eight weeks following the battle on the Ngalzang ridge, the Battalion was to see a great deal more action. Yet, all this was still to come, when I arrived, that morning, at our carefully camouflaged Battalion H.Q., at the end of a winding jungle track.

I found the Colonel studying a map, his habitual briar pipe clenched grimly between his teeth. I had come to hate that pipe; I had never seen the Colonel without it and I sometimes wondered whether he even slept with it in his mouth! Whatever the truth of the matter, the Colonel invariably gave all his orders without even thinking of removing his pipe, the result sometimes

*The Author in the Chin Hills/Burma border in 1943*

being a jumble of words that were often dangerously easy to misinterpret. This, as I myself had experienced, too easily led to quite serious disagreements, but at the time about which I am now writing, the Colonel was still being guardedly civil to me! On this occasion, he looked up as I approached and almost smiled. "Ah, there you are, Kinloch," he grunted through his pipe. "I have just received important orders from Brigade; they want us to attack that

Jap strongpoint, the one on the Ngalzang ridge which your patrols pin-pointed the other day. Urgent orders from above I believe." He looked at me enquiringly, sensing my surprise. "Well, any comments?"

I thought for a moment or two before slowly replying. "We've already established that it's a very strong position, Sir; it's going to be an extremely tough nut for anyone to crack. The ridge is a rocky knife-edge, a very narrow one, and it is covered with a really dense jungle, yet the only feasible line of approach, as far as I can see, would be straight along the top of the ridge, a frontal attack, in fact; but, under those conditions, it would be virtually impossible to deploy any force strong enough to do the job. Sounds like 'mission impossible' to me, Sir. Brigade must be mad to suggest it; who on earth do they believe would be crazy enough to tackle it?"

The Colonel studied me reflectively for a moment, then – "You," he replied. "The Brigadier wants you to do it, because of your battle experience, and because you happen to know far more than anyone else about the conditions and the Jap positions on the Ngalzang ridge … and you would have two rifle companies to do the job," he added hastily, "plus, of course, some gunner support."

"I have been talking to Brigade about it and they have promised to direct 12 Mountain Battery to support you and also to arrange for some dive-bombing by the R.A.F. I will tell Lionel Mead that his 'B' Company will be coming under your command," the Colonel continued. "And you had better warn Dougie Martin that he will be taking over your 'D' Company for this operation. Incidentally, the Brigadier is most insistent that this action must be completed by the middle of this month; today is the 2nd, so that gives you a couple of weeks to do any more reconnaissance you think you need before finalising your plans and to liaise with the gunners and the R.A.F. Any questions? No? Well, go away and think about it, and let me know your plans as soon as they are ready."

I left Battalion H.Q. with my mind in a whirl, and my emotions were very mixed as I made my way down the jungle track to my Company's position, at the top end of the Ngalzang ridge. As I walked, I had already started to think how I should plan the very difficult attack which I had been ordered to carry out, but it was not until I reached my own Company H.Q., that I realised that I had forgotten to ask the Colonel one all important question. Supposing, just supposing, we succeeded in overrunning the Jap position;

extremely unlikely, but not totally impossible and miracles have been know to happen – even in war! – then what?

It was clear that Brigade H.Q. expected this operation to be an in and out raid on a large scale, but supposing we caught the Japs completely by surprise and succeeded in capturing their position as a result. We would, by then, be literally miles ahead of any of our own forces and inevitably short of stores, particularly ammunition, while the Japs – always quick to react – would certainly counter-attack, swiftly and in force. Short of ammunition, we would then be unable effectively to resist any such attack, and would therefore face annihilation if we tried to do so. Having been taught that, when planning any operation, one should consider every possible eventuality and plan accordingly, I requested a ruling. The Colonel passed my query on to the Brigadier, whose reply was swift – "Should the circumstances you describe arise, you should first destroy all enemy equipment and then withdraw immediately, in planned stages, as swiftly as possible. Any involvement with counter-attacking forces should be avoided."

For my Company, the next ten days were frenetic. I led a reconnaissance patrol down a parallel ridge, in the hope of obtaining a flank view of the Jap position, but due to the denseness of the hill jungle, this proved abortive. However, my 'tiger-patrols' – operating down the Ngalzang ridge itself, under the strictest instructions to avoid, at all costs, being either seen or heard – obtained valuable information. They discovered that the Japs maintained a screen of lightly manned outposts and listening posts some 200 yards forward of their main position. Armed with this vital piece of information, plus some very recent aerial photographs showing Jap big gun positions at the end of the Vownalu Mual ridge, three miles north of Ngalzang, I laid my plans accordingly, Brigade H.Q. having agreed that the operation should be launched on the October 14th.

On 'D' Day minus three, I assembled my 'O' Group to explain the details of my plans and issue my orders. My 'O' Group consisted of 'B' Company commander, 'Whisky Mead'; 'D' Company commander, Dougie Martin; the battery commander of 12 Mountain Battery , with one of his gun section commanders, and his forward O.P. Officer; and the R.A.F.'s Liaison Officer from No 84 Squadron who were flying, at that stage of the war, Vultee 'Vengeance' dive-bombers. 'A' Company commander, Robin Bishop, also attended, because he had already been instructed to launch, on 'D' Day minus one, a mock attack – with noise effects only – on another strong Jap position on Vownalu Mual. It is interesting to note that this diversionary mock attack was so successful that, when we approached our own objectives at dawn the following morning, Jap counter-attacking troops could clearly be seen, several miles to the north, hastening like long dogs for Vownalu Mual!

I explained to my 'O' Group that my plan depended on us achieving complete surprise, and that this called for a silent night approach to our objectives. However, because of the very difficult nature of the terrain, our only feasible line of advance was straight along the top of the rocky, knife-edged ridge, until we bumped the Jap outposts at dawn. The order of march, I then told my 'O' Group, would be 'D' Company, followed by the section of the Mountain Battery, who would drop off when they reached the gun position selected by their Section Commander. Our start time would be 0500 hours, to enable us to reach the Jap listening posts in the half light of dawn.

'D' Company, I said, would be the first to contact the enemy; providing our timing was right, they would bump the lightly occupied Jap outposts about dawn and eliminate them. This would inevitably result in a fire-fight, of which the noise, however brief, was to be the signal for the mountain guns to bring down maximum concentrations for 15 minutes on the Japs' main position. After that, the guns were to lift on to the Jap mortar and gun positions at the rear of their main position, and during this period 'B' Company were to leap-frog through 'D' Company to assault the Japs' main position.

From then on, I admitted, immediate control of the battle would pass out of my hands and I would then have to 'play things by ear'. But the timing was planned, I said, in the expectation that the assault on the Japs' main position would go in at first light, at which time 'A' Company's mock attack on the Vownalu Mual feature, was expected to have drawn off appreciable numbers of counter-attacking troops, while the R.A.F. would have started dive-bombing the Japs' big-gun positions – for their 105mm and 135mm guns – at the end of the Vownalu Mual ridge, to neutralise them. Finally, before dismissing them, I told my 'O' Group that I had strict orders that this action was to be an in and out raid and that, should any circumstances arise which made it urgently necessary, signals for withdrawal would be sent by bugle. That was the end of the planning. What actually happened in fact, was a classic example of Robbie Burns' dictum '*The best laid plans o' mice and men gang aft a'gley!*', as the following account of the action vividly demonstrates!

Early in the morning on 'D' Day and still in the dark, 'D' Company, followed by myself, with the Gunner O.P. and my orderly in attendance, then 'B' Company, with the mountain guns trailing far behind, all advanced quietly along the ridge in the dark – with kuris drawn! Then came the first surprise, the Japs' outpost positions were empty, they had withdrawn them at night, a new tactic but an encouraging one. After briefly consulting me, Dougie Martin pushed slowly and carefully on until, as dawn broke, his 'D' Company reached a deep gully in the ridge, across which the main Jap position was plainly visible, the jungle around it having been cleared to provide fields of fire and bunkers having been dug.

At this point, Dougie wisely halted his men in the jungle and sent a runner to report to me. I crept forward and joined Dougie where he lay, hidden with his men on the lip of the gully. Everything was very quiet and, to my surprise, the Japs, the nearest of whom was less than 50 yards from where we lay, were blissfully unaware of our presence; they were moving around in the open, yawning and stretching, while one was sitting on top of his bunker, washing his feet in an enamel basin!

At that stage in the jungle war, all British officers, when going into action, were required to carry rifles, 'to confuse enemy snipers', according to an Army Instruction which caused much hilarity in Gurkha Rifle battalions, where the officers almost invariably towered above their stocky little Gurkha riflemen, sticking out like 'sore thumbs', a sniper's dream target! On this occasion, Dougie Martin, as 'D' Company commander, was carrying a rifle as usual, and as a fire-fight had to be started to trigger-off the mountain guns, I turned to him and said – "You had better shoot that one", pointing to the Jap who was still assiduously soaping his feet!

The effect of the rifle shot was impressive – and startling; the hygiene-minded Jap lost all interest in worldly things, but the slope in front of us erupted with leaping, bounding Japs, diving like startled rabbits into their bunkers and foxholes. Then came the swish and roar of the 19lb shells of the 3.7 inch Mountain Guns, as they burst – right among us; they had got the range wrong and the Gunner O.P. was frantically trying to get the guns to lift – through a dead wireless set damaged by a splinter from one of his own shells!

The Japs were seasoned troops; in moments they had recovered from their surprise and were pouring heavy and light machine-gun fire at us and saturating the area with their mortars. 'D' Company returned the fire with rifles and

*Surviving Officers of 1/3 Gurkha Rifles after the Burma campaign.*
*The author is in the centre*

L.M.G's, while 'B' Company, ignoring everything, stormed forward cheering and blitzing as they went. Then overhead, to our surprise, appeared the 'Vengeance' dive-bombers of 84 Squadron, whose map reading was distinctly weak; their target was the ridge three miles to the north of us, but they decided to bomb our ridge instead, and their dive-bombing was as accurate as their map reading was bad. Time after time, as we watched in fascinated horror, the planes banked, keeled over and dived, only pulling out as their 500lb bombs left them to burst among and around use with a shattering roar, while the planes circled and dived again and again; and the Japs' heavy guns to the north joyfully joined in, quite unhindered, the hiss and roar of their 105mm and 135mm shells adding to the now nightmare crescendo of sound.

The position was hopeless – and pointless. 'B' Company had got right into the Jap position, but the Japs were holed up comfortably underground in their deep bunkers, and the two rifle companies were pinned down by the intense shelling, mortaring, air bombing, and machine-gun fire from concealed bunker slits. There was only one thing to do, disengage and pull back, which we did – but only with great difficulty.

Although, by then, 1/3 GR was a battle-hardened battalion, the roll call was still a heartbreaking affair. 'B' Company commander, 'Whisky' Mead,[1] a young officer of twenty-one who was much liked in the battalion, had been killed while leading an attack on a strong Jap bunker; his Gurkha Subedar – who was his Company 2i/c – had also been killed, along with 23 riflemen, many more being wounded. Had it not been for the shape of the ground, our casualties could easily have been far worse, it was the rocky, knife-edged ridges which saved us from the worst of the air-bombing, shelling and mortaring. But for much of the action we were being bombed, shelled, mortared or shot at from every single direction – except underneath! In fact, we were literally blasted off our objective by our own bombs and shells, as much as those of the enemy.

And G.H.Q., New Delhi? Well, their Press Officers produced a dramatic, sanitized account of a hard-fought action in the Chin Hills, which appeared, a week later, in '*The Statesman*' and '*The Times of India*' dramatised account, which carefully and skilfully avoided any mention of errors and casualties, reads as follows:

## GURKHAS ROUT JAPS IN FIERCE HILL BATTLE

'Strongly-defended 'bunkers', in which the Japanese have entrenched themselves in the Chin Hills, were the scene of a fiercely fought engagement in the latest action reported from this area of the Assam-Burma front, writes an Indian Army observer.

---

[1] Lionel Mead, aged 21, was posted to the Indian Army in late 1942. On board ship he tried to learn a smattering of Urdu from a book, but on arrival in India he found that he had been posted to the 3rd QAO Gurkha Rifles. On his first night in 3GR Mess at the Regimental Centre he ordered a large whisky. Unfortunately he confused 'burra' (large) with 'bara' (12) and ordered bara whisky. His astonishment can be imagined when the Mess orderly arrived with a large tumbler literally brimming over with whisky. Whether or not he shared the whisky with his brother officers or did his duty and consumed the lot, no-one will ever know. But what is known is that two of his brother officers helped him to his quarters later that evening dragging him by his feet. Ever after he was known as Whisky Mead or just Whisky to his many friends.

'Two companies of Gurkhas took part, supported by mortars, machine-guns and mountain guns. The first glimpse of the enemy was a group standing on a ridge 200 yards away. The leading company crept to within 25 yards of their most forward position before a shot was fired. This was from the company commander, who dropped a Japanese. Covering fire was immediately brought down on all the enemy positions. Enemy machine-guns opened up with a heavy crossfire while Japanese riflemen crawled about their bunkers, firing wildly and hurling grenades. One camouflaged bunker was bitterly contested. The Gurkha section which was the first to locate it, remained in position within six yards of the enemy throughout and by covering fire kept the enemy's heads down. Repeated attempts were made to charge the Gurkha position, but were beaten back by heavy fire from the flanks and the centre, and grenades.

'On two occasions two section commanders, both of whom were wounded in the legs in the first charge, rallied their men and, kukri in one hand and stick in the other, limped on, leading their men. After the third attempt a rifleman braved the heavy fire, running up the slope he threw his grenade into a trench from which the Japanese were lobbying their own. All the occupants were killed and the Gurkha then made his way back.'

## SUCH IS THE NATURE OF PROPAGANDA IN WAR!

# Chapter XVI

# A Battery on a Shoestring

The explorers and big game hunters of the Victorian and Edwardian eras were intrepid characters, bold individualists who were wont to disappear for months or even years at a time into the wild bushland of Africa or the steaming jungles of Asia or the Amazon. But before they ventured forth into the unknown, these adventurous but prudent men spent time, care and as much money as the depth of their pockets would allow, in selecting and assembling a battery of assorted firearms designed to meet every foreseeable contingency.

The problems which faced those hardy characters were many and varied, ranging from raids by hostile tribes and marauding lions to close quarter encounters with such formidable adversaries as elephant and buffalo, quite apart from the ever present need to keep their porters supplied with meat. In consequence, their batteries consisted of a variety of light and heavy rifles, shotguns and sidearms, the cost of which made sizeable holes in their complex budgets. In this day and age however, few of us ever have either the chance or the wherewithal to try to emulate, even in a small way, those mighty Nimrods of a colourful era. For myself such an opportunity has occurred only once in my life and that was 'way back in the autumn of 1947, when I was dependent on a very shallow purse indeed.

In September 1947, I had found myself back in England with my chosen career in ruins at my feet. The British Government had already begun the sorry process of dismantling the British Empire, and British Imperial India, that Mecca for fieldsportsmen, had ceased to be; the old Indian Army – at the end of the largest volunteer army in history – had been split between the new India and Pakistan; and my own Gurkha Rifle regiment had been handed over to India. Having served only with Gurkhas during my Indian Army career, the opportunity to transfer to the British Army had not really appealed to me, so – but not without many doubts and great sadness – I had resigned my commission. Thus, at the age of twenty-eight, I had arrived at a major crossroads in my life. What next? As one of my main reasons for joining the

Indian Army – aside from family tradition – had been the fine opportunities for fieldsports which service in India had assured, and as that door had finally been firmly closed behind me, I had then decided to turn my thoughts to the opportunities offered by service in Africa. Eventually, after much deliberation, I had applied for a post as a District Officer in the Colonial Administrative Service. For once 'Lady Luck' had literally beamed on me; not only was I accepted but, as an early applicant, I had also landed near the head of the queue for postings.

"Where do you want to go?" The question fired at me at the Colonial Office took me by surprise. I had expected to be told where to go. "West Indies", promptly said my wife, who was with me. I looked at her pityingly. I was sure that there was only one part of the world which could offer us a life similar to the one we had enjoyed in the Indian Army and that was East Africa. For a split second visions of teeming herds of game and the great hunters of the past flashed through my mind, then – "The answer is Kenya", I replied firmly. "Right", said my questioner. "Kenya it will be. You will sail in three months time. Good luck!" I floated out of the Colonial Office in a dream, fondly imagining myself as a second 'Sanders of the River' and thinking of how such great hunter-explorers as Sir Samuel Baker, Selous and 'Karamoja' Bell would have armed themselves for such a venture. As far as my battery was concerned the hunt was on!

I had returned from India owning nothing in the way of firearms; before leaving, I had sold my two rather tired rifles and the Japanese Imperial Army had relieved me of my faithful old B.S.A. 12-bore at the Battle of the Sittang River in Burma in 1942, since then I had used a series of borrowed shotguns. Among the latter had been my father-in-law's Cogswell and Harrison side plate model 12 bore named the 'Avant Tout', a gun which I had liked and one which was probably the single most popular model of shotgun in India at that time. So my hunt started with a visit to Messrs Cogswell and Harrison's premises in Piccadilly.

Sadly, Cogswell's could not help me; their 'Avant Tout' was out of production and their other models were either way above my price range or else I did not fancy them. Disconsolate, I trailed around all the leading London gunmakers, but in every case the answer was the same – either their guns were far too expensive for me or else not my 'cup of tea'. Finally, I remembered my old friends Halliday's of 63 Cannon Street, traditional gunmakers of the old school with whom I had dealt regularly as a youth before the war, and when I walked out of Mansion House tube station I felt a pang of nostalgia as the familiar shop 'B. Halliday and Co Ltd' confronted me across the street.

Mr Benjamin Halliday and both Mr Kenneth Greenfield and his father Mr Watson Greenfield greeted me so warmly that I felt like the proverbial Prodigal Son! 'Where had I been?' That took a long time to answer. 'What was I doing now and what did I need?' That was easier to explain and as if by magic a beautiful sidelock, 12-bore hammerless ejector, with classic engraving and a glowing walnut stock, was reverently produced for my inspection. Ken Greenfield studied a massive ledger. "It's No 2 of a pair," he said. "It's a Holland and Holland 'Royal' and it was built in 1897," he added with a smile. I looked at the gun again in surprise and awe. The 30-inch barrels appeared to be perfect – later tests on the plate showed that they threw superb patterns – and I realised that here was a supreme example of the best in the gunmakers' art. I hesitated, then asked the price. "Ninety-seven pounds, I'm afraid," replied Mr Halliday apologetically. Moments later I walked out of the shop a happy man! That lovely gun handled like a dream and was a joy to use; it seemed literally to float at my shoulder and it gave me many happy years after duck, francolin and guinea-fowl in East Africa, but on that day in London it was only the first item in my intended battery, albeit the most important one.

My next objective was a magazine rifle for use on African medium game, and having read Lt-Colonel Stockley's book '*Stalking in the Himalayas and Northern India*', the idea of a .318 Westley Richards had caught my fancy. The .318, with alternative bullet weights of 180 grains and 250 grains, giving muzzle velocities of 2,700 and 2,400 feet per second respectively, seemed to me to be ideal for my needs, so the hunt for a .318 was on, my first visit being to the original makers of this famous rifle, Messrs Westley Richards and Co, themselves.

Regretfully, Westley Richards could not help me, but eventually, after diligent searching, I tracked down a very nice, secondhand, take-down model of the Westley Richards .318 in the showroom of one of London's top gunmakers, whom Halliday's had advised me to visit. The label on the rifle said that it had been tried and tested; my firearms certificate was in order and the price was a very reasonable £40. I left the premises very satisfied, but next day when I took the rifle on the range to test it myself, the bolt would not close

*The author demonstrates his double .470 rifle, made by William Evans.
The .470 has a large cartridge with a massive 500 grain bullet, making it a
favoured calibre for elephant hunting*

on the cartridges due to insufficient head space! When I returned, fuming, to the shop, the manager, with profuse apologies, promised to fix the rifle in a few days. This the firm did, but in the meantime I resolved to be more careful.

Having found myself a suitable medium rifle, my thoughts began to turn to something more powerful. "Do I really need a heavy rifle?" I asked myself. For dangerous game, such as elephant, buffalo and lion, nothing less than a .375 magnum was really suitable, particularly in the hands of a comparative novice. But heavy rifles were expensive and in any case, as a District officer, how often would I be called upon to deal with large dangerous game? (Little did I know at the time how very often it would turn out to be!). With my mind full of doubts and a rapidly shrinking purse, I began a half-hearted search. But it was then only two years after the war and heavy rifles were not only very expensive but also in very short supply and I rapidly became discouraged. Then I made a chance discovery.

I was searching for a really good split-cane flyrod, suitable for Kenya's trout streams, but at that time good rods were also both relatively expensive and hard to come by. One day however, Halliday's informed me that there was a flyrod listed in the catalogue of an Auctioneer with premises off the Strand. It was described as a 'Hardy 'C.C. de France', 8 foot, split cane', which sounded ideal, so I went to inspect it. The rod proved to be just what I wanted, so I left a bid with the Auctioneer's clerk – at the reserve price which was £8 – and then had a casual look around the saleroom. Suddenly, in a dark corner behind a dusty Victorian commode, I noticed a well worn, green canvas gun case with brass corners. My curiosity aroused, I opened it. Inside the lid was a label inscribed 'Manton and Son, Calcutta', and nestling snugly in the red baize interior, broken down like a sporting shotgun, was a heavy double rifle.

With rapidly mounting excitement, I took the rifle's well-worn stock section out of the case and examined the action; it was a hammerless non-ejector made by William Evans of London. Next I inspected the barrels; they were 28 inches long (too long for comfort in thick bush) and much of the blueing had gone, but the rifling was still good and the bore was .470, a calibre much favoured for elephant hunting in Africa since the .470 cartridge is a powerful one firing a 500 grain bullet at a muzzle velocity of 2,125 feet per second. Carefully hiding my excitement and as casually as I could, I again approached the Auctioneer's clerk. "No, not much demand for those sort of guns," he said. "The reserve price? Round about £30, I think." I couldn't attend the auction itself, so again I left a bid at the reserve price and walked out into the Strand with my fingers crossed. Two days later I telephoned the Auctioneer's. "Yes, they're both yours," the clerk replied. "When will you collect?"

As the gunmakers from whom I had purchased the .318 had a reputation as builders of top quality double rifles, I took the .470 straight round to them. "You owe me a favour," I said. "So I want these barrels cut down to twenty-four inches and the whole weapon refurbished." A month later I returned. The rifle looked like new, with shorter barrels it handled superbly and the bill

*Outside the premises of B. Halliday and Co., next door to
'The Sugar Loaf' Inn in Cannon Street.
Mr Watson Greenfield demonstrates a rifle.*

was a token one of £10; anyone who knows how tricky and time-consuming it is to adjust and correct the sighting of a double rifle will appreciate what a gift that was, but I still had to put the rifle to a final personal test.

Near my parents' house in Bucks' there was an old gravel pit where I erected a target with a four inch bull. Going back 50 yards, I fired both barrels of the .470, in turn, from the sitting position, each time ending up flat on my back. Dusting myself down, I walked over to examine the target; there were two large bullet holes, touching each other, slap in the centre of the bull. I smiled to myself, well satisfied. For the sum of £40 I had obtained a heavy double rifle which any hunter would envy, and in the years to follow it gave me sterling service when hunting crop-raiding elephants in the dense coastal bush of Kenya and in the papyrus swamps of Uganda.

Before I sailed for Kenya I added one more rifle to my battery. I was on a farewell visit to Halliday's when Ken Greenfield opened a display cabinet and took out a weapon. "Here's a rifle that will interest you," he said, handing me a pre-war Mannlicher-Schonauer carbine in perfect condition and with a detachable Zeiss 'scope sight. Like all Mannlicher-Schonauers of that vintage the rotary magazine was as smooth as silk. A beautiful toy, I thought, and then I remembered that, next to the .275, the .256 had been 'Karamoja' Bell's favourite bore and with it he had felled many an elephant. I sighed. "You win," I said and wrote out a cheque for 19 guineas.

A month later my wife and I sailed from Tilbury; among our luggage was my battery of three good rifles and a superb shotgun, a collection which had cost me a lot of hard searching, but in cash a shade under £200 – in other words a formidable battery assembled on a shoe-string budget! However, I owed a lot to the courteous help given to me by Halliday's and in the years that followed, whenever I was home on leave from Africa and in the vicinity of London, I made a point of calling at the old shop in the East End. B. Halliday and Co had been at 63 Cannon Street, next to the 'Sugar Loaf' Inn, since 1921 and at 60 Queen Victoria Street before that, and they seemed to be as permanent as the Tower or the Houses of Parliament. So, I was not prepared for the shock which greeted me when I arrived in London in September 1961 en route for a wildlife tour of the U.S.A.

Humming happily to myself, I walked out of Mansion House tube station and, as always, I glanced expectantly across the street; then my mouth fell open. The 'Sugar Loaf' Inn was still there, but what was that next door to it? In the window where the best guns and rifles by leading British makers had stood in regal ranks, surrounded by shooting sticks, gamebags and cartridge belts, were row upon row of sleek nylon stockings, diaphanous nightgowns and an assortment of female underwear. Sadly, I turned away; only later was my morale partly restored when I learnt that although Halliday's had closed in 1960, Mr Kenneth Greenfield had then opened a gun shop in Salisbury, Wiltshire, under his own name. But for me something of value and a link with my past had gone from London.

*The author with two pairs of fine tusks, both from Uganda.*

*The longer pair, 174 lbs and 155 lbs, are from the same elephant and one of the 'soft' (i.e. workable) variety. The smaller pair, 62 lbs and 60 lbs, are the tusks from a forest elephant and therefore of the ' hard' variety – difficult to carve.*

# Chapter XVII

# The Lure of the Elephant

Long ago it dawned on me that elephant hunting has a great deal in common with salmon fishing, a comment which will no doubt cause a sharp raising of the eyebrows among the aficionados of the exclusive fraternities of elephant hunters and salmon anglers. But before I am condemned, out of hand, as a mentally defective heretic, I must first stress that I am referring to the pursuit of the African elephant and of the Atlantic salmon. Having made that point, I will now try to explain how and why I consider the similarities to be so striking.

First of all, both the African elephant and the Atlantic salmon have long enjoyed a very widespread and well defined range, but also, sadly, a steadily decreasing one. Moreover, wherever either of them have occurred, it has usually been in large numbers and with noticeable regional variations in their physical size and shape, quite apart from the obvious influence of the age factor.

Next, just as certain rivers invariably produce salmon of a high average weight and with occasional outsize specimens, so do certain regions of Africa produce elephants with a high average tusk weight and occasional giant tuskers. Furthermore, any truthful salmon angler will admit that however much he enjoys salmon fishing for its own sake, it is his secret ambition to land at least one really big salmon during his lifetime. Exactly the same can be said of the elephant hunter, whose constant search is for a really big tusker. In both cases, in their dogged pursuit of these elusive leviathans there is that element of unquenchable optimism and undying hope which is the very hall-mark of the seeker after treasure trove!

To an elephant hunter a really big tusker is a 'hundred pounder', that is a bull carrying a pair of tusks each of which weighs one hundred pounds or more. In my reckoning, in salmon fishing this equates to a thirty pound salmon in the British Isles and a fifty pounder in Norway; and many – possibly the majority – of skilled, dedicated and determined elephant hunters and salmon anglers never achieve this ambition during a lifetime of intensive hunting and fishing.

Time and time again, when one of these leviathans does happen to fall to a rifle or rod, it happens when least expected and often when least deserved. Furthermore, all too often the lucky hunter or angler is a novice, possibly even out for the first time, and he or she then goes away thinking that it is all too easy, that there is nothing to it. In both elephant hunting and salmon fishing, 'Lady Luck' is indeed fickle, and from my own experience and from my knowledge of the experience of others, the answer is simple – the bagging of a 'hundred pounder' elephant, or of a 'thirty pounder' or a 'fifty pounder' salmon, is ninety per cent chance and luck, and only ten per cent determination and skill!

Africa is full of tales of legendary elephant, ancient bulls with tusks so long that not only do they sweep right down to the ground but they curve up again, leaving tell-tale grooves in the soil when the great beast is weary and his massive head droops. Some of these tales are true, and in twenty-five years as a Game Warden in Africa I had the good fortune to meet up with several of these mighty tuskers, secretive beasts often accompanied by one or more mature young bulls as sentries and bodyguards.

A few of these mighty but ancient beasts were true loners, and one of these inspired me to write the following verses, which I have entitled '*An African Night*'. I hope that the dedicated elephant hunter will find these verses evocative and that they will remind the salmon angler of the ugly threat of the poacher.

*'The Patriarch'*
*for years, this old bull with enormous tusks, made a home for himself*
*near the Murchison Falls in Uganda*

## 'An African Night'

Across the moonlit bushland came a lion's moaning roar,
The distant screams of elephants, a leopard's rasping saw.
At the water-hole below me there was scarce a sound until
Its peace was rudely shattered by hyenas on a kill;
Their frenzied madman's cackles would have made a banshee shiver,
While those raucous, grunting bellows came from hippos in the river.

As I sat beside my camp fire, its warming, flickering glow
Cast leaping, dancing shadows that wandered to and fro,
'Till imagination kindled and between the nearby trees
A stealthy, slinking movement brought my rifle to my knees.
But a moonbeam like a searchlight showed a jackal on the prowl,
Frustrated, hungry, searching, he departed with a howl.

Like diamond studded velvet far above me stretched the sky,
And across this star-lit backcloth the nightjars glided by
With trailing, fluttering pennants, unlike any other bird,
Their softly whispering pinions so quiet and seldom heard;
Yet they were also hunters, alert and on the seek
Their gentleness deceptive, catching moths in gaping beak.

Then suddenly I heard it, that sound which brings a thrill
To the soul of any hunter, whatever grade his kill.
Like muted, rumbling thunder, or a giant feline purr,
'Tho the mighty beast which made it was not adorned with fur.
I held my breath and listened for the sound to come again,
With adrenalin a'pumping speeding up my pulse and brain.

The noise was not repeated, but there came a different sound,
A rending, tearing, crashing – as a thorn tree hit the ground.
When the splintering subsided came yet another tone,
A steady, rhythmic chomping, massive jaws on wood like bone.
But still the beast was hidden by the shadows of the trees,
And still I tensely waited with my rifle on my knees.

My patience was rewarded, for like some giant snake,
Curling high above the thorn trees, yet another branch to break,
There rose a questing tentacle, a pachydermal trunk
So massive that I wondered could I possibly be drunk?
I looked again, this time the moon revealed a thrilling sight,
A fleeting glimpse of ivory – but could my eyes be right?

Then noiseless as a shadow and with cushioned, silent tread,
Out into the clearing stepped a shape all peasants dread,
A towering, massive elephant so tall it blocked the sky,
With tusks so long, so thick, so white, my throat and mouth went dry.
It was an ancient, mighty bull which hunters long had trailed,
A local native legend which I too had sought but failed.

One moment it was there – and then, as silent as it came,
The beast had gone, I knew not where, the jackal back again.
I waited for the dawn to break and at the sun's first gleam
I woke beside my camp fire – so was it all a dream?
But no, around my camp site the evidence was there,
The mighty tracks like giants' plates, the thorn tree smashed and bare.

With hope renewed I gathered up my rifle, pack and bearer,
The tracks were clear, we followed fast, our quarry ever nearer.
As noon approached the sun beat down, the pace we set was testing.
Excitement grew for well we knew our bull would soon be resting.
And so it proved, with sudden shock, in a fig tree's spreading shade
We found our bull, his heart quite still – from a drop-spear's
   poisoned blade.

# Chapter XVIII

# The Elephants of Knysna

When the first settlers landed at the Cape of Good Hope, more than 300 years ago, elephants existed throughout Africa, from the wooded slopes of Cape Aghulas, the southernmost point of the continent, right up to the edge of the Sahara. In Cape Province, an area considerably larger than France, these great animals abounded wherever suitable bush and forest conditions occurred. But both the bush and the forests, and the elephants with them, soon began to disappear before the sharp axes and ready guns of the ever-advancing pioneers.

Two hundred years later, elephants in Cape Province were mainly confined to the dense coastal forests and bush country between George and Port Elizabeth. Nevertheless, in 1868, when Thomas Bain (a famous road engineer) and Captain Christopher Harrison (then Conservator of Forests at Tsitsikama) explored the wooded country from Knysna to Witte Els Bosch, halfway to Port Elizabeth, they reported an abundance of elephant and buffalo.

When, eight years later, Captain Harrison had become the first Conservator of the Midland Conservancy, with responsibility for the forests of George, Knysna and Humansdorp, he estimated that there were between 400 and 500 elephants in these forests. But he was concerned for their future since they were remorselessly hunted both for sport and for ivory, and as often as not illegally, although free permits were readily available on demand in Cape Town.

Harrison's pleas for effective conservation measures fell on deaf ears until 1908, when an embarrassed officialdom awoke to the fact that the Knysna elephants had been reduced to a herd of some 20 individuals. Apart from the herd inhabiting the Addo Bush near Port Elizabeth, they were the only elephants left in the Cape Province, and were belatedly declared Royal Game.

For 12 years, no more permits for hunting were issued. Then, in 1920, Major P. J. Pretorius, the famous elephant-hunter, obtained leave to shoot one bull in the Knysna Forest for scientific purposes. He wished to prove his theory that the elephants were a distinct sub-species, the biggest in Africa. Unfortunately, what followed reflects little credit on this courageous man.

In the dense forest dogs were used to harry the elephants, and in the ensuing fracas two bulls and a cow charged and were shot. A calf was killed in the stampede, and another died as a result of its mother's death. The Knysna elephants had been dealt a blow from which they have never recovered.

Press reports of the time suggested that the bulls shot by Pretorius were enormous animals, measuring 12 feet 8 inches and 13 feet at the shoulder. However, the official museum records in Cape Town, where the elephants were finally measured, give the largest as being only 9 feet 4 inches at the shoulder. Any elephant taller than 11 feet 6 inches is quite outstanding, although larger specimens have been reported from various parts of Africa from time to time. In 1955, a gigantic bull standing 13 feet 2 inches at the shoulder was shot in Angola, and is now on display in the museum of the Smithsonian Institute in Washington. So, despite the efforts of Pretorius, the mystery about the size of the Knysna elephants remains unsolved.

The remnants of the herd now inhabit the Gouna, Deep Walls, and Kafferkop sections of the Knysna Forest, to the north of the Port Elizabeth–Knysna road, and the Noetsie and Harkerville sections to the south of the road. The Forest lies between the Outeniqua Mountains and the Indian Ocean, at an altitude which varies from 1,000 to 3,000 feet above sea level, and it consists of about 200 square miles of very broken, irregular terrain, intersected by numerous deep, narrow valleys with clear running mountain streams. Most of this area is covered with very dense forest, made up of an almost continuous canopy of lofty, indigenous trees, hiding a tall carpet of thick undergrowth. The latitude is 34ºS, which makes the Knysna herd the most southerly elephant population in the world, although it is now no more than a pitiful remnant of the great herds which roamed this region from Palaeolithic times.

For reasons which are unknown the threat of extinction still hangs over the Knysna herd, despite more than 60 years of legal protection. That they have survived at all has been entirely due to the tolerance and sympathetic interest of the Forestry Department and private forestry concerns.

Such then, was the extent of my knowledge when, late in January 1968, I set out at the request of the Cape Province's Department of Nature Conservation to find out more about the elusive elephants of Knysna. They wanted some photographs, and some idea of the numbers and composition of the existing herd. Time was short before the date of the conference for which my report was required, and so I was only allowed 10 days to complete the project. It was only when I arrived at Knysna itself that I realised the impossibility of the task which I had been set.

Once there, I was promised the help of the forestry staff by J. W. Steyn, the Chief Regional Forest Officer, and Dr F. Von Breitenbach, the Chief Research Officer for the Indigenous Forests. They told me that even their men were uncertain about the number of elephants in the forest, and they passed me on to meet Hjalmar Thesen, a keen naturalist and head of a big timber concern, Thesen Industries, which owns the Brackenhill section of the Knysna Forest. From Hjalmar Thesen I picked up a great deal of useful information on the elephants, and I was promised the assistance of one of Thesen's woodcutters, John ('Aapie') Stroebel, as a guide. Aapie was reckoned an expert on the forest and its elephants, but even he didn't know their exact numbers, nor could he say how many bulls and cows there were.

I also made contact with a young forester, André du Plooy, who put me up at his base at the Deep Walls Forest Station in the heart of the forest, promising that the other stations would report immediately if they found fresh signs of elephants.

For the first four days, the search was concentrated in the sections to the north of the national road. It was only on the third day, at the Gouna station, that the trail started to get warm. The forest workers had reported an elephant close to the station at dawn a few days before, and in the area we discovered the two-day-old tracks of two adults who had been digging for bracken roots.

Next day, I returned to Gouna with Graham Wiltshire, a keen young member of the Wildlife Protection Society, together with Aapie Stroebel and his nephew Willem. Aapie was a bit dubious about me to begin with, having had some frightening experiences with novices out in search of the elephants. Graham reassured him that I did know quite a lot about elephants, and Aapie and his nephew quickly showed themselves to be good trackers, with a thorough knowledge of the Knysna Forest and the habits of the elephants. With their help we found fresh droppings, tracks, and broken trees on a path to the north of Gouna. It was early afternoon, and the signs were of an adult elephant, probably a solitary bull.

Later on, while we ranged farther ahead, we found even fresher droppings, and the tracks of two more elephants, one obviously a large bull, the other either a cow or a small bull. The signs were so new that we decided to leave the trail and follow them.

The forest presented a solid, leafy wall, dark and menacing. The trail led through dense, head-high undergrowth, and overhead the canopy of great trees seemed to blot out the light. We could only move along the meandering trail bulldozed by the elephants. For a moment we hesitated – we were armed with nothing more lethal than a pocket-knife – then slowly and carefully we moved ahead.

Every few paces we halted to listen, while I carefully checked the direction of the wind with a little bag of wood-ash. In the still air of the forest, what breaths of wind there were swirled and eddied as if in some mad waltz. Finally we realised that dusk was fast approaching. All around us the forest lay still and silent as the tomb. The time had come when it would not only have been pointless but also foolhardy to continue, so we turned and made our way hurriedly back to the Land Rover on the forest road.

Tracking elephants under such conditions is a hazardous operation calling for strong nerves, common sense, and cool judgement. The Knysna elephants are inclined to be vicious and react strongly when human beings are near. For an unarmed man in dense forest, the odds are heavily in favour of the elephant, and on that day near Gouna I would have been happier for my old double-barrelled .470 as some sort of life insurance, but the elephants were far too rare to run the risk of a shooting incident.

We now knew that there were at least three adult elephants in the Gouna area, and since we had found no fresh signs elsewhere in the northern section, I decided to switch my attention to the south, to the Harkerville Forest. Daily I checked all the places where the elephants might cross the national road, and to my relief I found no signs of any such movement throughout the time I was in the forest, a fact which helped my census considerably.

The following day, André du Plooy and I set out in his Land Rover to search the forest tracks in the Harkerville section. Between dawn and dusk, we covered them all, and as far as actually seeing elephants or their fresh tracks were concerned, we again drew a blank; but old droppings of all sizes were plentiful. These and the many broken trees showed that the area had been regularly used by elephants of all age groups for a long period. I therefore decided to concentrate my efforts on the Harkerville section.

February 6th dawned cool and overcast with intermittent drizzle – conditions that tend to keep elephant on the move and drive them out of the constantly dripping forest into the open. I decided to search the Harkerville section again, in the company of André du Plooy and Aapie and Willem Stroebel. En route we checked all the elephant crossing places along the national road, but found no fresh signs.

At 9.00am we found broken trees and very fresh droppings and tracks on a forest road three miles west of Harkerville Forest Station and only half a mile from the national road, south of the area known as the 'Garden of Eden'.

Following the tracks carefully through thick forest, at 10.00am we finally located three elephants in very dense cover in a valley bottom. The animals were feeding noisily, but, although we crouched within 30 yards of them for nearly an hour, listening to a discordant symphony of gargantuan rumbles and belches, the massive breaking wind, and the irregular plop of mighty faeces, all to the accompaniment of the squeals of tortured roots and the thunderous, rending crash of falling trees, of the elephants themselves we could see nothing.

Then, without any warning, all was still. I felt a breath of air on the back of my neck – the wind had changed.

Instantly a savage scream vibrated and echoed through the forest, shaking the nearby trees. Stunned by the deafening noise we crouched lower and waited apprehensively. Nothing happened. A cathedral-like hush descended on the forest.

Five minutes later I nodded at Aapie. Very cautiously we crept forward until we reached an area which looked as though it had been hit by a small cyclone. The ground was littered with broken branches and uprooted trees. Of the elephants themselves, there was no sign. They had vanished like ghosts. Only their mighty footprints, with the muddy swamp water still trickling into them, remained as proof that the animals had ever been there.

For nearly two more hours we trailed the elephants through dense forest, until in the early afternoon we caught up with them again, feeding in the bottom of another valley. Virtually the same performance was repeated, and as before it ended with a terrifying scream followed by complete silence. After that we decided to leave them. I was fairly sure that next time they would charge, and we had at least established that there were three elephants in the group – two adult animals and one half grown.

I had an idea that there might be more elephants in the area of the 'Big

Island', the largest of the grassy glades which occur throughout the Knysna Forest, varying in size from a few square yards to a hundred acres or more. Such places are frequently visited by elephants in search of a change of diet, particularly in wet weather when they like to escape the persistent dripping of the rain-sodden forest.

It was already late in the afternoon when we found our way back to the Land Rover, and as we headed for the Big Island, we were frequently held up by fallen trees, which had been pushed over by elephants. We had to make several long detours, but we felt that the omens were good.

The Big Island lies in the southern part of the Harkerville section, near the sea, and as we approached it the forest began to thin. Then, suddenly, I caught sight of elephant droppings by the side of the track. They were obviously from a big bull, and so fresh that they were still steaming. In an instant we were out of the Land Rover and listening intently. Soon, a tree groaned and fell with a crash in the forest nearby. We doubled along the track to get down wind, and then cut into the forest at a point where it had been partially cleared. All the time we could hear the elephant moving slowly but steadily towards us, feeding as it came. We stopped and waited. Carefully I tested the wind.

Aapie was afraid that the bull we had discovered was 'Aftand', an old elephant with a notoriously vicious temper. Several years ago it had come off worst in a contest with a bulldozer, breaking the end of its left tusk in the process. This bull terrorised the forest workers, and on several occasions had chased Aapie, who had no wish for this experience to be repeated.

At last, like a slow-motion film, the grey-brown shape of an elephant slowly began to materialise out of the forest some 50 yards to my front. Although it was still partly screened by bushes and small trees, I glimpsed a truly massive bull with long, curving tusks. And I could just see that the end of the left tusk had been broken.

One look was enough for Aapie, "It's 'Aftand'", he gasped, and he and his nephew made off at speed for the Land Rover. Andre stood his ground, taking the precaution of locating a climbable tree. The elephant was now thoroughly suspicious, and turned back into thicker cover. Cursing my luck I started to follow, my camera ready with its controls pre-set.

First I thought that the bull had vanished, and then I saw a great dark mass standing motionless in the forest about 40 yards away. Photography would have been hopeless; there was only one thing to do. I snapped my fingers.

*'Aftand' the rogue bull of the Knysa Forest*

Quick as a cat the bull whirled round to face me, ears out, his trunk reaching for the wind. But he was still only a dark shape in the gloom, so I snapped my fingers again.

The elephant's response was instantaneous – a lightning rush which brought him 10 yards closer, right to the edge of the bush-filled clearing. He stood partly screened by the bushes, angrily scenting with his trunk. As I raised my camera I was thankful that the wind was blowing strongly in my face. The clicking of my shutter infuriated him. For a moment he hesitated, then, curling his trunk between his tusks, he cocked his ears menacingly and launched himself violently in the direction of the sound. I snapped a picture of the charging elephant, dodged behind a tree, and made a careful note of my safest line of retreat.

The bull halted 20 paces away, puzzled and annoyed at finding nothing. He stood with his head raised, his trunk searching, and his eyes glaring myopically. I stared, fascinated, at his sweeping tusks. They must each have weighed at least 80 pounds. His gigantic ears, spread like the sails of a square-rigged ship, seemed to fill the sky. Teetering on a rotten tree-stump, I snapped away, my camera clicking like a typewriter.

The elephant angrily tried to pin-point the source of the noise. Twenty paces separated us, and my only cover was a flimsy tangle of fallen branches. Suddenly, with a quick crouching rush, almost feline in its vicious silence, he tried to outflank me. I doubled back along a small game trail, expecting him to follow me into the open, but he was too cunning. At the edge of the bush he stopped and hid, ready to ambush anything that moved along the track. I could just see the tips of his tusks where he lay in wait. I was relieved that I was now 50 yards away. I didn't trust 'Aftand' any more than Aapie did, but I had got my pictures, unique photographs of a rare and little-known race of elephants.

The next day I went down with fever, so my survey was abruptly terminated. However, it had achieved something. I could state categorically that, at the time of my visit, there were at least seven elephants of varying age groups in the Knysna Forest, indicating slow but regular breeding over the years. On all the evidence my estimate of total numbers was at least ten. The old bull, of which I had been lucky enough to get some unique photographs, though a massive elephant, was no bigger than other fine specimens of *Loxodonta africana africana* that I have seen elsewhere in Africa. I was satisfied that little more could have been achieved in the time and that what was needed to solve all the mysteries of the Knysna elephants was a really prolonged survey by a co-ordinated team of experienced people.

One thing still puzzles me. Every time I look at the picture of 'Aftand' I am struck by the size of the eyes. Can the camera lie – or not?

But that is not the end of my tale of the elephants of Knysna, although it was the end when I first wrote this story – illustrated by the numerous photographs I had taken of the rogue bull 'Aftand' – for publication in the September 1968 issue of *African Wildlife*, the journal of *The Wildlife Protection and Conservation Society of South Africa*.

However, on May 12th 1971, three years after my survey of the small, remaining herd of elephants in the Knysna forest, the body of 'Aftand', the rogue bull of the herd, was found, rotting, deep in the Harkerville section of the forest.

As 'Aftand's' tusks had been removed, it was immediately thought that the old bull had been the victim of ivory poachers. But there were suspicions, and a very thorough investigation by the police, in George, revealed the surprising truth – 'Aftand' had not been shot by poachers. The rogue bull, a dangerous menace to all who met him, had been assassinated, in secret and by a skilled marksman, on the direct orders of a senior official of the Forestry Department!

For years 'Aftand' had terrorised all those who worked in the Knysna forests. He would attack on sight and without warning, as I myself had experienced, and on one occasion he had even attacked a bulldozer, breaking the tip of his left tusk in the process. On another occasion he actually succeeded in catching a terrified forest worker and the latter's remains, when they were found, were so badly crushed that they were hardly identifiable. 'Aftand' in fact, was a very dangerous rogue, and it was therefore inevitable that, sooner or later, he would have to be destroyed.

'Aftand's' tusks were recovered from the office of the Forestry official who had ordered him to be shot, and I was interested to hear that 'Aftand's' right tusk had been found to weigh just under 80lbs, while his left tusk, the tip of which had been broken when he attacked the bulldozer, had still weighed 65lbs.

Like many others, I was sad but not surprised to hear of the death of 'Aftand' of whom I have many vivid memories. The old rogue had given me much interest and great excitement when I had been searching for elephants in the Knysna forest, while the dramatic photographs that I had taken of 'Aftand' as he charged me, I have since used to illustrate several articles and also in my book *The Shamba Raiders*. So, although I do not know whether it is appropriate to say this about an elephant – 'Aftand', rest in peace!

# Chapter XIX

# A Truly Royal Fish

Norway is famous for its mighty salmon and Sweden for its giant sea-trout, but how many people consciously connect the lakes and rivers of Scandinavia with brown trout of aldermanic proportions? I confess that until recently I, for one, did not.

I am what might be called an omnivorous fisherman and in the course of a somewhat varied career have had the opportunity to fish for a variety of species, from chub in England to mahseer in India, from pike in Scotland to barracuda off Zanzibar, from bass in Devon estuaries to Nile perch and tiger fish in the great lakes and rivers of Africa; there have been days with hard-fighting rainbow and brown trout in Kashmir, Kenya and the 'Old Country', and even the odd 'red-letter' day after salmon; but although I would much rather catch one really large specimen of any species I fish for than a number of smaller ones, this ambition, until the summer of 1953, had never even approached being realised.

Where shall we go? That was the question my wife and I were pondering on our return from Africa on home leave in July, 1953. We wanted to spend part of our leave seeing new countries and I, as usual, hoped to combine this with wetting a line in strange waters. I had by then been well and truly bitten by the salmon 'bug' although my opportunities for salmon fishing were very few and far between and, until then, I had only had two of these fascinating and elusive fish to my credit. Both had been caught spinning and my ambitions were fired to catch, first of all, a really big salmon, secondly a salmon on fly, and thirdly a good sea-trout, a fish with which up to that time I had not come to grips.

After much investigation and discussion, we decided on a sight-seeing-cum-fishing trip of three weeks by car to Norway, Sweden and Denmark. We realised that limited funds and the fact that we would have to go very late in the season were against us as far as the chances of Norwegian salmon were concerned, but by going direct from Norway to Denmark and ending up our trip in southern Sweden we hoped to coincide with the best time of year for a mighty sea-trout of the Baltic.

We landed at Bergen in the second half of August, blessing the comfort of the crossing in a ship fitted with stabilisers, and headed north for a hotel at the head of a small fjord which had some salmon water. The proprietor, himself a keen fisherman, was charming and helpful but warned us we were late in the season, and so it proved. The water did not have a reputation for numbers but of those salmon which were caught each season a high proportion were mighty fish, and from the walls of the hotel photographs of successful anglers holding enormous salmon leered down at us, apparently contemptuous of our unskilled and unsuccessful efforts.

It was not until our last day that I yielded to the proprietor's suggestion that I should try instead for some of the big cannibal trout to be found in parts of the river, and then only after seeing a 5lb specimen caught by a local angler. I found them, yes I found them, and finished my last evening sadder and wiser after three great trout had broken my light spinning tackle on under-water snags where the river flowed through a deep, precipitous gorge. I then began to realise that there were worthy antagonists among the Scandinavian brown trout!

We left regretfully and continued on our way, casting envious eyes at the tunny-fishing in the straits between Sweden and Denmark, finally finding ourselves on the Morrum River in southern Sweden in the first week on September. It was a lovely river, with on its banks a state-run salmon and sea-trout hatchery of absorbing interest, but luck was again against us. The weather had been dry, the river was low and the normal big early September run of sea-trout had not materialised. Again we were mocked by photographs on the walls of our hotel showing sea-trout as large as the average British salmon, and as in Norway the local people of all walks of life were genuinely concerned at our continued ill-luck. Eventually when we were left with only one clear day and not a fish to show, they intervened.

Through the kindness of a visiting Swedish angler from Stockholm and the 'Fishing Master' (or water bailiff) on the Morrum, I was put in touch with the Secretary of the South Swedish Angling Club, who gave me permission to fish for brown trout on the Bolman River at Skene. This was a very great privilege for the club is the most exclusive angling club in Sweden, with a strictly limited membership, and the Bolman River was famous for the size, numbers and fighting quality of its trout. I say 'was' advisedly, as will be seen later.

It was a long run to Skene and we decided to fish there in the afternoon and evening, returning to our hotel late at night, ready to pack up and move on to Gothenburg the following day, to catch our boat to England. The weather had changed suddenly and there was a cold, blustery wind and occasional squalls of rain.

We arrived eventually at the Club's delightful old wood-built fishing-lodge on the banks of the river, and to our surprise were met by a charming young Swede, who greeted us in perfect English with typical Scandinavian courtesy, explaining that he had been warned of our visit and that he was to look after us as guests of the club; his name was Borje Verlander.

Borje turned out to be a lawyer from Halsingborg, and the youngest member of the Club. He told us the sad news that, owing to a big hydro-electric scheme, this was the last season that anyone would fish this river. The fishing-lodge which had stood there for over 50 years, and on the walls of which were the tracings of mighty fish and the caricatures, signatures and pictures of famous anglers from all over the world, was to be dismantled; and the Bolman River itself, which flowed between two great lakes and which had already been diverted into a new course, would disappear forever.

Fly only was the rule and we lost no time in getting to the water, but yet again ill-luck dogged our footsteps, and by dusk we only had one smallish fish between the three of us, caught by my wife. Borje was most upset for our sake and blamed the sudden change in the weather. He insisted that we stay the night at the lodge and try again the following day, and after a conference, in which my wife gallantly volunteered to drive back herself in the morning to fetch our luggage from the hotel so that I might fish, we agreed. Luckily Skene was well on our way to Gothenburg, and, barring accidents, an early start on the day after would get us to that port in time to catch our ship. That being fixed we settled down in front of a roaring log fire to a magnificent meal of fat, pink-fleshed trout caught by Borje that morning, washed down with good Swedish schnapps and beer, while he regaled us with stories of fishing in the Club waters. Apparently in May and September very big trout entered the river from the lakes, and small or medium sized salmon flies were the right medicine for them. He himself, he told us, had caught the Swedish record fly-caught brown trout in this river a few years before.

*Caught by the author in the Bolman River, Sweden (on a hand-made salmon fly).*
*This Brown Trout weighed 14lbs 12½ ounces, and a plaster cast of this fish now*
*hangs in the hall of the author's house.*

Next morning, after an early breakfast, my wife departed in the car, and Borje and I set off for the top of the best remaining stretch of fishable water, passing on the way the long line of fixed eel-traps which spanned the river. I had a nine foot trout rod, and on Borje's advice had tied a No 2 'Silver Doctor' on my cast. Borje, to my surprise, was using a twelve foot double-handed light salmon rod and a large peculiar looking fly, and was carrying a salmon gaff. He bade me start, saying that he would fish down after me. The weather had settled; the river, which was some thirty or more yards across, ran in its artificial course with a strong current, deep and of a good colour; my hopes rose as I placed my first cast.

It was not long before I was into a nice fish, of just over a pound, which put up a really good fight before being netted. I had lost two more, lightly hooked, and landed a second of about the same size as the first, when I heard a shout from Borje. Looking back I saw his big rod well bent and realised he had hooked a good fish. Despite his strong tackle the struggle, though dour and unspectacular, was a long one, and it was some time before I could slip the gaff into a very dark coloured trout which turned the scales at 4 kilos (8¾lbs).

"There you are", said Borje, "that is the sort of fish you can expect here, but it is getting too bright now, I know this river. We will go back to the lodge for lunch and try the rest of the stretch later this afternoon. When we come back I want you to try this tackle of mine". I thanked him and examined his 'fly', which was really a bucktail or streamer tied on a 3/0 hook. It had a silver body with a red feather tail and the hair 'wings' were natural buck-hair above and yellow below. Borje claimed that this was his own invention which had proved most successful.

Throughout a rather leisurely lunch I was fretting to get back to the river and eventually Borje declared that the time was ripe. We returned to where we had left off in the morning and I soon found myself with Borje's tackle in my hands, covering the river in long even swathes as if I was fly-fishing for salmon.

I saw several large fish move but by the time I had turned the bend at the top of the final short stretch above the eel-traps, which now hove in sight, dusk was near, and I had not had a touch. I was within fifty yards of the traps and casting almost mechanically, when my fly was taken with a bang in the middle of the river. I tightened to drive the hook home, and as I did so my rod bent double and my reel screamed as the fish went off in a mad rush upstream. After some 50 yards I managed to turn it and by this time I realised I was into a really heavy fish.

It came back again fast and I only just managed to stop it entering the eel traps and breaking me. This time it again set off in another long, mad rush upstream, tearing line off the reel and ending in a magnificent leap. As it soared upwards, the evening sun glinting on its great golden sides, it dawned on my awed senses that here was not only the biggest trout I had ever set eyes on but one bigger than any I had dared dream of. At that moment I heard the panting voice of Borje behind me – "Don't lose it", he said. "For God's sake don't lose it, that's the biggest trout I've ever seen!".

The struggle went on without respite, long heavy runs ending on three occasions with mighty leaps that flung that great trout three feet and more clear of the water, revealing its size and bringing my heart into my mouth each time lest I should lose it. But I felt it was securely hooked and the greatest danger was that it would get me tangled in the eel traps. It made one last effort to reach this sanctuary, but putting on all the pressure I dared, I managed to turn it and it began to roll.

By this time the fish had been on for over half an hour and I was sweating profusely from sheer nerves and excitement, my arms were aching, and Borje was crawling about on the bank like a red Indian, behind every available bit of cover, waiting excitedly for the first opportunity to use his long-handled gaff. It was not long before the fish started to flounder in the shallows, giving Borje his chance. He made no mistake, and scooping the fish from the water he clasped it to his bosom, scrambled up and flung it to safety over the top of the high bank.

Lighting cigarettes with trembling fingers as reaction set in, we gazed in awe at our prize as it lay in the grass – a great, thick, cock trout, glistening brown and gold, shading to silvery white on the belly and spotted and flecked with red and black. "Do you know" said Borje in a hushed voice, "I think you have broken the Swedish records; let's get back to the lodge quickly and weigh it properly".

The water-bailiff weighed the fish outside the tackle room and I watched the scales with wondering eyes as they registered 6.7 kilos (14¾lbs) – "Just, but only just under the Swedish fly record, which is 6.75 kilos", said Borje with a grin. "Actually your fish, which measures 84cm is 2cm longer than my record fish, and if he had had a larger meal this morning the record would have been yours!" For my part I was relieved; it would have been a poor return for all my host's kindness and hospitality to have taken the record from him, and that with his own tackle and self-made fly!

This was the grand finale, and what a finale! Any further attempts at fishing would have been an anti-climax, so we settled down to toast the great fish which lay in state before us. Then it struck me – what was I to do with a trout that size? We were due to sail from Sweden the following day and I could scarcely take it with me. Suddenly Borje said – "I have an idea. This is the second biggest trout ever caught in Sweden on a fly, it is a truly royal fish; His Majesty the King of Sweden is a keen angler and the patron of this Club, he has often fished here, would you care to present the trout to him? I am returning this evening to Halsingborg, where His Majesty is staying for a few days on the Royal Yacht, and I could leave the fish with the King's private secretary". This was an ideal solution, and later that morning, my wife and I regretfully said goodbye to Borje, who departed with my great trout and a suitably worded note addressed to His Majesty.

I have many happy memories of that trip and the kindness and hospitality of the Scandinavian peoples, while among my treasured angling mementoes are a rather odd-looking salmon fly, a carefully traced outline and coloured photographs of a mighty Swedish trout – later skilfully made into a lifelike plaster cast by Messrs Rowland Ward, the world famous firm of taxidermists, formerly in Piccadilly – plus a charming letter of thanks and appreciation acknowledging the gift of this great fish. Signed personally by His Majesty King Gustav of Sweden, himself a keen angler and sportsman, the letter concluded by saying, he was sure I would be pleased to hear that my giant trout had been served as a main course at a special royal banquet!

# Chapter XX

# Stalking the Scottish Stag

My host stared at me in frank amazement, which must have been genuine enough since his hip-flask of whisky had halted abruptly, half way on its usual rapid and unerring journey to his lips.

"You mean to say you have never stalked a Scottish stag?", he queried in unfeigned astonishment, "and you a big game hunter, and a Scot born and bred; I can hardly believe it!".

He took a more than usually long pull at his flask to restore his normal composure, while with a strange feeling of guilt and embarrassment I had to admit that I had not, adding rather lamely that I had, of course, hunted most species of African and Indian game from elephant and tiger to dik-dik and chinkara, but that the opportunity to try my hand at Scottish deer stalking had unfortunately not come my way.

"But my dear fellow this is terrible!" continued my host earnestly, "something must be done about it. Although I expect you would find it pretty tame after hunting buffalo?" he added, as an afterthought, his usual diplomacy reasserting itself as he offered me a dram to soothe my injured feelings.

"I doubt it", I hastened to reassure him, accepting the whisky gratefully.

"In that case would you care to come up for a couple of days on the hill on my ground next month?" he asked.

This conversation took place during a lunch break on a grouse moor in the Scottish county of Perthshire. As we lay at ease in the heather which covered the lower slopes of the rugged Grampian Range, each munching his 'piece' (as a packed meal is called in Scotland) and with flasks ready at hand, our every move watched hungrily by an assorted collection of setters, retrievers and spaniels, the discussion turned from grouse and blackgame to stalking and deer poaching, and it was then, in an unguarded moment, that I blurted out my confession!

I had often delved deeply into the copious literature, both classic and modern, which describes in glowing terms the thrills and glories involved in

*The Scottish Stag*

the pursuit of the Highland stag, but as I had been whisked away from the land of my forebears long before I was able to carry a rifle, and have spent most of my life abroad, I had hitherto had no chance of experiencing and forming my own opinions of this much lauded sport. Now at last the opportunity had been presented to me 'on a plate' so to speak, and I was not slow to accept, for I had long wanted to see if the critics who described the sport of Scottish deer stalking as artificial were right. And I also wished to see for myself how it compared with the hunting of similar non-dangerous game in Africa and Asia.

Those two days led to further introductions, and by the end of the season I had stalked on three different deer forests situated in widely-separated parts of Scotland, and covering a variety of rugged Highland country. I had had the good fortune to be taken on the hill by some of the finest Highland stalkers, all men dedicated to their calling. And by the grace of the gods of the chase I had grassed seven red deer stags without losing my reputation as a hunter.

What was my conclusion? Briefly this – stalking the shaggy red deer of the Scottish Highlands is one of the finest sports to be offered for the rifle. But to appreciate it to the full one must have a streak of sentiment in one's nature and of romance in one's soul, for much of the pleasure in this sport is derived from the rugged grandeur of the country in which it is carried out; a country steeped in history and legend; some colourful, inspiring and romantic; some grim and macabre; but all of it intriguing and fascinating. What is more, from being popularly regarded as the special perquisite of kings and princes, maharajas and millionaires, and the chosen few, it has become a sport available to almost anyone keen enough to seek it out, without, moreover, necessarily demanding a bulging purse.

How can you get such stalking? – Well, if your time is limited, as well as your purse, the simplest, and in those circumstances also in many ways the cheapest way is to stay at one of the Highland sporting hotels which cater for this sport. Most of them are well run and own or have the lease of one or more deer forests, on which you can book your stalking by the week or even by the day. Board and lodging average out at about £35 a week, and the stalking will cost you around £20–£25 per day, which will include the services of a stalker, pony-man and deer-pony. Under this arrangement the hotel usually retains the right to the venison, although the sportsman can buy back as much as he wants at current market rates, and the antlers are his to do what he likes with. Many of these hotels advertise in British sporting magazines such as '*The Field*', and others can be located through various sporting agencies that also advertise in such periodicals, while the B.A.S.C., whose offices are at Marford Mill in Rossett, near Wrexham, in Wales are very helpful in tendering advice. But you must book well ahead to avoid disappointment, since it is becoming an increasingly popular sport, and some places are beginning to charge fancy prices.

If you can afford to, and have the time to arrange it, rent a deer forest for part or all of the season. The best are expensive, and the very best seldom available, but it is surprising how cheaply odd bits of stalking can be obtained, particularly on ground where sheep are also grazed, or on grouse moors which have deer on them and where the grouse shooting for the season ends early. Again the sporting agencies will arrange everything for you, and on application will send full details of suitable propositions. You can usually defray much of the cost by the sale of the venison you shoot, and you will have the pleasure of having the area entirely to yourself.

Finally tactful enquiries, and chance meetings on the spot, can often lead to generous invitations to stalk on really good ground owned by some old

Highland family, for the Scots are a hospitable race and justly proud of their heritage.

If the foregoing has been enough to whet your appetite, let us examine what actually comprises the undoubtedly fascinating sport of Scottish deer stalking. Remember 'stalking' is the term used, not 'hunting'! 'Hunting' in the British Isles refers solely to the pursuit of animals such as the fox, the hare, and the otter with hounds, and huntsmen and followers either mounted or on foot. The red deer is not 'hunted' in Scotland, although it still is in certain parts of England. And first of all, to be logical, we must study the country and the quarry – that romantic and almost legendary beast the red stag.

To the north of the narrow neck of Scotland which lies clamped firmly between the watery pincers of the Firths of Forth and Clyde, is situated an area of thousands of square miles of rugged, heather-clad mountain and moorland. This is the home of the red grouse and the ptarmigan, the hill fox and the blue mountain hare, the slashing peregrine falcon and the majestic golden eagle. And of the great red stag. These are the Scottish Highlands, stretching from the Grampian Mountains in the south to the North West Highlands which end at remote Cape Wrath and John O'Groats in the far north. In the major part of this wild region the red deer is found in greater or lesser numbers.

The Scottish red deer was once a woodland animal, as is his counterpart in England and other European countries, for at one time much of Scotland was covered with forest. In fact, deer land in Scotland is still referred to as 'deer forest', although the greater part of the 6000 odd square miles concerned, with its population of some 150,000 red deer, is now almost entirely devoid of trees. In some areas re-afforestation schemes have been started, and deer fences protect the young and tender conifers, but for the most part the vegetation has been reduced to heather and course grass, with occasional clumps of bushy rowans, or a few withered firs or stunted poplars huddled in some sheltered glen – all that remains of the great Caledonian Forest that once spread its protecting cloak over the Scottish Highlands.

"Aye, it wass a great forresst in yearrs gone by", your stalker may tell you in his soft Highland burr, pointing at some petrified roots revealed in a peat hag, "but they burrnt it down! For why? To smoke out the wolves and the robbers!"

No doubt he will be right, but the destruction went on as the greed for more grazing for cattle and sheep increased, and a halt was not called until most of the few trees that were left had disappeared as pit-props for the mines, and revets for the muddy trenches of Flanders during the first world holocaust. The red deer had to adapt to a rapidly changing habitat or die, and in adjusting themselves to their new conditions of food and terrain they developed into a smaller beast than their woodland cousins, but what they lost in stature they gained in cunning and stamina. As a result the Scottish Highland stag is now a fine, rangy beast standing, when adult, a good four foot at the shoulder, and weighing anything up to 300 pounds and more. Although there is considerable variation in colour, his coat, as his name implies, is commonly a reddish brown fading to yellow and light grey on the rump, while with age he develops an impressive mane. His horns in his prime may measure well over three feet in length, with almost equal span, and he may carry six, or even more points on each side. They are, in truth, his crowning glory.

It is as well to learn the local terms used to describe the red deer stag during various periods of his life, as otherwise you may experience difficulty in understanding your stalker at a critical point! A male calf is called a 'knobber' in his second year when he has just sprouted his first small single horns. He becomes a 'staggie' in his third year, and a 'stag' or 'hart" in his sixth when he reaches maturity. At twelve years, and sometimes earlier, he should be in his prime, while at eighteen he will begin to 'go back', although he may live to the ripe old age of twenty-five or thirty if he is so long denied the merciful release of the stalker's bullet.

To bag a 'royal' or twelve-pointer stag is, by tradition, the ultimate ambition of everyone who stalks the Scottish red deer, but there are good 'royals' and bad 'royals', and a head with fewer points but greater length, spread and symmetry will often be the finer trophy. Moreover it is estimated that not more than one red deer stag in a hundred that reach their prime will become a true 'royal'. The term 'royal', as applied to a stag, is frequently misused. A true 'royal' stag is one which not only has a total of at least twelve points on his antlers, but also has these points distributed on each antler as brow, bes and trez tines, and 'three on top', the latter forming a cup or 'crown' – hence the term 'royal'. A stag with these plus one or more additional points is a 'royal' of thirteen points, and so on. He is not an 'imperial', a name which though sometimes used has no place in the customary terminology of deer stalking.

On a forest where the deer are properly conserved and cared for it is not always the best heads which are shot. A certain quota of stags is shot each

*The quarry alert on the high tops*

season, and the majority of those chosen will be old beasts past their prime, or animals with weak or poor heads which are better out of the way in order to improve the breeding stock. A beast which has a fine head but is still in his prime will normally be spared, so that he will not only have a chance to grow even better antlers in subsequent seasons, but will also pass on his characteristics to the calves that he sires. Once he starts to 'go back' of course, he becomes a fair quarry for the rifle.

Hornless stags, or 'hummels' as they are called, and switch horned stags are always regarded as fair prey, since on the principle that like begets like they are not considered to be good sires. A hummel is also frequently a good beast for the larder, as all the nourishment that would normally go to horn growth helps to build up his body. As a result a hummel is usually a particularly heavy and powerful animal, capable of driving any normal horned stag away from the hinds.

A 'switch' is a stag whose horns have no extra points, apart from possibly the brow tines. The resulting long rapier-like horns are deadly weapons in a fight, and in consequence a switch will also defeat most normal stags in any competition for the favours of the females.

The social system of red deer is a definite matriarchy. The old legend of the mighty stag being the monarch of the glen is a pure myth! Red deer herds are ruled, led and guarded by hinds, the leader usually being a wise and cunning old hind with a calf at foot, the theory being that a female with young has the acute maternal instinct to protect others. Thus a barren or yeld hind is seldom a herd leader.

For the greater part of the year the full grown stags live by themselves in groups of a few beasts up to large companies of a hundred and more. During this period the main deer herds consist of the hinds, calves and immature stags, and each herd has its own comparatively restricted territory. There is much less movement of these herds than of the stag companies, although the individual territory of each herd may be several miles long and extend over more than one forest.

The stag companies form at the end of the rut, and the mature males are together when they cast their antlers about the first week in April. In many forests where there is a deficiency of lime in the soil, the deer immediately eat these cast horns for the sake of their calcium phosphate content. They are chewed from the points upwards, only the butts being left!

Directly the old antlers are shed the new ones begin to grow, helped by the fresh spring feed. They develop rapidly through the spring and summer, with their sensitive covering of 'velvet', and by about the third week of August the latter has been shed and the fine new sets of antlers have hardened. Through this part of the year the deer are much troubled by the unwelcome attentions of clegs, gadflies and midges, as a result of which they tend to keep on the high ground during the day, in an attempt to avoid these pests, only descending to the low ground at night.

In September the necks of the stags start to swell and thicken, their manes to grow and their larynx to develop, so that when they throw back their heads and start to roar at the beginning of the rut they are a most impressive sight. During the week or two before the rut breaks the stags appear to grow more restless. They flock more, travel more and start wallowing in real earnest, so that by the time the rut starts the rutting, stags are often almost black from rolling in the peat, in striking contrast to the light red summer coats of the immature and late beasts. This autumn wallowing is thought to be linked with sex psychology since deer are more afraid of dark objects than light ones, and a great black stag with swollen neck and flowing mane, wild with the rut, is a sight well calculated to deter a lesser opponent!

The start of the rut varies in different parts of Scotland, and is influenced by variations in the seasons, but traditionally the rut is expected to break towards the end of the second or third week in September. It lasts for some six or seven weeks, during which period the mature stags roar and fight between themselves, each attempting to gather together the biggest harem of hinds that he can. Individual beasts are only sexually active for about a month, and even during this time they will periodically leave the hinds they have collected and retire to the cold, bracing air of the high tops for two or three days to rest, graze and recuperate. This is apparently neutral ground, a sort of males only club where there is no fighting or roaring, and no females to disturb the peace! By about the end of the first week of November the stags are all spent, the rut is over, and the stag companies form again to complete the age old seasonal cycle.

The ecology of his quarry is always of absorbing interest to the really keen hunter, but in the case of the Scottish red deer it is only by understanding their life history that one can understand the choice and timing of the stalking season. Having had, until very recently, no legal protection as game animals, an unfortunate fact that I will discuss in detail later, the season for stalking the red deer is fixed by tradition based on purely practical considerations. The latter are twofold as far as the stags are concerned – trophies and meat. The stags' antlers are hard and clear of velvet by the end of August, at which time the stags are also in good condition after the spring and summer feeding. Therefore stalking usually starts at the beginning of September. By the middle or end of October, varying with the locality, most mature stags are spent and thin, and their flesh rank, as a result of the rut; they are then no longer fit to shoot for good venison. November therefore sees the end of the stag season. However, it is usually necessary to cull a certain number of hinds from the deer herds to keep the population in balance and at optimum level, and hinds only are stalked from November through to January, during which period also their meat is in good condition.

The stag season is thus a short one of some two months duration, but this is long enough to enable the normal quota of stags to be shot, and climatically it can be the finest time of year in Scotland. Some people do not like the idea of shooting hinds, but they are often more cunning than the stags, and unless their numbers are controlled the result is over-population, and death through starvation and disease in the winter snows. It must be remembered that apart from man there are no longer any predators in Scotland capable of controlling the numbers of red deer. A golden eagle will take the odd new-born calf, as will the hill-fox and the wild-cat, but since the wolves and the bears were exterminated the red deer has had few natural enemies. Considering these facts it is really rather surprising that they have remained so cunning and sagacious, but anyone who has stalked them on the high hills will testify, often ruefully, to their wildness!

Red deer have been liberally endowed by nature with aids of self preservation. Their sense of smell is acute and their eyesight and hearing outstanding, a formidable combination indeed! But of these three senses, scent is undoubtedly the major ruling factor in their lives, and in consequence their movements are to a large extent affected by the direction of the wind. They tend to move and feed up-wind, and when resting they will choose a place where scent and sight will give them ample warning of danger from any quarter. A change in the prevailing wind may draw them from one end of a forest to the other, or even into a neighbouring forest, but in the broken, mountainous country of the Scottish Highlands there is considerable air turbulence, and resulting local variations in the direction of the wind in the many steep-sided glens and corries. Success in Scottish deer stalking therefore, depends to a large extent on the local knowledge and experience of the professional stalker. He will know the parts of the forest in which deer are most likely to be found in given conditions of wind and weather, the best lines of approach to avoid difficult or impassable terrain, and the vagaries of the wind over the ground to be covered. The rest depends on physical fitness; a willingness and ability to have, at times, to crawl long distances through tangled heather and the mud and slime of sodden peat hags; or lie motionless in the icy water of a highland burn under the watchful eye of a wary hind; or slip and slither down the rocky face of some precipitous scree ending in a dark abyss; and at the end of it, with heart pounding and lungs bursting, eyes filled with sweat or driving sleet, to be able to hold a rifle steady enough to hit a beast that still appears very far away, is hardly distinguishable from its surroundings, and is probably already suspicious and on the move.

What about suitable weapons? That is a comparatively simple question to answer, for difficult as he normally is to approach, the red stag is not a hard beast to actually kill. He has not, in my opinion, the toughness and tenacity of life of many species of game animals of the African plains and the Indian hills. If you choose the type of rifle that you would select to hunt the open plains and mountains of western America you will not go far wrong. What you want is a rifle of reasonable high velocity, giving a trajectory flat enough for hill shooting and an adequate punch at the end of it – .30/06, .308, .300 Savage, .280 Remington, 7mm, .270, .257, they are all good, but the best is the one with which you can shoot straightest and with confidence, even when you are tired, excited, and panting like a broken-winded horse. And don't forget the weight factor. You will almost invariably have a stalker with you, and he will normally carry your rifle for you until the closing stages of the stalk, but there may be occasions when you will have to carry the rifle yourself, plus other gear, over miles of broken mountainous country, and you will then curse every surplus ounce!

If you find yourself in the British Isles without your own rifle, either by accident or by choice, and then decide to try some deer stalking, you can frequently borrow a weapon on the spot, or alternatively hire a suitable rifle from one of the many long established gun makers and arms dealers in London, or in the main Scottish centres such as Edinburgh, Glasgow and Inverness. However, if you are offered a rifle on loan, or even on hire, in Scotland, it is a virtual certainty that it will either be a 7mm (.275) Mauser, or a 6.5mm (.256) Mannlicher-Schonauer! These two types and calibres, which were the first high-velocity small bores to replace the old black-powder and low pressure cordite stalking rifles of low velocity and large bore, appear to have become almost a traditional part of Scottish deer stalking!

Should you prefer to take your own tried and trusted musket, make sure before you leave the States that you will not be held up on arrival by import and licensing restrictions. The United Kingdom police authorities are particularly strict in regard to rifled weapons, and you would be wise to write well in advance to the section of New Scotland Yard that deals with 'Firearm Certificates' – address Whitehall, London, SW1.

Telescopic sights are a distinct asset in Highland stalking, as long as their use is not abused. Remember in the art and sport of stalking the red deer the shot is only the finale, while the whole hunt can be regarded as consisting of four phases. First of all, depending on the direction of the wind, a likely part of the forest is selected for the day's operations, and having reached the chosen area, and gained a suitable vantage point, the stalker 'spies' (or searches) the ground with his 'glass' (or telescope). When a shootable or likely beast is

*Fallow Deer*

found the stalker, with his intimate knowledge of the ground, plans and carries out the approach. During this stage of the hunt he guides his 'rifle' (or client) across country up to a point where preparations will be made for the final crawl in. The latter is the most critical and usually the most uncomfortable part of the stalk. It normally involves a real belly-crawl, often for some distance and in view of a wary hind or two, up to the spot selected for the fourth and last phase – the actual shot. The spying and approach may take the greater part of the day in magnificent, rugged hill country, particularly if several groups of deer have to be circumvented and carefully examined in the search for a shootable stag, but having found the latter the stalker's object will be to get his rifle close enough to make as near as possible certain of a clean kill. This is where the 'scope sight should come in – to enable you to see clearly enough to place your bullet exactly in a selected vital spot, not to enable you to sit back and take a chance at long range, thus avoiding the fatigue and discomfort of a lengthy belly-crawl. Scottish stalkers are notoriously conservative, and many of them still look askance at 'scope sights, so if you want to display your prowess as a long-distance marksman, without losing your reputation as a hunter and sportsman, stick to sniping at targets on a range, don't give your ability a try-out on the red deer. The few occasions on which fancy, long-range marksmanship are likely to be applauded in a deer forest are when there is no other way to prevent the escape of a wounded beast, or ensure the destruction of an unwanted animal. In fact when stalking the Highland stag it is as well to bear in mind the old African elephant hunter's axiom – 'Git as close as yer can – then git ten yards closer'!

One thing I found to be important was to have the 'scope on my rifle quickly detachable, and good iron sights as a stand-by to use in emergency. The weather in the Scottish Highlands is notoriously fickle, and brilliant sunshine in the early morning may turn to driving rain and sleet in a few hours. Under these conditions your 'scope will become 'drowned' and virtually useless in a few moments, once the leather end-caps are off, and the only answer then is to whip off your 'scope and use your iron sights. I once nearly lost my only chance of a shot, after a long day on the hill, through having to rely on a 'scope-sight in driving rain. But more of that later, and in the interim what of the accusation that Scottish deer stalking is artificial? To reveal this as a calumny it is first necessary to consider the legal status of the Scottish red deer.

Until quite recently, red deer, and other species, had not been protected by any form of game law in the British Isles. Legally speaking they had been vermin, so they had not benefited from any legal close season. In recent years well organised poaching gangs, operating at night at any time of the year had been blasting them with shotguns, rifles and even sub-machine guns at the roadside, in the headlights of their vehicles, yet even when they had actually been found in possession of the bullet-riddled corpses of hinds and calves, it had not been possible to prosecute the members of these gangs. Only when a poacher had actually been caught in the act of killing on private ground, had the law been able to take action, and then only to charge with trespass. Hard to believe I know, but unfortunately true. Public outcry increased, and the Nature Conservancy, a Government sponsored scientific organisation, finally completed a detailed survey of the Scottish red deer on which suitable conservation legislation was framed. This, the Deer (Scotland) Bill, became law, and therefore it is to be hoped that it is now only a matter of time before these fine animals get the proper legal protection they deserve. In the meantime however, their sound conservation and very survival continue to depend on the goodwill and interest of the private landowner, as has been the case since time immemorial.

The lack of suitable game laws has largely been due to the fact that the protection afforded to the deer on private land has until recently been adequate. However, the improvement of roads in the Highlands, and the advent of the era of the people's car have brought even some of the remoter areas into closer contact with the larger centres of population. This, coupled with periods of meat shortages and high prices has made commercialised poaching a profitable business, and unscrupulous gangs have taken full advantage of the loopholes in the law. Thus the commercial butchers, the opponents of so-called 'blood sports', and the jealous-minded cranks point at the fact that deer are only kept on private land at the whim of the owner. 'They are no better than cattle or sheep', they claim. 'How can the so-called sport of deer stalking be regarded as other than completely artificial?' In fact deer, and particularly stags in the rutting season, may travel great distances. The latter can be on a certain deer forest one day and in another many miles away a few days later. They are as wild and unfettered as the heather-clad hills they inhabit. Wind and weather may move them from one forest into a neighbouring one overnight.

From the foregoing I think it is clear that Scottish deer stalking is only artificial to the extent that the hunter's operations are confined within the boundaries of the particular deer forest in which he happens to be stalking. But since this may cover an area of 100 square miles or more of rugged, mountainous country, I can see little difference in practice between a Scottish deer forest and one of the special controlled hunting areas that have been created in East Africa, or the long established 'shooting block' system in India. In each the sportsman is allowed a certain restricted quota of shootable beasts within a defined and restricted area, and the similarity is increased by the fact that the professional 'stalker' in Scotland, who, with his intimate local knowledge of the ground, takes his visiting 'rifle' on the hill, has his counterpart in the professional 'white hunter' who guides his client in Africa, and the Indian 'shikari' who leads his 'Sahib" in the jungles or on the mountains of his native land. In each case he provides the local knowledge of beast and terrain that is so essential for a successful hunt. Whether you agree with me or not, I can assure you that long before your first day's stalking has drawn to a close you will be convinced that there is nothing artificial about the wildness of the

Scottish red deer! And, to my mind, it is a sport that is only equalled or sur-passed in the field of non-dangerous game, by the hunting of the greater kudu in the foothills of Eastern Africa, and the pursuit of markhor, ibex and wild-sheep on the mighty Himalayan Range. But let me describe a typical day's stalking that I myself experienced some years ago, and then you can judge for yourself.

I woke to a cold grey dawn, in which light the only cheerful things appeared to be the dull glow of the peat fire in my room, and the plump and jolly wife of Jock the stalker who roused me with a steaming cup of hot, sweet tea. Two days before I had motored up from the south, travelling first the main road through the famous Glen Garry, and then bumping and sliding for miles over a rough moorland track which wound its way along the wild and beautiful glen of the Edendon River, until with most of my exhaust pipe missing, and my shock-absorbers punch-drunk and nearly useless, I arrived at my destination – the lonely hunting lodge at the head of the glen. Here, deep in the Forest of Atholl, was peace indeed and the real spirit of the Highlands. The majestic, heather-clad slopes of the Grampian Range towered above the old building, and the only sounds that filtered through the blanket of silence were the calls of the golden eagle and the peregrine, the red grouse and the ptarmigan, while from time to time the distant roar of a rutting stag was carried on the wind that sighed in the thin belt of stunted firs.

When I looked out of my bedroom window on that second morning of my stay my heart sank, for the clouds were down low hiding the hills in a thick white screen, while the glen was filled with drifting wisps of vapour. However, Jock was cheerful and optimistic. It was his opinion that with the wind in its present quarter the clouds would soon lift and that in fact by the time Robbie, the pony-man, arrived with the garron (or deer pony) the hills would be clear enough for spying. He proved to be a good prophet, for as I finished a hearty breakfast, the click of the pony's hooves in the courtyard coincided with the first weak shafts of sunlight striking the high tops.

While Jock gave Robbie detailed instructions as to the route he should follow with the garron, to fit in with our plan for the day, I slipped on my stalking clothes and checked my equipment. The traditional garb worn by Scottish deer stalkers consists of a tweed coat of neutral colour, and some form of knee breeches or plus fours in similar material. Head-gear consists of a tweed cap, or true 'deerstalker' hat of the type made famous by that legendary detective of fiction – Sherlock Holmes. Footwear is usually a pair of heavy brogues or leather boots with nail studded soles. I'm afraid I broke with tradition for I favour lightness! My substitutes were a warm sweater and whipcord trousers ending in knee-length light canvas gaiters, and light canvas ankle-boots with rubber cleated soles. On top I wore a loose fitting, hip-length, camouflaged, waterproof ex-combat jacket, with a zip front, plenty of large pockets, and a useful hood. My unruly locks were demurely hidden under a lightweight, waterproof felt cap of neutral lovat! This garb not only stood the test and proved entirely suitable, but my camouflage jacket in particular roused envy in Nock's conservative heart!

I slung my binoculars round my neck, looped my hunting knife on my belt, checked that my hip-flask was full of whisky not air, and went to the gun cabinet.

I was using a brand new B.S.A. 'Featherweight' model .30/06 magazine rifle, which has a modified Mauser type action, a twenty-two inch barrel, and a very effective muzzle brake. Fitted with an Oigee 'Luxor" 4 x 81 'scope sight in Park-Hale 'roll-on' mounts the whole outfit only weighs 7lb 5½oz, yet the recoil is not noticeable. With Remington 'Core-Lokt' ammunition loaded with the 180 grain bullet I found it to be very accurate and a real killer, while the Oigee 'scope was a delight to use, particularly under difficult light conditions. The only drawback was the factory fitted iron sights with which the rifle was equipped at that time. They were coarse, hard to see, and I was reluctant to use them even in an emergency. On other days I sometimes armed myself with one of the 'traditional' stalking rifles – a 6.5mm Mannlicher-Schonauer carbine, fitted with a 2½ x Gerard telescopic sight. This was a handy and accurate little weapon but lacked the killing power of the B.S.A. .30/06. However, it had one advantage – the 'scope was in a really quick-detachable mount, and its iron sights could be relied upon.

This day it was the B.S.A., and after loading the magazine I slid it into its loose canvas carrying case. These covers are important items of stalking equipment. They protect the rifle from rain, mud and accidental falls. The weapon should be left in the cover until the last stage of the stalk, and it is therefore essential that the case should be loose fitting, yet stiff enough to enable the rifle to be whipped out of it as quickly, smoothly and easily as a sword from its scabbard.

It was time to be off. Jock slung the cased rifle and his battered telescope on his shoulder, picked up his ash stick, handed another to me and stepped briskly into the courtyard. We each had a packet of sandwiches, and Jock carried a small coil of stout rope.

A good stick is a great asset in deer stalking. Besides being a boon when one is tired or crossing bad ground, it helps to steady the telescope when one is spying. Some stalkers carry a crummoch or shepherd's crook for this purpose. A coil of rope is another useful item which is invaluable when a stag has to be manhandled and dragged over ground inaccessible to a pony, since it does much to ease this back-breaking task.

As the low clinging clouds lifted and retreated before the slowly advancing rays of the sun, we made our way up the glen heading for the northern marches of the forest. The greater part of the previous day had been spent in pursuit of a big yellow stag who, guarded by his ever watchful harem of hinds, had finally proved too cunning for us. He was a noble beast, well known in those parts, and the last we had seen of him was when he had paused for a moment on the northern horizon to glance back, his wild, sweeping antlers silhouetted against the evening sky, before disappearing from view after his womenfolk. I had finally been reduced to shooting a beast with a miserable, weak head, since the Laird wanted some venison for his tenants and friends,

*Spying from the high tops.*
*(the author with the Stalker)*

226

and Jock had chosen it for the good of the stock. "Tak yon staag, surr," he had said, "the yin wi the sma' heid. He's an auld beast and well oot o' the way, though he's in guid enough condition for the larder." Now we were heading northwards up the glen in the hope of again finding the mighty beast whose deep-chested roars had rolled and echoed from the high tops the day before.

A stag's roar varies greatly, both in timbre and volume, depending on the beast itself and the stage of the rut. Sometimes it is a mere dismal moan, like the lowing of a love-sick cow, while at others it is a mighty, deep-throated bellow, than which there is no sound more stirring to the soul of the hunter, nor more wild and romantic when heard echoing over the heather-clad hills.

Leaving the valley we climbed slowly up a sheep track that traversed the face of Glas Mheall Mor, the Gaelic for 'big, grey, rounded hill', which towered three thousand feet high and more, and whose rocky, rolling summit was beloved of ptarmigan, that pale, ghost-like bird of the high tops.

As we climbed occasional covies of red grouse rose with a whir from the short heather at the edge of the path, while from time to time a black-faced Highland sheep, almost as wild as the red deer themselves, would sound its alarm note, an explosive, sneezing snort, before disappearing from view in a heavy, fleece rolling canter. As long as the birds swung below or behind us, and the sheep did not gallop ahead, Jock did not worry, but when a solitary cock grouse skimmed low round the shoulder of the hill, and glided on silent wings back over our heads, he dropped like a stone in the heather. Following suit I just caught a glimpse of a hind and a small stag trotting over the rise from which the grouse had flushed.

Jock took the small ash-bag from his waistcoat pocket and shook it gently to test the wind. Like most Highland stalkers nowadays he had to be a 'Jack of all trades', being responsible in season for the grouse, vermin control, and even some sheep, as well as the red deer and the butchering and marketing of their venison. Conservative to a degree he was still receptive to new ideas, and this was one that I had shown him. It was the old elephant hunter's trick of carrying some fine wood-ash from the camp fire in a small bag of loose-woven cloth, and shaking it to test the direction of the wind. The fine particles of ash that filter through the cloth will drift in a white cloud on the faintest breath of air. I had made one for Jock the night before, using the toe of one of his wife's discarded stockings, and ash from the peat fire in the hearth. He was thrilled with it, and used it vigorously on the slightest excuse!

Reassured by the puff of ash that drifted softly away behind us on the damp, misty air, Jock rose to his feet and beckoned me on. "Yon beasties were movin' onyway", he said.

Our first spy was along the north west face of the Am Dun, and revealed that it was literally covered with deer. There were so many that the whole hillside appeared to be moving, but our elation was short-lived for closer inspection showed there wasn't a shootable beast among them. They were all hinds and immature beasts, and they were heading steadily north eastwards out of the forest. Jock commented that the rut was late. "We'll be findin' the staags on the high ground, I doubt," he said confidently, closing his telescope with a decisive click. "There's a wee bittie climb ahead a' ye surr," he added with a smile, pointing with his stick, across the glen, at the almost sheer face of Vinegar Hill, which very English name contrasted oddly with the Gaelic names of the surrounding features.

A long time later, winded and leg weary, I flung myself down in the heather beside the cairn which marked the boundary. Time and again I had been thankful for my stout ash stick, but we hadn't seen another beast. Jock had at first been puzzled, then suspicious. Finally he found tracks that evidently confirmed his fears. His face darkened, and he swore quietly to himself before explaining to me what was wrong. This was sheep ground as well as deer forest, he said, but to prevent disturbance of the deer during the stalking season, and also sheep stealing, the latter were only allowed to be gathered during approved periods. However, the tracks before us clearly indicated that someone had very recently been through gathering the sheep, and in consequence there wasn't an animal of any sort left in the area.

By this time the clouds had started to bank up again, and a cold wind was blowing across the high, exposed plateau. We found a sheltered hollow where we ate our pieces and discussed the next move. Prospects were not good, but a half-hearted survey of the ground with my binoculars revealed a small party of hinds lying down on the forward slope of a hill about a mile away to the west. Visibility was bad, and the icy rain squalls which scudded across the exposed ground made me more than thankful for the hood on my jacket. It was not possible to see if there were any shootable stag with the hinds, but we decided to find out. An hour or so later, wet, cold and tired, we watched with disgust as a dozen hinds, not a stag among them, grazed quietly past not fifty yards below us.

*Stag's Head*

Jock was still not discouraged. He believed there was a good chance that we might find a shootable stag in some low ground further to the west. Being low-lying, and full of peat hags, it provided good shelter from bad weather, such as had now set in. We started off at a brisk pace for it was getting cold as well as late.

Jock was right, though being taller than he was I saw them first as we carefully breasted a gentle rise to look down into a great shallow basin nestling among the hills. At the bottom of the depression, some half a mile below us, a small group of hinds were feeding quietly among the peat hags, and close to them two stags were having a sparring match. The larger of the two was unusually light in colour.

Jock steadied his telescope then exclaimed in excitement. "It's himsel, tes the auld warrior himsel!" As I rapidly adjusted my binoculars the magnified image of a great yellow stag swam into focus. He had paused for a moment with his head held high, and on each massive spreading antler the white tips of six well defined tines could clearly be seen. I checked them carefully – brow, bez, trez and three on top – a true royal, and a massive one. It was my turn to shake with excitement!

We studied the ground slowly and thoroughly to decide on the best line of approach. Finally it became apparent that we would have to make a detour so as to reach the lip of the depression at a point further to the west. From there a line of peat hags would give us some cover on the forward slope. It was chancey, and would mean a long, wet crawl, but it was our only hope. "It wull be a vurra deeficult staalk," said Jock, slowly and gloomily, as we wriggled back out of sight.

For once I blessed the weather. A series of blinding rain squalls helped us to by-pass two covies of grouse, and slide into the first of the peat-hags without being seen. Had we flushed the birds they would almost certainly have gone straight over the deer and given the alarm.

Then began a nightmare crawl. Inch by inch, flat on our bellies, we eased ourselves forward through the peat slime. From time to time we lay motionless for minutes on end, while an old grey hind, forever on the alert, gazed suspiciously in our direction, her bat ears twitching and nostrils quivering in search of the faintest sound or scent of danger. At these times we dared not move, though the hollows were running with water from the rain, and icy streams flowing through our garments froze us to the very marrow. Even under these conditions I was glad of my lightweight clothes, for they weighed less when sodden and dried quicker than heavy tweed.

Finally we reached a small knoll within a hundred and fifty yards of our quarry. It was covered with coarse grass and long heather, and had the luxury of being comparatively dry. We sank into it thankfully.

Jock slid the rifle quietly from its wet and grimy case and handed it to me. The cover had kept it as dry, clean and bright as the proverbial new pin, despite the shocking weather conditions. At a nod we wriggled forward to the top of the knoll and gently parted the heather stems.

"Watch oot for yon auld grey butch," whispered Jock, indicating the old hind which was again staring intently in our direction. I nodded and eased the rifle forward until I was in a comfortable firing position. I slowly slipped off the leather lens-covers of the telescopic sight, and lined it up on the big, yellow stag. He was now lying down, broadside on to me. I could see him clearly but the lower half of his body was hidden.

"Dinna try and tak' him lying' surr," hissed Jock in my ear, "wait till he rises."

Many Highland stalkers, used to iron sights and poor light conditions, will not shoot at a lying beast, and in deference to Jock's wishes I held my fire. I studied the great beast carefully through the 'scope. He appeared to be half-asleep, but I knew he would be on his feet in a moment if his rival appeared again, or if any of his hinds strayed too far. I was ready for him, and confident.

A sudden whir of wings low over my head made me duck involuntarily, and the big stag was on his feet in a flash as a pack of grouse skimmed past him and away into the glen. A startled glance in our direction and with a bound he had disappeared among the peat hags before my flustered finger had even started to tighten on the trigger.

For a moment we were stupefied, then before our horrified gaze Robbie and the garron appeared over the hill behind us, like some dreaded apparition.

Robbie was almost in tears. He had seen the covies of grouse, and had quite reasonably concluded that we could not possibly have passed that way without flushing them. He kept explaining this and apologising in his soft Highland accent, at times breaking into pure Gaelic. Jock was nearly as distressed. "I should ha' let ye tak' him lyin' surr," he repeated time and again. I confess I was nearly as depressed myself, and it took the greater part of my large hip flask of whisky to restore our combined morale, after which we held a council of war.

"He'll be headin' for the Cama Choire, I doubt," said Jock finally, after examining the tracks, "but yon's a cannie beast or he wouldna ha' lived as long as he has. We can follow the corrie doon to the heid a' the glen, but its gey late and we ha' no time to lose."

The Cama Choire was a long, very deep corrie, with steep, almost precipitous sides, that cut into the high ground like the fierce slash of a sabre. Along its bottom tumbled a turbulent burn, the Allt a' Cama Choire, which formed the headwaters of the Edendon, the river that flowed down the big glen. It was a sheltered spot beloved of deer in wild weather.

We went off at a brisk pace that was almost a run, keeping the pony with us, and it was not long before we reached the lip of the corrie. Here we turned eastwards to follow along its rim until we reached the main glen above the lodge. Robbie and the garron kept well away from the edge, while Jock and I moved as rapidly as we could along the top, stopping at suitable vantage points to study the slopes stretching far below us.

It had started to rain again, another wind-blown squall, when a reddish form, followed by another and another appeared from a hollow far down the slope on our side of the corrie. The light was poor, but they were stags, we could see that, eight of them, and the one bringing up the rear was noticeably larger and lighter in colour than the rest.

Jock and I looked at each other with rising excitement. The deer were moving at a fast walk in our direction, but at a level that would take them past a long way below us. There was no time to waste. Waiting until they had again disappeared momentarily into dead ground, we slid over the edge and down a loose scree, lying on our backs and breaking our descent with our heels and elbows, the while Jock admonished me fiercely to keep my knees down.

By a miracle we reached a shelf within reasonable range of the deer without being seen, but here again ill-luck beset us. As the stags again came into view the rain squall hit us with full force. The rifle was out of its case and I had the lens-caps off the 'scope sight ready to fire, but in a moment the lenses were drenched with water. I could see nothing through the 'scope and even if I had had time to remove it, I didn't trust the iron sights. It taught me a lesson I was never to forget!

"For God's sake hold your cap over the sight, Jock," I hissed as I frantically wiped the lenses with a half-sodden handkerchief, "I can't see a damn thing!" Then, digging my heels into the loose scree, I sat up and attempted to aim. With Jock crouching beside me valiantly trying to screen the 'scope with his old tweed cap, I just managed to make out the form of the yellow stag, the last in the line, appearing from the hollow behind the rest. Breathing a silent prayer I aligned the blurred sight on what I guessed was the centre of his shoulder, and squeezed the trigger. At the shot he staggered and fell back, disappearing completely from view.

"Guid shot, surr!" hissed Jock, in delight as the remaining stags milled in momentary bewilderment, before streaming past below us, misled by the echoes of the report. "Tak' anither for the larder, surr," he urged, pointing out a heavy beast with a poor head, which went rolling down the hillside, its heart shattered by the 180 grain 'core-lokt' bullet. "Aye, the Laird will be gey pleased," he concluded with a broad grin as he stood up and slid down the loose scree towards the last resting place of the big stag. He paused for a moment at the edge of the hollow, then drew his knife and plunged out of sight to perform the gralloch.

A short time later he re-appeared wiping the blood from his hands. He looked depressed.

"What's wrong, Jock?" I asked.

"This is no oor lucky day after all, surr," he sighed. "Yon's a bonnie beast in the body, but he's a puir heid; he's no the auld royal. I'm verra sorry, surr, but wi' the rain I couldna see his heid at a'."

At that moment there was a piercing whistle from Robbie, and looking up we saw him pointing towards the distant ridge of Glas Mheall Mor, away across the glen. There on the skyline stood a great stag with mighty, sweeping antlers, who, even as we watched, turned and trotted out of sight behind a small group of hinds.

I lifted my cap in salutation, then turned to the disconsolate stalker. "Never mind, Jock," I said. "He has won this round, and the one before, but there will be another, the third and last, and it's an honour to be bested by a beast like that."

"Aye, you're richt thre, surr," he replied, brightening, "and we'll no be going hame wi an empty saddle, onyway!"

As we wound our way slowly homeward down the darkening glen I relived the events of the day, still lost in the thrall of the big stag, and when we finally stretched our tired limbs gratefully in the warm glow of the peat fire in the lodge, comforted by the caress of a hot whisky toddy, I glanced through the pipe smoke at the old stalker dozing in the battered armchair by the hearth, his faithful collie at his feet, the horns of a fine 'royal' in the shadows of the wall above his head.

"Jock", I said, "there's no sport like it."

"Aye, surr," he sighed, "I wouldna be here if there wass!"

*Homeward bound at the end of a successful day*

# Chapter XXI

# Desert Lake

*An account of an expedition to Lake Rudolf in the wild desert country
of Kenya's Northern Frontier Province – including a hazardous voyage
to Crocodile Island, a volcanic islet lying far out in the storm-lashed waters
of the lake.*

'With 'is silly neck a bobbin' like a basket full o' snakes!' – These words
from Rudyard Kipling's poem '*Oonts*' came vividly to mind as a string
of camels shambled slowly past, their great circular feet padding silently on
the hot sand. They eyed us disapprovingly and bubbled through their rubbery
lips in unconcealed disgust. Perhaps there was some justification for their
supercilious expressions for, as the Arabs will tell you, the camel knows the
hundredth name of Allah, whereas we – mere humans – could know but
ninety-nine!

We were sprawling, hot and dusty, in the welcome but scanty shade of
*mswaki*, the 'toothbrush bush' whose fibrous twigs are used universally by
Africans to scrub and polish their teeth to their customary immaculate
whiteness. Around us stretched the Turkana desert, a thirsty wilderness of
shimmering yellow sand and lava, dotted here and there with weird cactus –
like plants and occasional stunted bushes such as the one under which we lay.

Turkana is a part of the 117,000 square mile Northern Frontier Province
of Kenya, – a desolate tract of wild, sunscorched country bigger than Arizona
and nearly as large as New Mexico, which separates the fertile agricultural
lands of southern Kenya from the rugged Ethiopian highlands to the north.
With a human population of less than two per square mile, and peopled by
wild and warlike nomadic tribes, of which the Turkana are one, it is still a
primitive, and at times troubled region, beset by inter-tribal strife and bloody
border raids.

Africa is a land of contrast but, nevertheless, looking at these seemingly
arid lifeless wastes, it was a little difficult to believe that they could conceal a

*Loading boats onto truck*

*Journey across sandy plains*

vast expanse of turbulent alkaline water teeming with fish and bird life. Yet in the middle of this desolate land lay a mighty inland sea – Lake Rudolf.

Lake Rudolf was first discovered in 1888 by the great Italian explorer Count Teleki. It is one of the largest of the string of lakes which lie scattered, pearl-like, along the length of the great Rift Valley. Some 185 miles long by 20 wide, its waters are notorious for their violent storms, built up by the howling winds which sweep down upon it from the surrounding desert.

Thus pondering, we reluctantly left the isolated shade of our *mswaki* and clambered once more into our heavily laden trucks to continue our safari, – grinding eastwards across the sandy plains, into the dancing heat haze which concealed the distant lake.

For most of our party of seven this expedition was the realisation of a long standing ambition. Despite their discomforts, deserts have a strange fascination. Perhaps it is their very hostility, their harsh uncompromising austerity, and the feeling they give of pitting oneself against untamed nature at her cruellest. It is this paradoxical attraction, combined with the primitive savagery of its wild tribes, which lends to the Northern Frontier much of its magnetic charm.

Falling under its spell we had long planned an expedition to Turkana and, in particular, to Lake Rudolf where, as keen naturalists, we hoped to study the fabulous wildlife of its shores and islands. The party consisted of Dr Jeffrey Kenyon, a geologist, and his wife; 'Tash' Crossley, his partner; Mrs Elizabeth Kinloch and her 12 year-old daughter, Bydie, on vacation from school; John Blower, game warden, Karamoja, plus the author, at that time, Chief game warden of the Uganda Protectorate.

Turkana is a closed district which no-one may enter without special permission – necessary restriction since inexperienced or ill-equipped travellers might easily land themselves in a deal of trouble. However, Mr Whitehouse, the District Commissioner, kindly gave our projected visit his blessing and towards the end of August 1957 we assembled at Moroto, a remote administrative station in the Karamoja country of eastern Uganda, not far from the borders of Turkana.

Equipped with three vehicles, two boats, petrol, food, photographic gear and a swarm of African helpers, we at last set off, winding our way along the rough road beneath the towering cliffs of Moroto mountain and then plunging down the 2000 foot escarpment, which here forms the boundary between Uganda and Kenya, into the volcanic wilderness of the Great Rift. At the top

*Notice at border*

an amusing notice board erected by a road engineer with a sardonic sense of humour, warned us of the dangers of the track ahead. At the bottom a larger and more battered notice board warned us that we had reached the Turkana District border, and that entry without the necessary authority was strictly prohibited.

In the border region we had passed through a zone of thorn bush and tall acacias rich in bird life, and intersected by numerous water-courses. Small herds of Grant's gazelle had bounded away from the road from time to time, and in the early morning light we had seen two of nature's 'sanitary corps', a spotted hyena and a silver-backed jackal, returning from their night-time scavenge hunt. Now in a few miles we were transported from the familiar olive green landscape of the typical African bush country into a strangely colourful sun-tortured wilderness of sand, black basaltic hills and wandering camels. The latter immediately drew shouts of glee from our 'boys' who had never seen such strange beasts in their own country. Quaint euphorbias, wait-a-bit thorn, some of it covered with beautiful white blossom, cacti and the lovely red and white blossoms of the Desert Rose fringed the track, with here and there the pale green fleshy leaves of the Dead Sea Fruit with its slightly obscene bladder-like seed pods. Birds were still surprisingly numerous, the Abyssinian roller, with its varied shades of lavender, blue and chocolate, and its long graceful tail feathers, and the chanting goshawk with its powder blue habit and brilliant yellow legs, probably being the most colourful and striking of them all. Turkana herd boys, naked and wiry, tended their goats and camels and watched our convoy as we ground slowly through the loose sand. They doubtless wondered at the long red and white motor launch lashed atop our big truck. No doubt they had heard of the great water far to the east but, even so, they would not have realised any connection with this strange monster crouching on the white men's lorry.

As we continued eastward the country became progressively more arid and the vegetation more sparse. Fantastic anthills reared up in 15 to 20 foot high pillars of baked red earth. From time to time we would pass a cluster of primitive beehive shaped huts. The Turkana do not live in villages, but in small family groups. Their huts are of two types; a smaller, more or less weatherproof, variety, built of grass or palm fronds, which is used at night, and a considerably larger type, loosely constructed of branches, which is used in daytime as a shelter from the burning sun.

The Turkana are nomads, whose simple lives are centred round their domestic stock; cattle, camels, donkeys, sheep and goats, which comprise almost their entire worldly wealth. Their year is divided into two seasons, the *Agiporo*, or rainy season, the time of plenty, when water is readily available and the green shoots of grass sprout miraculously from the earth. And the *Akumu*, or dry season, when the waterholes dry up and life for man and beast becomes a desperate struggle for survival.

It seems probable that the Turkana had a common ancestry with the Masai and other Nilo-Hamitic tribes, such as the Nandi, and that their forebears originally came as invaders from the north-west. Even today there are many similarities of dress, custom and language between Masai and Turkana.

*Lorry carrying the Motor Launch*

*Dead Sea Fruit Plant*

*The author's wife
admiring a desert cactus*

*Grant's Gazelles*

*Spotted Hyena*

*Silver Backed Jackal*

*Tribal Village*

Indeed one Turkana clan, the Ngithigirr, have a tradition of Masai ancestry and still maintain that tribe's custom of daubing their bodies with sheep's fat and red ochre. True to the Hamitic type they are tall and slender, though well built, and apart from a length of dark cloth, which has a variety of uses but is usually flung casually, cloak-like across the shoulders, the men go virtually naked, although with the advance of civilization more and more are taking to wearing a brief cloth kilt. This lack of decorative clothing is more than made up for by a variety of ornaments such as ivory or metal lip plugs; bangles, amulets and necklaces made of ivory, brass, or beads; and intricate head-dresses built up of various coloured clays, feathers and ostrich plumes of many hues. In addition no Turkana warrior is complete without his long, metal-shafted spear, his carved wooden neck rest cum stool, and his vicious circular wrist-knife. The women, who are shorter than the men, are cheerful and comely. Full breasted and graceful they wear a long half skirt of skins behind with a shorter apron in front, both ornamented with designs and patterns of cowrie shells and coloured beads, plus an often fantastic weight of necklaces, ear-rings, bangles and other assorted decorations.

Like the Masai the Turkana live mainly on blood and milk drawn from their domestic stock, although those living on the shores of Lake Rudolf have become fishermen and fish-eaters, with a keen liking for crocodile meat. Of their animals, the donkeys alone are used as beasts of burden. The camels, only introduced into Turkana some 70 years ago, probably by a neighbouring tribe, the Boran, are strangely enough not used as transport animals, except by the District Administration and the Police. In fact the latter had to bring in Somali camel-men to train the local camels as riding and transport animals, and the Turkana tribesmen in the proper handling of them.

The Turkana are a hardy, brave and upstanding race, but live in constant fear and hatred of their traditional enemies the savage and well-armed Merille warriors just across the border in Ethiopia. Only recently Merille raiders swooped down to massacre over a hundred Turkana men, women and children, and this border incident eventually involved reinforcements of armed police and units of the Kings African Rifles. In an attempt to prevent these clashes and endless blood feuds a policy of disarming the border tribes has long been in force, but large stocks of small-arms which were abandoned by the Italians in the last war fell into the hands of tribes in the southern Ethiopian region, and in consequence gun running is hard to stop. It is said that in the border areas a rifle can be traded for eight cattle, while a bandolier containing 30 rounds of ammunition is worth three cows, and even five rounds can be exchanged for two sheep and one male goat!

At last a somewhat menacing noticeboard at the side of the track warning us to 'Halt When Challenged' announced our arrival at the outskirts of Lodwar, the administrative headquarters of Turkana District.

A group of tribal police snapped smartly to attention as we passed. These must surely be the most colourful policemen in the world, with their magnificent helmet-like headdresses fashioned from the pinky-white breast feathers of pelicans and topped by long waving ostrich plumes

*Halt When Challenged*

243

*Camel train*

dyed in a variety of brilliant hues. The rest of their 'uniform' consists of a collar of red and yellow beads, a brief red and blue loin cloth, marked with the letters 'T.D.' for Turkana District, and leather belt and ammunition pouches. Some wear bracelets of ivory or metal on their arms while the real dandies favour plugs of ivory or aluminium stuck through the lower lip. Every man carries an immaculately clean Lee-Enfield rifle, his proudest possession, from which nothing will part him for a moment.

As we drew to a halt outside the District Commissioner's house the sun was sinking behind the frieze of stark basalt hills which dominates the town. Overhead, against the steely blue of the sky, a few vultures wheeled aimlessly, and from somewhere echoed the thin notes of a bugle, marking the end of the day.

The District Commissioner, Mr Whitehouse, welcomed us hospitably. We sat for some time on the broad colonnaded verandah of his delightful Moorish-style bungalow, enjoying the cool of the evening and washing the dust from our throats with long draughts of delicious iced lager and, at the same time, plying our host with a stream of questions about the country and its people.

*Turkana Police parade*

In the morning we loaded the trucks and, after watching the tribal police parade in all their finery for inspection by the District Commissioner, and the changing of the combined guard of regular and tribal police, we continued our journey eastwards towards the lake. The country became progressively more arid and desolate. Sometimes we would see a few Grant's gazelle or a flock of sandgrouse, and once we passed a desert hare, crouched wide-eyed and motionless at the edge of the track, but apart from these and one or two parties of wild-looking Turkana, the country was apparently empty and lifeless, although what desert is ever really so?

More than once a silvery sheen ahead raised our hopes and made us think that we were, at last, nearing our destination, only to find a mirage which melted at our approach. At length, however, threading our way through an unexpected belt of Dom palms, we saw pelicans skimming like miniature flying boats low over the surface of yet another 'mirage' and knew that this time it really was the lake.

We feasted our eyes on the vegetation which, though scanty, seemed luxuriant after the country we had come through; graceful palm trees, the familiar Dead Sea Fruit and even green grass and reeds along the edge of the lake.

Soon we were on the shore of Ferguson's Gulf, the narrow inlet on which

*Author with Tribesmen of the Turkana in 1959*

we planned to make our base camp. Clouds of birds rose noisily into the air and wheeled overhead; snowy white egrets and spoonbills, the brilliant black and white sacred ibis, several different species of heron, long undulating lines of pelicans planning low over the water, and V-formations of duck, flighting up and down the shore-line protesting loudly at our intrusion.

The boats were soon unloaded with the eager assistance of some Turkana fisherman who appeared to welcome us, and we began ferrying our clutter of assorted gear across the mile wide entrance to the gulf.

*Women of the Turkana Tribe*

We established ourselves comfortably in some picturesque palm leaf huts at the end of the long sandspit which separated the gulf from the main lake. This was the District Commissioner's permanent camp, and well built in consequence. It was only a few yards from the lake shore on the one side and

*Turkana Tribesman*

the still lagoon-like waters of the gulf on the other. Sacred ibis, Caspian terns, spoonbills and numerous small waders thronged the sandy beach, while a little way out in the lake two or three crocodiles cruised up and down in sinister fashion, and flocks of scissor-billed terns, or African skimmers as they are also

*Turkana Tribesman*

called, swooped in graceful undulating flight to dip their long red bills in the floating algae.

Our first three days were spent in exploring the lake shore, bathing, shooting a few duck for the pot, and enjoying the fabulous fishing. We soon discovered that tiger fish abounded close inshore beside our camp and the anglers of the party lost no time in getting out their rods and tackle. The tiger fish is a fighter; handsome in appearance, with his streamlined body barred with dark longitudinal lines and his formidable rows of razor-sharp teeth, he strikes like a torpedo and, once hooked, the battle is on! Tearing out line, rocketing from the water and, as often as not, hurling the hook from his mouth with a sudden defiant shake of the head. Spinning for 'tiger' with light tackle is certainly one of the most sporting forms of fishing which Africa has to offer.

Nile perch, voracious monsters which lurked in the deeper waters further from shore, gave us a lot of fun too and kept the whole camp in food throughout our stay. These mighty fish sometimes run up to over 300lbs in weight and are usually caught by trolling from a boat with an artificial bait. Our biggest was a mere forty pounder landed by Bydie Kinloch, the youngest member of the expedition, after an exciting battle.

Rudolf is so rich in fish that it could supply the requirements of most of Kenya. But, apart from a few scattered settlements of Turkana and El Molo fishermen who operate along the shore, the waters of the lake remain virtually

*Tribesman in small raft*

untouched owing to their inaccessibility and the difficulty of getting fish to the markets.

Recently seine-netting from the shore was introduced with considerable success, the local Turkana soon becoming experts in this method of fishing and producing large catches of Nile perch, Tilapia (East Africa's premier food fish) and various other species.

We tried both seine-netting and set-lines at night as experiments, both of which produced good results. But the crocodiles usually found the Nile perch which had taken the baited hooks of the set-lines long before we did. However, working at night with a torch and never quite knowing what was on the end of the line, or in the purse of the seine was a thrill not to be missed! The traditional method of fishing among the Turkana entails the use of rough circular baskets woven from the fibres of the Dead Sea Fruit. The fishermen wade in the shallows, holding their baskets open end downwards and periodically plunging them vigorously down to the bottom. There being so many fish about, some are inevitably trapped in the baskets. Primitive and inefficient as this method is it seems to produce enough fish for local needs. Equally primitive are their 'boats' which are merely two or three logs of the fibrous Dom palm lashed together with fibre. On these simple rafts the Turkana fishermen squat in a kneeling position, propelling themselves along with the help of long slender poles. Needless to say these rafts can only be used in shallow, sheltered waters, and in consequence, the Turkana have no knowledge of the islands in the centre of the lake which are shrouded in mystery and legend.

The fish of the lake provide a valuable clue to its past history, for they number several species which occur elsewhere only in the Nile and its tributaries. This seems to confirm the generally accepted theory that Rudolf, though now some 2,500 feet lower than the Nile's source in Lake Victoria, must at some time have formed a part of the Nile system.

Old beaches, some of them many hundreds of feet above the present level of the lake, indicate that it is steadily growing smaller due to the high evaporation rate, which considerably exceeds the inflow from the few rivers emptying into the lake. As the volume of water is thus reduced its salinity is inevitably increasing and, as this process continues, the concentration of salt and other dissolved minerals must eventually become so high that fish will no longer be able to exist.

*Desert Hare*

*Pelicans on Lake Rudolf*

*A herd of Goats at a waterhole*

*Camels at water's edge*

*The morning's catch of Nile Perch*

From the windswept sand dunes above our camp we could see on the horizon the barren volcanic cone of Central Island (or Crocodile Island as it is locally known). Few humans have visited this mysterious islet, for the 11 miles of water separating it from the main-land are frequently whipped into a foaming cauldron of tumbling waves and flying spray in which few boats could survive.

We remembered the tragic disappearance of the two members of the Cambridge University Rudolf Expedition of 1934 while trying to reach a similar island further to the south, and we wondered what chance our little 15 foot dingy would stand if we were caught in a real Rudolf storm.

However, the island was our main objective and we were determined to reach it if humanly possible. Studying the weather for several days, we found that the mornings were usually rough, with a considerable swell running, but that the afternoons and evenings were comparatively calm. We were warned to watch for black cloud banks rolling down from the Ethiopian highlands to the north which would be a sure sign of bad weather.

We decided to make a dash for it during a calm afternoon and, if the weather held, to complete our explorations and return the following day.

With four of us, all fairly large, in a little boat, equipment had to be kept to a minimum if we were to maintain a safe margin of freeboard.

Fresh water, petrol, food and camping gear were loaded into the forward part of the boat and covered with a tarpaulin, while the four of us who were making the crossing crammed into the stern. The 18 h.p. Evinrude outboard was checked over and we were ready. We arranged to fire a white signal flare at 8 o'clock that night to indicate our safe arrival. A red flare would mean that we were in trouble!

The ladies of the party, who would remain at the base camp until our return, waved us farewell from the beach, the outboard engine purred contentedly and we headed out towards the open lake. In the sheltered waters of the gulf we made good progress but, rounding the point, we started butting into a steep swell which rolled up from the south-east and forced us to reduce speed.

The flared bows smacked into the waves and showered us with spray, making us a little apprehensive at first, but heading into the wind we shipped little water and our confidence was soon restored. After about 2½ hours we were in the lee of the island, sheltered from the wind by the great crumbling pink coloured cliffs which formed its northern coast. With the aid of a rough sketch map made by the 1931 Rudolf Expedition we found a sandy cove, where we were able to run the boat up between jagged blocks of lava to a narrow beach at the foot of the cliffs.

*Triumph: Turkana boys landing a crocodile*

At our approach a number of large crocodiles flopped into the water, where they lay watching us balefully with only their protruding eyes and the tops of their snouts visible above the surface, while a reception committee of long legged spoonbills lined up nervously on the beach. A flock of the graceful red-beaked Caspian terns, visitors from Europe for the breeding season, rose screaming in protest at our intrusion. Cormorants, spoonbills, herons, pelicans and Egyptian geese took off from the cliffs and flew in noisy confusion above our heads as we unloaded the boat and humped the gear up the beach.

With only a few precious hours of daylight left we lost no time in starting to explore the island. Two of us decided to go inland, whilst the other two skirted the rocky coastline in the boat in the hope of catching some fish for supper.

The island, which is some 2–3 miles in diameter, is the top of a submerged volcano. Five large craters pit its domed surface, their bottoms, now flooded, forming deep circular lakes abounding with crocodiles, fish and bird life. Also scattered about the island are smaller explosion craters and still active blow-holes, which periodically emit jets of steam and sulphurous fumes.

Progress was slow over the steep slopes of loose grey ash and pumice of which most of the island is composed. Clambering up to the ridge above our landing place we found ourselves on the rim of the northernmost crater, a great mile-wide cauldron containing a lake of deep green water.

It was an astounding sight, for the lake shore beneath the beetling cliffs of the crater wall was fiery pink in colour. Through binoculars the pinkness resolved itself into thousands of lesser flamingos, many of them perched on their pedestal-like nests of mud. This was a discovery indeed, for a good deal of mystery surrounds the breeding habits of the lesser flamingo – extremely shy birds, they nest only in the most remote and inaccessible places where they are seldom seen by man. Here, hidden away on this barren islet and effectively guarded by the storm-swept waters of Lake Rudolf, was a great colony of them!

Armed with our cameras and binoculars we eagerly glissaded down a chute of loose ash to the crater floor, and began to pick our way cautiously through a jumble of sulphur-coated boulders towards the flamingos, standing in their gaudy ranks along the edge of the lake. At first they were nervous, rising in clouds and circling the crater with a chattering roar which reverberated from its towering cliffs. It was an incredibly beautiful sight; thousands upon thousands of these great birds, their long graceful necks outstretched, with the

*The Turkana fishermen heft a mighty Nile Perch of some 60lbs weight,*
*while the man in the left foreground clasps a Tilapia*

pink, scarlet and black of their plumage brilliant in the evening sun.
Wheeling round and round the crater for a few minutes, they gradually lost
their fear and settled again, some on the shore and others swimming in
massed flotillas on the limpid green water.

There were many nests clustered along the waters edge, each consisting of
a compacted pillar of mud nine inches or a foot in height with the top slightly hollowed to prevent the eggs from rolling off. Most of the nests contained
one single egg, pure white in colour and some three inches in length, though
some had already hatched into gawky long-legged chicks covered in fine grey
down, which ran about among the nests or swam out adventurously to join
their parents on the lake.

By the time we had taken some photographs of the crater and its birds the

*Fishing on Lake Rudolf*

sun was sinking and it was time to return. We reached the landing place just as darkness was falling and found the others with half-a dozen fat Nile perch which they had caught from the boat.

They had found the fish in amazing concentrations off a small headland at the mouth of the cove. Off this point, using spinning tackle and plug-baits, nearly every cast had brought a strike, and the bait was sometimes seized the moment it hit the surface. The perch were not unusually large, varying from 20 to 35 pounds in weight, but hard fighters which gave great sport and frequent thrills with mighty head-shaking leaps and savage, thrashing surface flurries. Approaching darkness and the loss of several plugs eventually forced our anglers to tear themselves reluctantly away from this fisherman's paradise, and return to our camp site.

This part of the island was practically devoid of vegetation, but nevertheless we managed to find sufficient twigs and withered roots to make a small fire and cook our supper. At the prearranged time we fired a white signal flare to let the rest of the party on the mainland know that all was well, and then settled down beneath our mosquito nets on the narrow strip of shore.

It was a disturbed night: several times we were awakened by the rush of wings as great flights of birds flew overhead, dimly seen in the moonlight as they headed for distant feeding grounds. Once, a minor landslide from the cliffs above brought us to startled wakefulness. A sudden rain squall at 4 am was the final straw, hissing down with tropical intensity and leaving us, soaked and shivering, to await the dawn, and the problem of starting a cooking fire with our meagre supply of now sodden fuel.

The next morning was spent exploring the rest of the island and photographing the innumerable birds which crowded its cliffs and beaches. Nearly all were nesting and young birds were everywhere. Newly hatched chicks of the Caspian terns squatted in shallow hollows in the black volcanic sand; fluffy baby pelicans overflowed from inadequate nests in the bushes; and incredibly ugly young spoonbills staggered away from us on long gawky legs. Crocodiles lay on every sandspit and strip of beach. Sinister and watchful, they regarded us with malevolent yellow eyes until we were within a few yards of them, when they would raise themselves, lizard-like on their short crooked legs, and lumber ponderously into the lake. Even when thus disturbed they never went far, but lay half submerged a few yards from shore, waiting until it was safe to land again. Flocks of Egyptian geese with their attractive fluffy goslings, spoonbills and numerous other birds stood at the waters edge, often within a few feet of a somnolent crocodile, at whose proximity they appeared blissfully unconcerned.

We landed on the western side of the island and crossed the narrow strip of lava and ash separating the largest crater lake from the main lake. Formed by three large overlapping craters it was about 1½ miles long and half a mile broad, overhung on the inland side by the towering cliffs of the crater walls. Birds were everywhere, including busy colonies of pelicans and cormorants nesting in the stunted trees along the crater's edge. We could see numbers of crocodiles, some of monstrous size, lying log-like in the still water beneath the cliffs. Far below us, out beyond the crater's rim, the broken windswept surface of Rudolf stretched away to the remote shore of the mainland shimmering yellow in the heat haze. Then, looking northwards towards the distant mountains of Ethiopia, we saw a towering bank of sinister black clouds – the storm warning of which we had been urged to beware!

There was no time to lose if we were to avoid being marooned on the island so, hurriedly, we slithered down the loose slopes of ash – now burning hot under the vertical sun – back to the beach where we had left the boat.

We hastily loaded the gear and were soon heading out from the shelter of the island. The rollers were now coming up behind us so that we had to be wary of being pooped, however the little boat rode them well and we made good progress. With the storm fast approaching we ran for the nearest point on the mainland and then followed the coastline, so that, in the event of a sudden squall, we should have time to beach the boat before she was swamped.

Heading into the rising wind we were soon drenched with the flying spray, but, surprisingly, the boat took in little water and eventually we rounded the sandspit at the entrance to Ferguson's gulf and, a few minutes later, reached the base camp just as dusk was falling – wet and shivering, but not a little relieved to be ashore again.

During the night the storm swept down the lake with hurricane force, sending great waves boiling up the beach, bending the sturdy palm trees to its fury and lashing our camp with driving spray. In the morning the heaving white-capped water looked more like the Atlantic than an inland lake in the heart of Africa. We were thankful to be safely back on the mainland, for our little boat could never have survived in such a storm.

The following morning the local Turkana staged a dance both in our honour and to celebrate our safe return from the mysterious island which they regarded with such awe and dread. Men and women circled and twisted in complex manoeuvres, chanting monotonous dirges to the accompaniment of the rhythmic stamping of their feet. On and on they swayed and sang until dust clouds dimmed the scene, and one by one they fell out exhausted to rest in the shade of the palms before our huts. We chatted with the watching elders and showed our appreciation with gifts of tobacco, salt and beans, until the various groups of tired men and women rose to their feet, and with cheerful farewells moved off in happy laughing parties to their homes.

Our expedition was now nearly at an end, so reluctantly we said goodbye to the friendly Turkana fishermen, and ferried our belongings from our sandspit camp back to the opposite shore of the gulf where we had left the vehicles.

The trucks were finally loaded up, everyone climbed aboard, and, with a last glance at the now turbulent waters of the lake and the wheeling clouds of birds, screaming their noisy farewells, we headed sadly westward towards distant civilization. But our return journey was not to prove so easy as our outward one. When it does rain in Turkana there are no half measures, and the dry river beds in which the loose, shifting sand presents something of an obstacle to any but four-wheel drive vehicles, become raging torrents of foam crested, chocolate coloured water, which may take two or three days to dry out. This we soon found to our cost as time and again the lorry stuck in loose sand when we branched off the main track to try and find a fording place at some water-filled nullah. Finally it stuck so firmly that all our efforts at towing, pushing and digging out failed to move it, and we had to abandon it for the night. 'Tash' made himself comfortable on his camp-bed alongside the lorry with a crate of beer to console him, while the rest of us crammed into the Land Rover and pushed on to Lodwar to sleep and bring help in the morning.

At dawn we returned with a truck full of palm fronds to use as sand tracks, and some cheerful Turkana labourers kindly lent by the District Commissioner, to find 'Tash' already hard at work jacking up the lorry's

*Turkana Tribal dance*

wheels. At last with engine roaring and amidst loud cheering the heavy vehicle slithered, slipped and bounced on to firm ground. Twenty minutes later it was again firmly stuck, but this time in the layer of sticky red mud left behind by the flood in a wide riverbed!

The tedious and back-breaking performance of jacking up the wheels and laying tracks had to be repeated all over again, while passing Turkana herdsmen dallied to watch curiously, or laughingly lend a hand, as their herds of camels, donkeys, sheep and goats crowded down into the river bed to drink their fill at the steadily shrinking pools.

At long last we were away, and pushed on again through Lodwar with a brief halt to say goodbye and express our thanks to the District Commissioner. Then with a lingering backward glance at the flooded Turkwell river, we turned our faces reluctantly to the west and the rugged line of the distant escarpment. As the sun dipped finally behind the hills we reached the top of the pass, and looked back for the last time to see the Turkana desert bathed in a strange blood-red glow. We had little doubt that one day we would return.

# Chapter XXII

# Kismet

## *Or the Hand of Fate*

A s I wrote in the Preface to this book, it was due to a quite extraordinary coincidence – or a quirk or trick of fate if you would prefer me to use these alternative expressions – that led to the creation, on the slopes of Mount Kilimanjaro (at 19,340 feet the highest mountain in Africa) of my personal brainchild, the College of African Wildlife Management.

Although the full implications of it only dawned on me much later, the actual timing of this extraordinary coincidence was, in itself, coincidental with Julius Nyerere's decision to resign from the premiership of Tanzania, in order to drum up support for his campaign to become the first President of Tanzania. What is even more coincidental, is that of all the elected ministers to whom Nyerere could have handed the reigns of premiership, he chose a minister who was the son of a man who happened to have been one of the finest Game Scouts that the Tanganyika Game Department had ever had!

I originally told this fascinating story in my book '*The Shamba Raiders*', which was first published nearly twenty five years ago, but for the sake of new readers, or those who may have forgotten it, I have decided to repeat the story, in rather more detail, in this chapter of '*Tales from a Crowded Life*'.

The original story (as told in '*The Shamba Raiders*') began on August 10th

*The College of African Wildlife Management*

1960, the day I entered my office in Dar es Salaam, for the very first time, on transfer from Uganda. This I recorded in the chapter entitled '*The Grand Finale*', which continued as follows:

"My first day in office in Dar es Salaam sobered me up with a jerk. As a result of the unpopular move from Tengeru the morale of many of the Game Department staff was low, ranging from resentment through depression to apathy, and I discovered, to my concern, that although Tanganyika's first, post-independence, three year development plan was in the course of preparation – and only a few days remained before the closing date for submissions – no proposals for any expansion and improvement of the Game Department had been prepared or submitted by the Ministry.

Perhaps even more significant, in the circumstances, was that, not long before, the Game Department had proposed that most of its finest game areas should be considered for re-classification as national parks, which, in turn, meant handing over full responsibility for their control to the National Parks Trustees.[1] At that time there was still only one national park in the whole of Tanganyika – the Serengeti, while the Game Department was responsible for all wildlife management matters throughout the remaining 357,000 square miles of the country, including over 70,000 square miles of game reserves and game controlled areas. Although the extension of the national park system was therefore obviously important and had my full support, the timing and circumstances of the Game Department's proposal were such that it bore the scent of abdication.

When I examined the Tanganyika Game Department's organisation, it immediately struck me that its main defect was that for a country the size of Tanganyika it was too centralised, with insufficient delegation of responsibility. It was also grossly under-staffed. The inevitable result was that some of the remoter game warden stations were very seldom visited by a senior officer and the game wardens concerned tended to regard themselves as 'forgotten men'. When the Department's headquarters was at Tengeru, one of the areas so affected was the Selous and south to the Ruvuma river. There, the late George Rushby, a famous game warden and elephant hunter, once had an arresting notice displayed in his dusty, ramshackle little office. In protest at what he felt

---

[1] The Chief Game Warden was an ex-officio member of the Tanganyika National Parks Board of Trustees.

was a particularly petty and officious headquarters reprimand for the manner in which he drafted official memoranda – on the infrequent occasions that he felt compelled to do so – he posted up in large letters, evenly spaced around the four walls of his office, a notice saying:

'IF YOU WANT TO BE . . . A GOOD ELEPHANT HUNTER . . . YOU MUST NOT FORGET . . . TO NUMBER YOUR PARAGRAPHS!'

George Rushby's action was amusing, but it was a bitter humour that revealed the dislike and mistrust of headquarters felt by many game wardens in the outposts at that time.

Burning the midnight oil, I managed, with the help of my patient deputy, Keith Thomas – an ex-paratroop gunner and qualified vet – to produce a comprehensive document; entitled '*A Review of the Wildlife Situation in Tanganyika in 1960*', it contained detailed recommendations not only for doubling the size of the Game Department and its facilities over a period of three years, but also for reorganising the Department on the basis of four game 'regions' with their headquarters at Arusha, Morogoro, Tabora and Mwanza respectively. Each of these game regions was to be under the control of a 'Senior Game Warden' (a new rank) with considerable local autonomy but ultimately responsible to the Department's headquarters in Dar es Salaam.

In addition to the reorganisation and expansion, I included a plan for the creation of a training school, an establishment to produce men qualified to fill what I had long referred to as 'the missing middle ranks' – the massive rank gap between the game guards or game scouts on the lowest rungs of the ladder and the game rangers or game wardens at the top. This gap had always appeared to me to be a serious weakness in the organisation of all African game and national park departments. It was like having an army with private soldiers at the bottom and commissioned office at the summit, but no non-commissioned or warrant officer ranks in between – yet the latter have always been recognised as the 'backbone' of any disciplined force. In Uganda I had created the rank of 'Game Assistant',[2] but suitable training had continued to

---

[2] An ugly, clumsy title not of my choosing but one ordained by the Public Service Commission (P.S.C.) and the Establishments Division of the Secretariat, who, between them, decided such matters as titles and salary scales for the Civil Service.

be a problem and with independence and 'Africanisation' coming nearer, the advent of this new rank was not, in itself, enough. Hence the vital importance of starting a wildlife management school, an institution which just did not exist anywhere in Africa at that period – and time was running out fast.

Most of my proposals for the development and reorganisation of the Game Department were approved with remarkably little pruning; and within eighteen months the four new game 'regions' were established with the four Senior Game Wardens appointed. The latter were Bill Dick, a steady and valuable old-timer, now retired; Bill Moore-Gilbert, ex Indian Police and a particularly able game warden, later killed in an air crash; Peter Achard, one of the best, most dedicated and most likeable game wardens I have ever known, a man who worked himself literally almost to death and is now an invalid as a result; and Brian Nicholson, a tough, versatile, amusing character and outstanding hunter-naturalist who was a protégé of the great Ionides. Of the four only Brian Nicholson is still in Tanzania at the time I pen these words; he is in charge of a special wildlife development project for the area to which he and Ionides were drawn above all others – the Selous Game Reserve, a project the foundations of which he and I laid together. By then Keith Thomas had also left; a quiet, determined man, tough but courteous, he was missed by all.

Tony Mence, one of the Tanganyika Game Department's most experienced game wardens, now became my deputy as Assistant Chief Game Warden. A strong, wiry, little Welshman with a degree in zoology, quiet, unflappable and a most efficient administrator, he was a tremendous asset. As an ex-Royal Marine Commando, with the swarthy good looks of a popular screen star, Tony had been pestered with requests for his services by the American 'Paramount Film Corporation', a Hollywood company whose high-powered field unit, directed by Howard Hawkes, had descended like a whirlwind on the surprised inhabitants of Arusha late in 1960, to make on location, with the help and guidance of the Game Department, a dramatised game-catching film called *Hatari* – Swahili for 'danger'. Impressed by his appearance and his ability to ride a wild rhino with the carefree nonchalance of a bronco-busting cowboy, Paramount had wanted Tony to double for one of their highly paid stars – but neither his wife nor the Government had shared Paramount's enthusiasm for the idea.

Scarcely had the dust settled on the departure of the Hollywood galaxy –

taking with it into orbit such celebrated personalities as John Wayne, Elsa Martinelli, Hardy Kruger and Red Buttons – than another event disturbed the lives of the bewildered, starstruck people of Arusha. This time it was a top level, international wildlife conference to be attended by leading scientists and wildlife conservation experts from all over the world.

The Arusha Conference[3] took place between the September 5th and 10th 1961. It became not only the launching pad of IUCN's 'African Special Project', but a turning point in the annals of African wildlife conservation. That Arusha was chosen as the venue, spotlighted its world-wide recognition as the centre of some of the richest and most varied wildlife areas in Africa.

The Conference was opened by Sir Richard Turnbull, K.C.M.G., the Governor of Tanganyika, a brilliant man with an infectious sense of humour, well known as a strong but humane administrator.

During his opening speech he appealed for realism in the approach to wildlife conservation, quoting an earthy rhyme which he claimed to have learnt during his school days:

East is East and West is West
Though this may not seem relevant
You all know how to milk a cow
But you can't muck about with an elephant

My own contribution to the Conference consisted of a paper on training entitled *'The Urgent Need for Formalised Training Facilities for Wildlife Management Personnel in the Africa of Today'*. I had written the paper, at the request of IUCN, after a discussion I had had with Monsieur Claude

---

3 A Symposium on the Conservation of Nature and Natural Resources in Modern African States' sponsored by the Commission for Technical Co-operation in Africa South of the Sahara (C.C.T.A.) and the International Union for the Conservation of Nature and Natural Resources (I.U.C.N.), supported by the United Nations Educational Scientific and Cultural Organisations (U.N.E.S.C.O.) and the Food and Agricultural Organisation of the United Nations (F.A.O.), and organized by I.U.C.N., C.S.A. (C.C.T.A.'s Scientific Council for Africa South of the Sahara), and the Tanganyika Game Department – representing the host government, Tanganyika.

Cheysson, Secretary General of CCTA, in which he had expressed enthusiastic interest in the training school project that I had prepared for Tanganyika's 'Three Year Development Plan'. We had agreed that it would be an ideal regional project, if Kenya and Uganda approved, since the problem was clearly the same in all three territories. It was on this basis, therefore, that my paper was prepared, and what was probably the key paragraph in it was quoted by Sir Richard Turnbull in his address. "May I read you," he said, "what Major Kinloch has to say in his paper – 'It is clear that the time is long overdue for wildlife management to be regarded in Africa as a true branch of natural science comparable with forestry and agriculture. It has long been so treated on the North American continent; why not here? The foresters and agriculturists have always considered it necessary to have a high percentage of both scientifically and technically qualified officers; why should we continue to consider that those responsible for managing our wildlife resources are in a different category?'"

My detailed proposals and plans for a regional wildlife management training school, an establishment to be sited somewhere in the Arusha region, were finally discussed and universally approved by a special session of the Conference (See Appendix I). At the same meeting, at the request of the delegates, Dr Jacques Verdier, Scientific Secretary of CSA, accepted the responsibility of approaching the American Agency for International Development (AID) for the financial assistance necessary for the project. Not unnaturally I was delighted at the outcome of my efforts, and when the 'Arusha Manifesto' – a clear declaration of the Tanganyika government's unqualified support for wildlife conservation – was presented to the applauding delegates, my cup was full. It was a fitting conclusion to an outstandingly successful conference.

The Arusha Manifesto can justly be described as a beacon in the history of wildlife conservation in Africa. In this impressive declaration, Tanganyika, one of the finest game countries on the African continent and the first of the British East and Central African Colonial Territories to become independent, came out solidly in support of wildlife conservation by making an official and most solemn pledge; drafted as a formal document of state, it was signed by the Prime Minister, Julius Nyerere, and two of his Ministers[4] responsible for wildlife. Kenya was swift to follow this example, and the pessimists – the dismal prophets

---

4   Chief Abdulla Fundikira, hereditary Paramount Chief of the Wanyamwezi and El Haj Tewa Saidi Tewa.

of doom who had forecast the dissolution of the national parks and the game reserves and the massacre of the great herds of game, immediately the countries of East Africa became ruled by elected African governments – were forced to eat their words. When the time came the contrary was the case, the truth being that there was greater support, both moral and material, for wildlife conservation by the countries of East Africa *after* they became independent than was ever the case before. I had always been one of the optimists, but when, at the end of September 1961, Elizabeth and I flew to America on my United Nations Fellowship, things seemed to be going much better than even I had dared to hope.

For four glorious but hectic months Elizabeth and I toured Canada and the USA, thrilled by the wonders of those two great countries and overwhelmed by the never failing courtesy and warm hospitality of their vital peoples. On our return journey London seemed suddenly to have shrunk, like a gracious old lady who is feeling her age; and when we reached Dar es Salaam at the end of January 1962, it took us some time to come down to earth.

During my absence from East Africa there had been important developments and significant changes. To begin with it was clear that Tanganyika was well set on the shortest possible road to becoming a republic. To further this end Julius Nyerere had resigned from the post of Prime Minister and had withdrawn, like John the Baptist, into the wilderness. Although he did not say so publicly at the time, it was immediately obvious that his object in going into the highways and by-ways was to round up political strays; to rally the faithful of Tanganyika African National Union – TANU, the ruling political party – behind him; and to return to power as the first, popularly elected President of the Republic of Tanganyika. In the interim, into Nyerere's shoes as Prime Minister had stepped a close friend and political ally of his, a tiny, bouncy, little man by the name of Rashidi Kawawa. For an ironic and little-known reason, this latter single factor was soon to have a profound effect on developments in the wildlife field.

Shortly after my return to Dar es Salaam, an advertisement appeared in the *Government Gazette* and the East African press calling for applications for vacancies in the post of Game Warden in the Tanganyika Game Department. The newly independent Tanganyika Government had agreed that we should continue to recruit suitably qualified Europeans, on short term contracts, until young Africans had been properly trained to take their places, it being clearly understood and accepted by all concerned that this would inevitably be a slow process. There were, at that time, a handful of academically qualified and physically suitable young Africans whom we were sending on four-year courses, at selected American universities, to study for degrees in Wildlife Management, while my training school project for the 'missing middle ranks' was still in the early stages of protracted financial negotiations with American AID. Into this carefully conceived dream world there dropped a bombshell which threatened to shatter my most cherished plans; taking the form of a letter to my Minister, Tewa Saidi Tewa, from the Prime Minister, Rashidi Kawawa, the contents of which I am unlikely ever to forget, it arrived on my desk with a request for my comments.

The text of the missive is graven on my mind to this day. 'Dear Minister,' it said. 'I have noted with great interest the advertisement for game warden vacancies. With my personal knowledge of this type of work, I consider that it is just the sort of post for young Africans with their experience of the bush. You are aware of the need to accelerate the Africanisation of posts in Government service, a policy which TANU has promised to the electorate. I consider, therefore, that we could select suitable Standard 8[5] schoolboys, place them under a game warden, or possibly a senior game scout, for a year and then let them take over the game warden posts in the Game Department. I would appreciate your comments.' The signature revealed the letter's origins; it did not reveal the crucial fact, known to few people, that Rashidi Kawawa was a son of Mfaumi Ali, one of the finest senior game scouts who had ever served in the Tanganyika Game Department! Had this not been the case it is doubtful whether Rashidi Kawawa would even have noticed the advertisement; it is certain he would not have been moved to comment on it.

Mfaumi Ali, a grand old man and fine hunter who had worked for both Ionides and Brian Nicholson, had been killed while setting a trap-gun for a man-eating lion. If the accident had not occurred *after* Rashidi Kawawa had been conceived the history of the Game Department might have taken a different course. Alternatively, if the game warden vacancy advertisement had appeared *before* Julius Nyerere vacated the post of Prime Minister, it is also unlikely that Rashidi Kawawa would have been in a position to take formal

---

[5] Standard 8 was four grades *below* School Certificate level (now called 'O' levels) which was Standard 12!

notice of it and to act accordingly. As it was, the timing and circumstances were such that the hand of fate was clearly apparent. Overnight the son of a senior game scout had become the most powerful man in the country; a man whose brother, Saidi Kawawa, was still only a senior game scout, had suddenly been made Prime Minister of Tanganyika; as such his opinions and wishes could not lightly be brushed aside.

Without waiting a moment, I sat down and drafted a closely reasoned letter to my Minister, carefully listing the serious drawbacks and dangers of the Prime Minister's proposal and citing the horrors of the Congo as a sobering example of what can happen when discipline goes, training is forgotten, and armed men go on an extended rampage. I stressed that there were over six hundred, tough, well armed game scouts in the Tanganyika Game Department; a force which could terrorise the countryside if they got out of control. And what of the effect on Tanganyika's increasingly valuable tourism, an industry which was almost entirely dependent on proper care and management of the country's wildlife?

A month later I received my Minister's reply. It consisted of four words at which I stared in growing disbelief. 'The Prime Minister insists,' they said; no more, no less, just that!

For a few moments I was stunned. 'So much for the Arusha Manifesto,' I thought to myself bitterly. Then suddenly I realised that I had been naïve to expect the Prime Minister to retract his proposal for this could have been regarded in political circles as loss of face. Given time, and provided I played my cards with care, the Prime Minister's instruction might be suitably modified, but to achieve this I would have to provide some convincing alternative – and fast. If not, then the Game Department, with its proud traditions, would soon be in real trouble and the National parks would not be far behind. My training school project, the real answer to the problem, was still in the early stages of protracted negotiations with AID; it would be months before even the money might be voted, let alone building started and staff recruited. Something else had to be thought of in a hurry to fill the gap.

My first idea was to press again for the amalgamation of the Game Department and National Parks to form a unified wildlife service, a policy I had always strongly and openly advocated ever since my earliest days in Uganda. This move would not only have cut overheads by having one wildlife department headquarters instead of two, but would have made fuller use

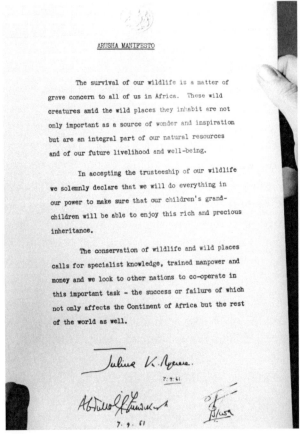

ARUSHA MANIFESTO

The survival of our wildlife is a matter of grave concern to all of us in Africa. These wild creatures amid the wild places they inhabit are not only important as a source of wonder and inspiration but are an integral part of our natural resources and of our future livelihood and well-being.

In accepting the trusteeship of our wildlife we solemnly declare that we will do everything in our power to make sure that our children's grand-children will be able to enjoy this rich and precious inheritance.

The conservation of wildlife and wild places calls for specialist knowledge, trained manpower and money and we look to other nations to co-operate in this important task - the success or failure of which not only affects the Continent of Africa but the rest of the world as well.

*Julius K. Nyerere.*
7. 9. 61

7. 9. 61

*Arusha Manifesto*

of available staff, thus enabling us to stall on further recruitment to senior posts until proper training facilities were ready and operating. Ironically, the motives behind my outspoken opinions had frequently been misrepresented by others as a personal bid for power. If amalgamation was to be achieved in a hurry, therefore, there was only one possible proposal I could make.

I went to see John Owen, Director of Tanganyika National Parks, whom I knew to be firmly opposed to any policy which might infringe on the complete independence of national parks. After explaining the problem in detail and emphasising the threat it posed to wildlife conservation in general, not merely to the Game Department, I presented my proposition. "John," I said, "I suggest the time's come for the National Parks and the Game Department to get together and form a strong, unified 'Wildlife Service'; and in case it'll persuade you and convince you that I'm being entirely sincere, I want to say that if you agree to this amalgamation I'll be willing to step down in your favour. You can take over the combined department. I'll just pull out."

John Owen stared at me in surprise. I think he realised what a tremendous effort it had been for me to make the offer to step down, for there is scarcely a national park in the length and breadth of Africa that did not start life as a game reserve, or similar protected area, conceived and developed by the game department concerned, before being handed over to a newly created national parks organisation; and invariably the latter owe their existence to having been initiated by one of the old, traditional game departments. This was certainly the pattern in both Tanganyika and Uganda, where the national parks organisations had been granted special status and given only the choicest of the game departments' preserved wildlife areas to look after. When I went to Tanganyika in 1960, the Serengeti was the only national park; by the time I left, four and a half years later, there were five national parks,[6] all of which the Game Department had been largely instrumental in converting to national park status. In the circumstances, therefore, my offer to hand over control of the remainder of the Game Department's widespread responsibilities was a bitter and indigestible pill for me to swallow.

For a few moments John Owen was silent, thinking hard. Then he replied. 'I appreciate your offer very much, Bruce,' he said. 'But I feel I must refuse. I don't think it would benefit the National Parks to become involved with all the extensive and complicated wildlife management problems with which the Game Department has to deal throughout Tanganyika. The National Parks have their own problems, but at least they are clear-cut and concentrated and I think it's best to keep them that way.' Somehow I felt relieved. It would have been a sad day if the characteristic paratroop-red berets and glistening, brass, buffalo head badges of the Tanganyika Game Department were to disappear from the scene. However, there was still one other person to whom I felt I should present a similar proposal – Robert Sangster, Chief Conservator of Forests in Tanganyika. Robert was an ex-officio Trustee of the Tanganyika National Parks and, like many professional foresters, keenly interested in wildlife. Furthermore, in certain other parts of the world it is still the government forestry department which is responsible for wildlife conservation. Would an amalgamation of the Tanganyika Forestry and Game Departments be a possible answer? After all, we were already in the same Ministry. When I put the suggestion to him, Robert Sangster also thought hard about the idea

---

[6]  Serengeti, Lake Manyara, Ngurdoto Crater (now Arusha National Park), Ruaha (part of the great Rungwa Game Reserve) and Mikumi National Parks, all previously game reserves or game controlled areas developed and managed by the Game Department.

before politely turning it down. His reasons were similar to John Owen's. He had enough problems on his plate already, he said regretfully.

The most immediate possible solutions having been tried and failed, there appeared to me to be only one answer left. I had to get a suitable 'crash' training programme under way as quickly as possible. This meant staff, equipment, funds and suitable buildings for a permanent base.

Wasting no time, I went straight to the Permanent Secretary of my Ministry and obtained authority to side-track the minimum necessary requirements from the projects already approved in the Game Department's three-year development plan. Then I sent an urgent circular letter to all Provincial Commissioners in Tanganyika, asking if they could offer me any empty buildings suitable for a training project, preferably in the Northern Province. One by one the answers trickled in, each more depressing than the last, and by the time I flew to Nairobi, at the end of March 1962, for urgent discussions on 'Africanisation' training problems with Dr Jacques Verdier and the Chief Game Wardens on Kenya and Uganda, it appeared that there were no suitable buildings available anywhere. The only bright spot in this otherwise depressing period, was the advent in the Kinloch ménage of a young banded mongoose; 'Pipa', as he was called, soon proved to be a strong character who quickly dominated the household and his colourful life story was eventually published in my first book.[7]

The first sign that my luck was changing came at Arusha, on my return trip. On landing there I was met by Bill Dick, Senior Game Warden for the Northern Game Region, and he and I paid a courtesy call on the Acting Provincial Commissioner of the Northern Province, Tony Golding. With little hope I asked Tony Golding again about possible buildings for my training project. He shook his head regretfully, but when I rose to leave he had a sudden though. "I've just remembered," he said. "There are some old school buildings on the lower slopes of Kilimanjaro in an area called Mweka, a few miles from Moshi. They were built by German farmers in the area, between the wars, as a school for their children. During the last war they were used as a nurses' training school, but they've been empty for some time and I believe they're now in need of a fair amount of repair. I don't suppose they would be of much use for your purpose, but you might like to inspect them."

---

[7] *Sauce for the Mongoose* by Bruce Kinloch, published by the Harvill Press, London 1964.

"I can't afford to pass up any chances," I replied. "Bill Dick and I'll drive down there straight away and have a look."

Late that afternoon, Bill Dick's old Land-Rover clattered up the rough, winding road leading from Moshi to Mweka. Climbing steadily through mile after mile of coffee plantations of the Chagga country, we eventually passed between the old, stone pillars of what had once been an impressive entrance gate, on to a long-neglected drive. On our left was a small but adequate playing field, over which a number of scrawny chickens were fossicking industriously. On our right was a group of old but imposing and obviously very solid stone buildings; shabby they might be, with grimy stonework, blistered paint and here and there a broken window, but it was the threadbare shabbiness of a well-made suit which has seen hard and worthy use – worn but not worn out. As we stared our excitement grew. Then, suddenly, the clouds behind the school rolled back like a curtain drawn by an unseen hand, and through the last filmy wisps, high in the sky, there thrust a great towering, white-capped dome, pink-tinged and glistening in the dying rays of the evening sun – it was the snow-capped peak of Kibo; what the Masai call *Oldonyo Oibor,* 'the White Mountain', the tallest peak of Kilimanjaro; at nearly 20,000 feet, the highest mountain in Africa.

Slowly I turned to Bill Dick. "We've found it at last, Bill," I said quietly. "This is the end of the search."

The next day I was in Dar es Salaam and went straight to see the powers that be. "The school is ideal for our purpose," I said. "Not only are the buildings suitable, although they need some repair, but the site itself could hardly be better. It's the centre of, or close to a number of major game areas of varying ecology, all of which would be essential for field demonstrations and practical training. May we have it please?"

The man behind the desk smiled. "Certainly!" he replied. I rocked back on my heels. He had not even bothered to glance at his files!

As soon as I could I returned to have a closer look at the school. Elizabeth accompanied me and we were joined by Oscar Charlton, the Game Warden from Tanga. Armed with chalk, tape-measures, pencils and paper, the three of us crawled about, on hands and knees, among the accumulated dust and cobwebs of years, planning and marking out such refinements as cubicles in place of former dormitories and staff quarters where none had ever existed. By the time we had finished, dirty and dishevelled, I reckoned that, with the liberal use of hardboard partitions, we could just about manage to adapt the existing buildings sufficiently to meet our major needs. The next problems to solve were money for basic running expenses, staff and equipment. I could drain off some of the Game Department's always slender resources, but very little without crippling it. Whom could I approach for financial help?

Fortunately, I did not have to think very hard. Two old friends immediately sprang to mind – Professor Bernhard Grzimek, Director of the Frankfurt Zoological Society; and Judge Russell Train, at that time a judge of the United States Tax Court by profession, but a dedicated hunter-conservationist by interest and inclination. Bernhard Grzimek, internationally known conservationist, author, television personality and hard fighting, philanthropic champion of wildlife in Africa, needs little introduction. Russell Train, on the other hand, despite his subsequent meteoric rise to power and fame in the wildlife conservation world,[8] was a comparative newcomer to such circles at that time. However, young and dynamic he had just been instrumental in forming the 'African Wildlife Leadership Foundation' – of which he was President – a body dedicated to the important cause of educating young Africans to appreciate and care for their great wildlife heritage, a body whose members I had been asked to address, only the year before, at a luncheon they had given in my honour in Washington, DC. I was soon to discover that my words, mainly on the urgent need for proper training, had not fallen on deaf ears.

I wrote to both Bernhard Grzimek and Russell Train, explaining the crisis in detail and saying that I needed £10,000 urgently, to get the training school launched and to keep it going until the hoped for American AID project materialised. In both cases their response was immediate. Bernhard Grzimek wrote from Germany to say that the Frankfurt Zoological Society had made an initial donation to the value of £2,000 and more would follow. Russell Train cabled from Washington saying that the 'African Wildlife Leadership Foundation' was sending $25,000 and to whom should it be paid?

To whom *should* the money be paid? This was a poser. If I allowed it to be swallowed up in the ever-hungry maw of the Tanganyika Treasury, its regurgitation and effective use would be gagged by a tangled mass of red tape and

---

[8] In 1965 he became President of the Conservation Foundation; in 1968, Under Secretary for the Interior; and in January 1970, he was appointed Chairman of the newly formed, United States 'Council on Environmental Quality'.

civil service regulations. Such a prospect was so ominous that I immediately suppressed my never very active civil servant's conscience and sought a more workable alternative. Happily, in cases like this I had a well established standby in the East African Wildlife Society, that immensely valuable and effective organisation conceived and created in 1956 by the efforts of Noel Simon, one of those truly dedicated individuals who has done so much for wildlife conservation behind the scenes. The Society was always willing to act as banker for any worthy wildlife conservation project financed from private sources, and on this occasion again it readily came to my aid.

Later, I rode rough-shod through further civil service principles by authorising the opening of a private bank account in Moshi, in the name of the training school. In so doing I laid myself open to severe official censure – or worse – but there was really no alternative since somehow the school had to be enabled to pay its day-to-day expenses during the critical construction period. It was a risk I just had to take.

With the buildings and basic running expenses assured, the next problem to be settled was the question of staff and particularly the instructional staff, for it was on the latter that the success or failure of the whole project would ultimately depend. Here I was fortunate in having several game wardens who were not only suitably qualified but – equally important – keen to try their hand at training. First I needed a good administrator, a game warden who could not only organise and supervise the day-to-day management of the school and its subordinate staff, but also instruct as well. For this post I chose David Anstey. As a general instructor in a wide variety of subjects from basic zoology to anti-poaching measures, I picked Gilbert Child, a versatile East African born game warden with a degree in zoology. Finally, I was left with the problem of selecting the key man – the head of the establishment.

I jotted down the attributes for which I was looking in the person to be selected as 'Principal' of my wildlife training school. The ideal incumbent had to be a firm disciplinarian but diplomatic, for it was important that he should both inspire confidence and command respect. He had to be a good organiser and an able administrator. His approach had to be scientific but strictly practical at the same time. He had to be both a scholar and an athlete, a good teacher, physically tough, ingenious, adaptable, and a good mixer with people of all races. Above all he had to have a more than normal interest in wildlife and considerable practical experience of the many thorny problems associated with its management. Where could I find such a paragon? There was one person in the Tanganyika Game Department who went a long way towards filling the bill. His name was Hugh Lamprey, he was thirty-four, and he was the Game Department's Biologist.

Not only had Hugh Lamprey an outstanding academic record, but he had served for two years as a gunner subaltern in Palestine and Egypt – valuable discipline training – before going to university. While an undergraduate at Oxford he had been a member of three university expeditions, including one to the Tehri-Garhwal region of the Central Himalayas in 1952, when he had taken part in the first ascent of the 21,560 foot Mount Gangotri III. He had graduated in 1952 with 2nd Class Honours in Zoology, and had then joined the Tanganyika Game Department as its one and only Research Biologist. From that time on he had been employed on a variety of tasks – including that of acting as a game warden – until finally he had managed to hide himself away in the Tarangire Game Reserve to complete his research work for a doctorate! Before he had finished his research he had learnt to fly, as a valuable aid to his work, and by the time I reached the stage of looking for a head for my wildlife management training school, Hugh had become not only a most competent pilot, but was back at Oxford in the final process of obtaining his degree as a Doctor of Philosophy.

I now had two problems: would Hugh Lamprey accept the offer of the post of Principal; and would the British Government be persuaded to pay the salaries of the school instructors if the officers concerned were seconded to the job? The people who could provide the answers where Hugh Lamprey and the Department of Technical Co-operation,[9] the successor to the old Colonial Office. Both were in England. Letter writing on the issue would be slow, tedious and very liable to lead to misunderstandings. Somehow I had to find the means to fly home and talk to those concerned. But where could I raise the money for my return airfare to London? Suddenly I had an idea. I picked up my telephone and asked for a Nairobi number.

On the September 11th, 1962, I found myself somewhere high over north Africa, the focus of row upon row of frankly curious brown eyes set in a sea of dark, bewhiskered faces. I felt like Gulliver in Lilliput for most of my travelling

---

[9] Later re-named the Ministry of Overseas Development (O.D.M.) and now the Overseas Development Administration (O.D.A.).

companions were under two feet tall. I was aboard the weekly British United Airways 'animal freighter' aircraft flying between Nairobi and London, travelling officially as a 'monkey attendant'. The firms exporting the vervet monkeys – animals needed for such vital medical research purposes as the production of poliomyelitis vaccine – were required to provide one person to assist the steward on these journeys; and, through the courtesy and kindly help of Allan Lambert, Freight Manager of BUA, it had been arranged that, on this particular occasion, the Chief Game Warden of Tanganyika would travel aboard, not only to help the steward but also to experience and see for himself the conditions under which the monkeys were being transported. There had been some very vocal but often misguided public criticism of the export of monkeys for medical purposes at that time, and in particular of the handling and shipping arrangements involved in such export, so this gave me a chance to kill two birds with one stone – see officially how the monkeys fared; and get a free rid to London and back at the same time!

When I had boarded the aircraft at Nairobi I had been met by a cheerful cockney steward. Having greeted me like a long lost brother, he had led me courteously between closely packed rows of cages to a cramped canvas seat at the rear of the aircraft. "Mind your 'ead on the corner of that there parrot's cage, sir," he had said, malevolently eyeing a lemon-crested cockatoo and sucking a blood-stained thumb. "It's sharp and 'is beak's a bloody sight sharper! – think you'll be all right there, sir? Not exactly four star comfort, but I'll bring you some coffee and sandwiches once we're airborne." So saying he had disappeared like a wraith up the narrow, murky alley-way leading to the bows of the aircraft, leaving me the centre of attention of several hundred excited and uninhibited primates, a few curious birds, several rather sad and bewildered looking dogs, and a couple of very bored cats.

By the time we were over the Sudan I had discovered that my responsibilities were not arduous. My chief duty appeared to be to keep out of the way. At the same time, I had to ensure that my fellow passengers were kept well supplied with water, and that the lashings which held the cages remained secure. At Khartoum and Malta I was let out for a run, escorted by a large and friendly Alsatian who seemed to enjoy the exercise as much I did. When I arrived in London and reported favourably to the RSPCA on the care of animals in transit, I was feeling remarkably perky.

Hugh Lamprey was at the airport to meet me. The warmth of manner, the old world courtesy, the quiet confidence which, in turn, inspired confidence – all were there. I had written ahead to warn him that there was an urgent and important matter which I wanted to discuss, but I had thought it wiser not to mention what it was. Travelling in Hugh's car to London I explained the situation in detail. Later, over a pint of draught beer in one of my favourite pubs – The Red Lion tucked away in that ancient, narrow alley called Crown Passage, between St James's and Pall Mall – I put the final proposition to him. "Hugh," I said, "I know you're a research man and that's where your heart really lies. But, to my mind, to get this training school running smoothly and on the right lines is the most urgent and important wildlife task in Africa today. I think you're the ideal person for the job. Will you take it on? Wait – think hard before you answer. I must have a 'willing horse', Someone who is really keen on the idea, not just a friend who is tackling it from a sense of duty."

For a few moments Hugh was silent, staring into his tankard; then he looked up and smiled. "I'll be glad to take it on, Bruce," he said.

The next day I called at the Department of Technical Co-operation, whose Permanent Secretary was my old friend and ally from Uganda days, Sir Andrew Cohen. I had not seen him for seven years, but, despite his tour of duty in the difficult and testing diplomatic post of Britain's Permanent Representative to the United Nations, I could detect little change. The same youthful energy, the same rather mirthless, almost wolf-like smile, both were still there. He greeted me warmly. "What can I do for you, Bruce?" he asked. I told him the whole sad story. By this time I knew it off by heart, like the glib patter of a practised travelling salesman. What I was hoping, I said, was that the British Government would agree to meet the cost of the Principal and Bursar who would also double as an instructor. Sir Andrew thought for a moment. "How long are you in London for?" he asked eventually. "About ten days," I replied. "I'm waiting for the return freighter flight." "Come and see me at the end of the week," he said. "I'll give you an answer then."

Sir Andrew was as good as his word and I climbed aboard the return BUA freighter with a light heart. Not only had Hugh Lamprey's reaction cheered me, but my spirits were buoyed up by the knowledge that the Department of Technical Co-operation had agreed to meet the costs of the school's Principal and Bursar for a period of three years in the first instance.

Shortly after I returned to Dar es Salaam, I was able to give the school project the final push that really started it moving. Like a snowball it gathered size and momentum as it rolled and, by December 1962, the necessary building modifications were well advanced, repairs and renovations were in hand. David Anstey was firmly installed in what had been the matron's cottage at the school – with a nucleus of subordinate staff such as drivers, game guards and a clerk – and Hugh Lamprey and Gil Child had moved into houses in Moshi. Between us we had also worked out a provisional syllabus for a two-year course, a syllabus for which I had laid down the guidelines. It had to have a simple but sound scientific basis, and it had to cover all facets of a game warden's many-sided duties – from elephant control to office administration; from anti-poaching measures to the supervision of tourists and the safari hunting industry; from map reading to vehicle maintenance; from road building to court work and prosecuting under the game laws; from game population assessment to the capture, marking and translocation of animals; from the care and use of firearms to the collection and preparation of scientific specimens; and so on and so forth. Above all, I stressed, at least fifty and preferably seventy-five per cent of the training had to be practical work in the field; the rest could be lectures, demonstrations and instruction in the class room.

In January 1963 a climax was reached, for during that month a high level meeting was held in Moshi to make formal recommendations on the estab-lishment of the training school. It was attended by the Chief Game Wardens and Directors of National Parks of Kenya, Uganda and Tanganyika; represen-tatives from the East African Common Services Organisation and from the relevant ministries in the three East African countries; and also a Senior Game Warden from Northern Rhodesia. The Chairman was Dr A.C. Evans, who, by then, had succeeded Dr Jacques Verdier as Scientific Secretary of CCTA/CSA.

The proceedings were opened by the Regional Commissioner of Tanganyika's Northern Region, who said, "This is a very special occasion. This meeting marks the beginning of the last phase of a project which is not only unique, but of far reaching importance. I refer to the creation in Africa of an institution to train Africans in the modern techniques of conserving wild animals as a natural resource." ... "With these few words," he concluded, after reviewing how the school had come to pass and thanking those benefactors who had made it possible, "I wish you success in your deliberations, the results of which will be of long term importance to the economy of Africa."

The Moshi meeting set the final, official seal on the training project, giving the school the security and respectability of formal recognition. A number of important practical administrative matters were thrashed out and decided, including the formation of a governing body, the details of courses, and the charges to be levied per student. A course fee of £400 per student per year, to be paid by the governments concerned, to provide the basis of funds required for recurrent expenditure, was agreed as fair and reasonable, since the capital costs involved were already covered by substantial grants of both money and equipment received or promised from outside sources.

By the time the Moshi meeting was held, in addition to the actual school buildings and staff provided by the Tanganyika Government, the money sent by Russell Train's African Wildlife Leadership foundation (later followed up by a further $16,000 for a laboratory) and by Bernhard Grzimek on behalf of the Frankfurt Zoological Society, as well as the aid promised by the British Department of Technical Co-operation, further promises of firm assistance had been received from abroad. These included $50,000 from American AID (later increased to $95,000), while the West German government made a most valuable contribution of Mercedes 'Unimog' four-wheel drive lorries and essential safari equipment and clothing, as well as the services of an additional instructor. To my delight the latter was Anno Hecker, a qualified German forester-game warden who had not only served with the Tanganyika Tsetse Control Department for several years, but had also been one of my honorary game wardens; and due to the television broadcast appeals of the indefatigable Professor Grzimek, the generous public of West Germany donated £4,500 towards the cost of a house for Anno Hecker. Later still the Ford Foundation offered $30,000 for recurrent expenditure and the Rockefeller Brothers Fund provided $36,000 for scholarships. In fact, in the course of a few months, an enterprise based on little more than inspiration, faith and hope, had become a well endowed project which had aroused widespread international interest and support.

The concluding actions of the Moshi meeting were to approve the draft syllabus which we had drawn up – with emphasis on the nearby Mkomazi Game Reserve as the main working area for basic field training – and to agree that the first, two year course would commence in June 1963. Finally, the meeting formally decided that the training school should be given the title of 'College of African Wildlife Management', with the authority to grant a Diploma of Wildlife Management to all students successfully completing the senior, two year course designed to produce men capable of filling game warden posts, and a Certificate of Wildlife Management in respect of the shorter, one year, middle-grade courses for game assistant ranks, which were planned for the future.

The first course started on the June 24th, 1963. The old buildings shone from their recent face lift and from the flagstaff proudly floated the college flag, emblazoned on it the symbol of a lion encircled with the words 'COLLEGE OF AFRICAN WILDLIFE – WE HOLD IT IN TRUST.' As if to mark the occasion the normal cloud blanket had lifted from Kilimanjaro, and the gleaming, sun-lit face of Kibo, the ice and snow of its glaciers sparkling like a birthday cake, looked down happily on the scene. And a novel scene it was, for parading on the sports field, awkward in their new uniforms, were twenty-three cadet wardens; one Arab the rest Africans; men of varying ages and education hailing from three different countries and five different organisations: the Game Departments of Tanganyika – ten, Kenya – seven, Uganda – three; the National Parks of Tanganyika – two, Uganda – one. Later they were joined by one African from the Forest Department of Nyasaland and a second from the Forest Department of the Cameroon Republic, making them twenty-five in all, from five different countries. They were the first non-Europeans to be trained as game wardens in Africa. Some were young, just out of school; others were men of long service. For the inexperienced a School Certificate pass had been the minimum educational qualification accepted for selection. In all cases a tough physical test had had to be passed. The oldest was one of the first two game assistants I appointed in Uganda, an ex-warrant officer of the King's African Rifles, an Acholi by the name of Daniel Otim. Our pleasure at meeting again was mutual.

From that day on, although my interest in it remained as keen as ever, my official connections with the management of the College virtually disappeared. In due course, the Tanganyika Government passed a special ordinance to establish the legal status of the college, which was followed by the formal appointment of its governing body. The latter included the names of a variety of persons; some venerable; a number resident overseas; a few who had been associated in some way with the creation of the College. My own name was not on the list!

Some years later still, after the College had been included in the United Nations Development Programme, I listened to a United Nations official holding forth on the subject. To my surprise his version of how the College of African Wildlife Management came into being was a new one. It reminded me of the occasion when the State Opening of the British Parliament was first televised. To millions of viewers Her Majesty the Queen was shown reading the 'speech from the throne' – the miscellany of pious platitudes and grandiose promise which every government produces, at this time. One little girl – so I was told – after watching enthralled, turned excitedly to her father and said, 'Look Daddy, the Queen's reading a fairy story!'

The United Nations man was charming; it was not his fault that he had been fed only half the true facts. And so I told him the story I have repeated here.

January 1964 – six months after the start of the first Mweka course – was a dark month in the annals of East Africa. The horrors of the Zanzibar revolution, when the streets of that old Arab city ran red with blood, were followed by the army mutinies in Tanganyika, Kenya and Uganda. Like the shock waves of an earthquake the repercussions of the troubles rolled far and wide across the face of the land. The staff of the Game and National Park Departments of East Africa stood firm; they held their old, traditional loyalties and so, I was relieved to find, did the students at the College of African Wildlife Management. But the ominous thunder of revolution revealed the writing on the wall; the days of the European game warden in Black Africa are numbered, it said. The College at Mweka had been started only just in time.

In the quiet after the storm, the Tanganyika Government issued a courteous but definite edict. The process of Africanisation of the Civil Service must be accelerated, particularly in the higher posts. I just had time to complete the christening of my final brain-child – The Tanganyika Wildlife Development Company[10] – a government owned tourist safari company, designed to operated carefully controlled wilderness safaris in the 20,000 square miles of the Selous Game Reserve, under the watchful eye of Brian Nicholson. Then I packed my bags and, in August 1964, Elizabeth and I set out on our last, nostalgic tour of our old happy hunting grounds.

Late in September, we visited Mweka. The students were intelligent, interested and desperately keen; they were the game wardens of the very near future, and how my beloved elephants would fare under their control, only

---

[10] Now called Tanzania Wildlife Safaries, an idea which originated in Uganda with Uganda Wildlife Development Limited, started by John Blower and Ernest Juer.

time would tell. As I watched the students being instructed, I thought of the old time game rangers and wardens they would be replacing. In my pocket was an almost visionary poem written while I was still in Uganda. Its author was T.R.H. Owen, C.B.E., a one time Governor of the Bah el Ghazal Province of the Southern Sudan, a brilliant, human and generous man with a gift for writing what he humbly called 'doggerel', witty verse with which he was wont to lampoon any truly farcical situation. On his retirement from the Sudan, reluctant to leave Africa he had elected to fill a comparatively humble post as a 're-tread' as he dryly called himself – in the headquarters of the Uganda Game and Fisheries Department. At one period, when we were receiving a spate of official requests, from exalted and influential overseas scientists, for obscure and complicated scientific specimens, requests blandly passed on by the Secretariat but which drove our game rangers and wardens to distraction, Richard Owen had come to our rescue and restored our sense of humour, with a delightful, but sadly prophetic poem which he dubbed 'The Triumph of Science'.

I sat down in the sunshine, on the steps of the College of African Wildlife Management and studied the poem again, for the hundredth time, to refresh my memory. As always it brought a smile to my face as I read:

Sam Scroggins was a naturalist and hunter from the nursery;
His maths were poor, his Latin weak, his grammar-studies cursory.
At three he was a graduate of field and forest lore,
And broke his father's windows with a catapult at four;
Could ride and shoot, - just sign his name, and loved a spice of danger;
Equipped in fact by Nature for the duties of a Ranger.
So when he grew to manhood and they offered him a billet
As a Ranger in Uganda, he was very glad to fill it.

He entered on his duties with efficiency and zeal;
Would face marauding lions with a nerve as true as steel;
Could deal with raiding elephants; could follow any track;
And Heaven help the poacher who felt Sam upon his back.

He lived in tents; he liked it tough; his beer was never iced,
And if the dukas hadn't gin then waragi sufficed.
His letters might be in arrear – his Guards were brisk and neat;
In fact he was 'The Ranger' as you might have said 'Compleat';

And everybody liked him, for depicted in his face
Was that hardy, horny kindness which transcendeth creed or race.
His prospects were unpromising; that didn't make him quail.
He liked the life, and didn't seem to bother with his Scale.[11]
Accountants, secretaries, clerks and all the inky crew
Were eligible for A1 (or anyway B2);
In the eyes of Mr Whats-his-name (the Establishments' Grand Chan)
Z7 was considered to be adequate for Sam.

But things are never static; Father Time is apt to canter;
Some dismal ancient poet has it '*Tempora mutantir*'.
The Warden told his Rangers (though it seemed a trifle tough)
The old bush-whacking qualities no longer were enough;
We must join the March of Progress, and he looked for some compliance
From subordinates in meeting the demands of Modern Science.

A letter followed presently – there wasn't long to wait –
From the USA containing application from a great
Demonstrator in Biology (God send he never tutor us!)
For a sample pregnant female Black Rhinoceros's uterus;
And Samuel, who when peevish was too honest, far, to mask it,
Read, shrugged, then tore it up and threw the fragments in the basket.

But short indeed his respite, for there followed an appeal
From a (Swiss) Monsieur le Professeur le Coq de Bogusville,
Requesting him to forward (here he grew a little flustered)
The tape-worm from the colon of Neotis (Denham's Bustard).
Sam wrote a rude epistle, and he hadn't much to say,
But he called the worthy professeur a Bustard with an A.

---

[11] For the uninitiated, salary scales in the Civil Service were graded by letters and numbers finally decided by the Establishments Division of the Secretariat and the Public Service Commission (P.S.C.).

He had scarcely mailed his letter when again the postman came
With a large forbidding envelope addressed in Scroggins' name;
A letter from the Warden, in which he could discern
A letter from the minister, which forwarded in turn
A letter from the Governor, of slightly earlier date,
Conveying a direction from the Secretary of State

To assist our politicians in a tricky situation
By acceding to a foreign scientific application –
A certain Dr Bunckheim, who was asking to be lent a
Hyaena (female)'s endotheliochorial placenta.
Sam scratched his head and spelled it out; he turned a little pale,
Then ground his teeth – his attitude was definitely male;
At length he firmly gripped his pen, and moved by wrath primordial
Wrote a letter which was rather less than endotheliocordial.

And that was Scroggin's downfall; for alas there's no specific
To cure a brain which wallows in a bog unscientific.
They sacked him; and a firman came from out the P.S.C.
That rangers must possess a University degree.

The post has been upgraded now, since applicants were few
And Bachelors of Science may aspire to enter Q:
And if they raise it to P3 we rather hope to get
Some Doctors of Divinity (we haven't hooked one yet).

By the time I had finished, my smile had assumed a wry quality. Read at this time, the penultimate verse in particular, was so near the hard truth as to be uncanny. I went inside and watched the African students at work. By a weird coincidence one was actually preparing a study skin from a greater bustard, and doing it remarkably efficiently. I was tempted to ask him if he had found any tape-worms in its colon! It dawned on me that I was looking at the scientifically trained game wardens of the future, that the brightest might go on to obtain a university degree, and that not one of them was a European. In East Africa the day of the old time game ranger and warden – those colourful, tough and entertaining characters who achieved so much – was fading; it was foolish to pretend anything else. Sadly and with strangely mixed feelings I turned away; I was on the way out myself.

A week later, Elizabeth and I sailed from Dar es Salaam in a small, Holland-Afrika Lijn, cargo ship heading for England. For as long as possible we remained on the upper deck of the *Oosterkerk*, sadly watching the coast of East Africa fade slowly in the distance. All too soon we could see no more than the waving tops of the coconut palms which lined the coral-fringed shore. At last even these disappeared beneath the horizon and quietly we went below. For the time being I did not want to think about the future.

# Chapter XXIII

# In Search of the Fish God

*A Tale for the dedicated angler*

It was on November 21st, 1949, that I arrived, with my wife and daughter, in Entebbe, the Administrative Capital of the then Uganda Protectorate; the reason for my journey had been to fill the newly created post of Deputy to the Chief Game Warden who, in turn, was the Director of the Uganda Government's combined Department of Game and Fisheries. It so happened that the Chief Game Warden at that time, Captain C.R.S. Pitman, D.S.O., M.C, was, like myself, formerly an officer who had served in the old, Imperial Indian Army, so my new career started off firmly on the right foot!

A little over nine months later, on the August 31st, 1950, Charles Pitman – by then a world renowned herpetologist – retired from the post he had filled with great distinction for twenty-five years – and, to my delight, I was allowed to slip quietly into his shoes! From that moment I became responsible not only for the protection and management of Uganda's varied and abundant populations of mammals and birds, but also for the development and management of the country's budding and potentially valuable fisheries industry.

Since I have been a dedicated angler for as long as I can remember, one of the first things I did when I arrived in Uganda, was to find out what species of sporting fish are native to the numerous lakes and rivers of the Uganda Protectorate. It didn't take me long to discover that there are really only two species in Uganda that can fairly be described as being top quality sporting fish; these are the world famous tiger fish (Hydrocyon spp), renowned for it's savage fighting qualities, and the Nile Perch (Lates spp), famous both for the size it so often attains and also for the superb quality of it's flesh. It is therefore the latter species that I now intend to discuss in more detail.

The Nile perch is found in most of the main lake and river systems of tropical Africa, with – until very recently – the notable exception of Lake Victoria and its tributaries. In Uganda it was previously confined to Lake

*Elizabeth and her leopard cub at the Game Dept Entebbe in 1955*

Albert, the Victoria Nile downstream of the Murchison Falls, and the Albert Nile and its tributaries such as the Aswa River in Acholi. It does not occur in Lakes George and Edward, but in the course of 1955, as a result of a very thorough and complex stocking operation that I had carefully thought out and planned, Nile perch were successfully introduced into Lake Kyoga and the Victoria Nile downstream of the Owen Falls dam. However the dam did not impose the impassable barrier that everyone had expected, because, in 1958 small specimens of Nile perch began to appear in Lake Victoria, up stream of the dam!

Concerned at this unexpected development, scientists at the East African Fisheries Research Organisation's headquarters in Jinja, close to the Owen Falls dam, carried out a very thorough investigation, in conjunction with the engineers at the dam; together they arrived at a surprising and, from the scientists' point of view, not very welcome conclusion. They discovered that, on those infrequent occasions when one or more of the turbines in the darn had to be shut down briefly for cleaning or maintenance, it was possible for small specimens of various species of fish to by-pass the dam and enter Lake Victoria.

For me this was a welcome development, for, in the nineteen thirties, the Worthington expedition had discovered fossilised remains of both Nile perch and tiger fish on some of the islands in Lake Victoria. Dating back to the great upheavals of the Ice Age, these remains proved that Lake Victoria, once a much deeper lake than it is now, had contained flourishing populations of oxygen dependent predatory fish, such as the Nile perch and tiger fish.

This theory was supported by evidence from Lake Albert where – as I will explain in more detail later – during the ten years that I was Chief Game Warden of Uganda, there were half a dozen occasions when there were mass mortalities of Nile perch in various areas of Lake Albert, due to temporary de-oxygenisation of the water in those areas.

The Nile perch, which, as its name implies, looks in shape like an outsize edition of the common European perch, has been regarded with esteem since time immemorial. The ancient Egyptians venerated and actually worshipped it as a fish god. According to Hurcombe it was named Latis in the Grecian Ptolemy dynasty, and the city of Esmeh, the centre of its worship, was then called Latopolis. Graeco-Egyptian coins of Latopolis bore its image, and it was portrayed on tombs and temple walls, mummified and ceremonially interred.

Locally called 'Mputa' in Uganda, the Nile perch grows to a great size, the largest recorded from Lake Albert weighing 360lbs. The latter was caught in a seine net and, although it was an exception, fish of 150lbs and upwards are regularly caught every year in nets and on long lines by commercial fishermen. Specimens of 60lbs to 80lbs are quite common, and can be expected by anglers. The largest fish are females, the males seldom exceeding a weight of some 50lbs. The biggest landed to date on rod and line in Uganda weighed 243lbs, and was caught in January, 1999, by Mr Marco Magyar, when he was fishing from a boat in Hippo Pool below the Murchison Falls. This fish took him two kilometres downstream before it was finally gaffed an hour later.

In colour the Nile perch varies, but it is usually a silvery fish dark on the back and white on the belly, and when freshly caught it often has a beautiful purplish-violet sheen reminiscent of a fresh-run spring salmon. After death the colour rapidly fades to a dirty brown grey. Fish caught off reed-beds, particularly over reedy bottoms, are often golden-yellow instead of silvery-white.

This is presumably a case of camouflage, adapted to environment, for the Nile perch is a predator which lies in wait for it's prey, hanging almost motionless in the water until an unsuspecting small fish swims by, when, with a lightning dash and a snap of it's cavernous mouth, it secures another meal; but it is also cannibalistic.

Perhaps the most striking feature of the Nile perch, however, is it's eyes, which have an unearthly, luminous, incandescent yellow glow, as if a fire was burning within it's head, the light from which is reflected through two glassy orbs!

The '*Mputa*' is excellent eating but some blasé anglers tend to decry it as a sporting fish. True, size for size there are many species elsewhere in the world that normally fight harder and longer, but the Nile perch is no mean antagonist, particularly if fished for with reasonably light tackle, and once hooked the outcome is by no means certain. It usually takes the bait with a bang, notably when the latter is being trolled behind a boat, and goes off with a mighty rush of 50 to 100 yards ending with a leap or a head shaking flurry on the surface, when the discomforted angler may see his bait sail into the air, and reel in to find his hooks buckled and bent. Don't attempt to stop the fish when it makes its first or subsequent runs, but keep a medium tension on the line and when its first rush slows up, and if possible before it breaks surface or jumps, tighten up and drive the hooks home. Remember the Nile perch has a hard and bony mouth and is adept at throwing the hook in its head-shaking flurries and leaps.

The fight is not normally very prolonged but this is not always the case. Alec Anderson, at the time Fisheries Officer in charge of Lake Albert, once hooked a Nile perch which he soon thought must be the mother and father of all the '*Mputa*' in the Lake. It fought stubbornly and deep without showing itself for 5 hours when, exhausted and with night coming on, he decided he must finish the contest one way or another. Putting on every ounce of strain his tackle would stand he finally boated the fish, which came in stone dead. He was using strong tackle, and is not a believer in sparing his fish, but this proved to be a male fish of only 50lb. normally hooked in the mouth! On the other hand the biggest perch I have caught, a female of 127lbs. came to gaff in half an hour. However, she gave me a spectacular fight with a series of long powerful runs and twice hurled her great 5ft bulk clear of the water. Although I was using a medium weight 8 ft glass rod, 30lb breaking strain line and a strong wire trace, I was uncertain of the outcome until we got the big gaff into her the first time she came alongside the bat. I then found that she had been securely hooked in the corner of the mouth and the triangle of the 6 in plug that I was using had to be cut out.

*The author's daughter, Bydie,
at The Murchison Falls*

As far as Lake Albert is concerned recent experimental fishing and the use of echo sounders have shown that Nile perch are to be found almost everywhere. At one time it was believed that there were two sub-species in the Lake, and the scientific name of *Lates Athertiartus* was given to what was thought to be the larger shore-loving type, and *Lates Macrophthalmus* to the allegedly smaller, deep-water type. Investigations during the last few years however, have shown that perch of all sizes exist in all depths of water, and it is likely that there is really only one local race of perch in the Lake. However, as far as the angler is concerned the most important point is the best place to fish for them, and this is undoubtedly where the shallow water shelf starts to drop steeply into deep water, and preferably in sheltered bays or the leeward side of spits or islands, for the Nile perch does not like rough water. Here the perch lies in wait for its prey, the fry and smaller fish which frequent the shallows and reed-beds. They can be caught at any- time of day, but for the larger fish the evenings and early mornings are undoubtedly the best, for the big perch seem to come into the shallow water in the evenings to feed, and move back into deep water when the night is over. The distance of the edge of this shallow water shelf from the shore naturally varies with the nature of the coastline but is usually some 20 to 40 yards out. Unless an experienced person is with the boat, depth plumbing or trial and error are the only ways of finding it.

For trolling or spinning comparatively clear water conditions should be chosen, so that the perch can see the moving bait at a reasonable distance. By static live-baiting of course fish can be successfully taken in much thicker water. When trolling from a boat the latter should travel at a slow walking pace along the line of the shelf, keeping the correct distance from the shore, while the lure is trolled some 30 to 40 yards astern. I think that the wake of the boat must attract the fish who come in to investigate the disturbance, and when a fish is hooked its mate will frequently follow it in to the gaff, for the perch often appear to be in pairs, and when two rods are fishing it is quite common for both the male and female fish to be hooked simultaneously. On one occasion when four rods were fishing over the stern of a launch I saw two pairs of perch hooked at the same time. Despite much crossing of lines and profanity they were all four finally successfully boated!

Trolling from a boat is by far the most productive method of fishing for Nile Perch in the Lake, and on one occasion a friend and I caught 29 Nile perch weighing 570lb in an afternoon's fishing; but where the shelf is close enough inshore, and where there are no wide reed-beds in the, way, good sport can often be had by walking along the shore, casting out towards the edge of the shelf at suitable spots, and spinning the lure slowly in.

The Nile Perch will take almost any form of spinning lure that resembles a fish spoons, plug-baits or dead-baits on a spinning mount – but in the Lake I have found plug-baits to be both the most effective and the easiest to use. Colour and size do not appear to matter a great deal although a bright coloured plug on a light day, and a dull coloured one on a dark day are fair enough rules to follow. American made plugs I have found to be excellent, and these can now be purchased in Kampala. The colours I use in the 'Creek Chub Pikie' series are 'Natural Pikie' (a good all rounder and a proved killer), 'Silver Shiner,' 'Golden Shiner,' 'Blue Mullet' and 'Rainbow.' They are obtainable in Kampala in two sizes, 4¼" and 6". I usually use the larger for fishing in the Lake as although the smaller size will take large fish as well as small, its smaller hooks are more likely to buckle and tear out in a big fish. I therefore normally use them only when I am fishing with really light tackle, or in the rivers, about which more later.

When trolling for perch you will often see the beautiful white-headed fish eagle sitting on a tree at the water's edge, or sailing majestically overhead occasionally throwing back his head to make the hills ring with his wild, laughing cry. As likely as not he will make a stoop at your plug bait as it wriggles enticingly astern just below the surface, and you may well find you have hooked a bird instead of a fish! I have heard of this happening on several occasions, and it once happened to me. It was rather like flying a kite for a time, but eventually I won, and we rescued a distressed and bedraggled eagle which had crash-landed in the water. A coat was flung over its head and the hook removed from its talons, to which luckily little damage had been done. On being released it flopped slowly ashore, sat on a rock and ruffled its feathers in the sun, a picture of thoroughly outraged dignity. In a recent case however, neither the angler nor the eagle was so lucky. The bird, having been hooked, finally fell in the water, whereupon there was a mighty swirl and a snap as it was engulfed in the jaws of a large crocodile. The latter dived immediately with a jerk which tore the line, reel and rod right out of the angler's hands, leaving him to watch helplessly as his expensive tackle disappeared for ever.

You never know quite what to expect. A District Officer, and therefore a magistrate and truthful man (in any case his story was corroborated by a Fisheries Officer who was an eye-witness), was trolling for Nile perch at the southern end of Lake Albert a few years ago, when he hooked something really big which sounded. After much pumping on the rod, a strong one luckily, his catch broke surface in the shape of a crocodile, the plug-bait clamped firmly in its jaws. The croc stared balefully at the launch, then with a disdainful flick of its head threw the plug towards the astonished angler and submerged. A moment later it surfaced again closer to the launch, glared threateningly at the occupants and disappeared for good. I have heard of two other cases of crocodiles taking plug baits, but on neither occasion was the reptile apparently so annoyed at being fooled, and on both times it finally removed the unlucky angler's plug.

From time to time mass mortalities of Nile perch occur in various parts of the Lake, and the floating bloated carcases of many hundreds of perch of all sizes can then be seen covering an area of several square miles of water. This phenomenon has never been properly explained, particularly as these mortalities appear to be confined to the Nile perch, but the latter is certainly quickly affected by shortage of oxygen, and the latest scientific theory is that the deaths are due to de-oxygenisation of the layer of water in which the affected perch happen to be, as a result of a rapid reversal of the thermocline.

The most convenient base for fishing for Nile perch in Lake Albert is

*The author's wife, Elizabeth, with a 95lb Nile Perch*

Butiaba, where there is a very comfortable Railway Rest House and Perch fishing can be good in Butiaba Bay, and around Butiaba Island, but if you can spare the time and the money it is wiser to go further afield, preferably south-wards where there are many good stretches which always seem to hold perch.

I have already spoken about lures but a few words on tackle in general may also be of help. Don't rig yourself out with shark tackle if you want good sport. The very big fish are few and far between and even these can be taken on light tackle if the boat is used skilfully. For trolling a light sea-rod or heavy salmon spinning rod is quite adequate, preferably not longer than 9ft or it becomes difficult to manage in a boat. The reel can be of any sort as long as it will hold 200 yards of line, which need not be stronger than 30lbs breaking strain, although one with a big drum or a multipying action is an advantage to enable line to be recovered quickly. A strong check mechanism on the reel is advisable. The most important thing is to have balanced tackle. If you use a very light line with a strong rod and reel with a powerful drag, you will almost certainly be broken.

Always use a wire trace at the end of your line. A Nile perch has no large sharp teeth in its mouth but it has hard, sharp and bony gill-covers and a sharp dorsal fin. These may cut through a gut or nylon trace if the latter becomes twisted round the fish during the struggle, and the same thing can happen if the perch dives deep on a rocky bottom. In addition tiger-fish frequently go for a lure being trolled for perch, and even for the swivels on the trace if they are at all bright, and they will slash through gut or nylon like a knife through butter. The trace need not be longer than 3 ft, but it should have a link swivel at one end to facilitate quick changing of lures, and an ordinary swivel at the end of which the line is attached. If you are using a spinning bait, such as a spoon or a dead fish on a spinning mount as opposed to a plug, your trace should have at least one extra swivel in the middle to reduce twisting and kinking of your line. The strength of your wire trace should preferably be slightly less than that of your line, so that if you do have the misfortune to be broken you will probably only lose your trace and lure and not half your line as well. Wire traces, either twisted or single strand, can be bought ready made-up in Kampala, but they are inclined to be expensive and it is easy to make one's own. I personally use 'Alasticum' wire, which, as its name implies, is slightly elastic, and is very easy to make up into traces. It again is now obtainable in Kampala.

*Author with "Barbus nadeliffei" at Ripon Falls, Jinja*

A final word about lines and care of tackle. For trolling a braided as opposed to a twisted line is best, and for spinning it is virtually essential, as however efficient your swivels there is always some twist, and this will eventually open up the strands of twisted line. Braided lines can be of cotton, flax, silk or nylon. The latter has the advantage of being virtually rot-proof, and can safely be left on the reel when wet after fishing.

For spinning a special braided spinning line with a waterproof dressing is advisable, as without this dressing the line quickly becomes soggy and water-logged, and is then difficult to manage on the reel.

Nylon monofil (single strand), of which there are many makes, can be used for both trolling and spinning. I find it excellent in the smaller sizes, and I use it a great deal. It is cheap, strong and generally reliable, but in the stronger sizes around 20lb breaking strain and upwards, it tends to be very springy and unmanageable.

The last, but not the least important item of equipment is a strong, long-handled gaff. A big perch is a powerful fish, and you will feel somewhat non-plussed if you get one, alongside your boat with no means of getting it aboard,

To round off this tale, I would like to say a few words about what I consider to be the most fascinating and sporting form of fishing for Nile perch. I refer to spinning for them in certain pools and fast flowing stretches of the Nile and its tributaries. The place 'par excellence' is I think undoubtedly that stretch of the River Nile from the Murchison Falls downstream to the landing stage at Fajao. This is within the Murchison Falls National Park, but the Park Authorities allow visitors to fish. Accommodation can be had at the Paraa Safari Lodge, but as this is frequently booked up application should be made well in advance to the Park Warden, Murchison Falls National Park, Private Bag, P.O. Masindi.

Perch in the rivers seem more selective in their liking for various types and colours of lures than they are in the Lake. At the Murchison I have found the 4 in 'Pikie Minnow' plugbait in 'Natural Pikie' finish to be far the most effective all round lure, although if the water is at all coloured a 'Silver Flash' or 'Blue Mullet' plug in the same size is often killing. Funnily enough in the Aswa River (of which I have no personal experience) various keen anglers have found plug-baits to be of little use, and have had most success spinning slowly with a dead fish, live baiting and even still fishing with meat or guts! Admittedly in the Aswa conditions are different, for fishing there is mainly confined to the dry weather period when the river is a series of large pools linked by a mere trickle of water.

At the Murchison the water is heavy, and the fish are lively and fight well under these conditions. The perch lie in pools and eddies off the main current and it pays to know where these lies are. The guidance of a person who knows is invaluable here, although there is an angling record book in the Paraa Safari Lodge with a sketch map showing the main pools and runs. Water conditions make a lot of difference to the fishing. If the water is very coloured after heavy rain, perch fishing. is hopeless. When the river is low after a dry spell the perch will be found concentrated in the stretch nearer the Falls, but they do not appear to like rough, heavy water, and if the river is very full they seem to drop back into the quieter pools and stretches further downstream.

When fishing you should cast your lure into the main current, and allow it to be swept into the pools and side eddies, whence you should recover it at a medium pace. Fish your cast out carefully to the last moment, as a perch will frequently follow your line right in and take it with a splash right at your feet.

Owing to the strength of the current medium weight spinning tackle should normally be used. In the big side pools quite light tackle can be successfully employed, but there are some big fish here and if they get out in the main current you will surely be broken if your tackle is very light. The largest perch so far caught below the Falls fell to the rod of John Savidge, one of the Park Wardens, in December, 1959; this fish weighed 160lbs and is believed to be the heaviest fish ever caught on rod and line, from the land (as opposed to a boat) but let me repeat, here, in his own words, John's personal account of his titanic battle.

> I only ever enjoy perch fishing in retrospect – at the time I am too busy worrying!
>
> This was particularly true on December 20th, 1959, when my luck and 18lb breaking strain line held throughout an agonising 2 hours, 35 minutes, to land the heaviest perch ever taken at the Falls – a magnificent hen-fish of 160lbs. The monofilament line had been over the pick-up bale so many times that the spool was coated with fine nylon dust. The clutches of the reel were hot to the touch, and my right palm was blistered from gripping the cork grip above the reel. The fish had been active from the moment it took the plug, to the time it was gaffed in four feet of water at the end of the battle; and five minutes before the end I had thought it would never tire!

Fishing in these magnificent surroundings is a constant delight, and there is always something of interest to see. Crocodiles in dozens lying basking on the rocks in mid-stream, hippo snorting and grunting in the lower reaches, and from time to time elephant wandering down to drink and bathe on the opposite bank. They will not bother the angler as long as he does not interfere with them, although as a precaution the National Parks Authorities detail a Ranger with a rifle to keep watch over visiting fishermen. Only once have I had any unexpected excitement. On that occasion an old and crusty bull hippo suddenly appeared unexpectedly out of a pool and chased my companion up the bank. Thwarted by my friend's agility he turned his attention to me just as I hooked a nice perch in the next pool. I retired rapidly behind a bush, paying out line as I went, and a volley of stones and abuse turned the hippo at the last moment. He went off splashing and grumbling downstream and the Nile perch, I am glad to say, was successfully landed. However, this old bull started to make a habit of this sort of thing, and he eventually had to be shot as a danger to the public.

Well, there it is. If this tale has interested you enough to get you to try your hand at Nile perch fishing, then it has achieved its purpose. I do not think you will regret it and I am certain you will not forget the thrill of hooking, playing and landing your first big *Mputa*, the fish-god of the Nile.

To conclude my tale about the 'Fish God', I think that I can do no better than repeat, here, the contents of a circular letter written, in 1986, by Mr Arthur de Mello of Kampala, Uganda's commercial capital. The was 29 years since the completion of my successful plan to stock Lake Kyoga and the Victoria Nile with small Nile perch from Lake Albert. The result of this stocking can only be described as spectacular, for in the fourteen years since the completion of this stocking with small Nile perch, the annual commercial fish production from Lake Kyoga and the Victoria Nile, rose from 4,500 tons per year, to nearly 49,000 tons per annum – an increase of over 1,000%.

Mr de Mello was therefore writing after having just been appointed as Uganda's representative on the I.G.F.A. (the International Game Fish Association) and the text of his letter was as follows:

UGANDA

## NILE PERCH

The Nile Perch (Lates nilotica) originally occurred in the rivers and lakes of the Rift Valley, mainly in the River Nile and its tributaries, Lake Turkana in Kenya and Lake Tanganyika in Tanzania, but not in Lakes Kyoga and Victoria, or above the Murchison Falls.

However, in 1949, Major Bruce Kinloch, a keen and dedicated angler, was appointed deputy head of the Uganda Game and Fisheries Department. Lake Victoria, whose waters are shared by Uganda, Kenya and Tanzania, was then the least productive lake in Africa, and at that

*A Nile perch carried on the handle of a boat paddle.*
*From a painting on the south wall of the tomb of the priest,*
*Rahotep, at Medum in Lower Egypt.*

time contained no trace of predatory species of fish at all. At that time Nile perch and tiger fish did not exist in the waters of the Nile system up-stream of the Murchison Falls.

However, Major Bruce Kinloch found out that there were fossilised remains of both Nile perch and tiger fish on the islands of Lake Victoria, dating back to the great upheavals of the ice-age, when the upper waters of the Nile had become shallow and de-oxygenated in and around Lake Victoria. Supported by this evidence, it was Bruce Kinloch who planned and organised the return of this superb sporting and edible species to its former habitat.

Nile perch were first introduced above the Murchison Falls and into the Victoria Nile and Lake Kyoga in the fifties, and upstream of the Owen Falls dam into Lake Victoria in the early sixties. In 1967 anglers started landing large catches of over 200lbs of Nile perch, with individual specimens of over 150lbs being caught in Lake Kyoga and on the Victoria Nile at Namasagali, Bujagali and below the Owen Falls dam.

In those days Uganda Hotels with co-sponsors B.A.T., East African

Airways, Uganda Hunting and Fishing and Uganda Wildlife, organised a yearly three days fishing competition at Chobe Lodge, on the Victoria Nile, during the Easter weekend, fishing mainly from the banks of the Victoria Nile. This competition attracted anglers from not only East Africa, but also from Europe; but sadly Chobe Lodge no more exists since it was destroyed in 1979, during the despotic regime of Idi Amin.

I landed my first Nile perch in Lake Victoria in 1968, off Gaba Water Works on the outskirts of Kampala; this fish weighed 15lbs. Later, in the early seventies, perch of 100lbs and more were landed at Entebbe. In 1986 when I returned to Uganda from Mombasa, after a four year contract with Air Rwanda, I started trolling and casting off the Entebbe Sailing Club and landed a Nile perch of 110lbs. Many members of the Entebbe Sailing Club then took to fishing and in 1988 we had our first fishing competition which attracted eleven boats; a total of 2,218lbs of perch were landed, the heaviest being 128lbs.

I then wrote to the I.G.F.A. asking them to officially recognise the Nile perch as a Game Fish. I am happy to say that this was agreed to and since 1989 records have been claimed, 191lbs being the all tackle record caught by Andy Davidson off Rusinga Island in Kenya, and the fly-rod record is 110lbs caught by Wayne John Hoselau off Rubondo Island in Tanzania. Specimens of over 330lbs have been landed by nets and long lines around Jinja.

The phenomenal spread and growth of the Nile perch throughout Lake Victoria was, however, at the expense of some other indigenous species. On balance the outcome has been beneficial in terms of greatly increased production of fish for the local market and export, and also for the sportsman.

Over 12 fish factories have mushroomed in each of the three East African countries and the export of Nile perch fillets is now a big foreign exchange earner for these countries. Furthermore, charter boat companies have started operating, and this will attract anglers and tourists for the benefit of these three countries.

From records you will note that in the early nineties anglers landed several big fish, but these days you are lucky to catch a really big one. The fish factories do keep to the law and catch a certain size, but it is the local fishermen who break the law by fishing close to the shore, where the fish breed, and also by using long lines and small mesh nets resulting in the landing of perch which are just 20cms long. The water hyacinth has also spread rapidly in the last three years, which at times blankets the bay making navigation and fishing difficult.

However hope springs eternal and good fishing can still be had around the Sesse Islands, although getting there can be difficult. The main method is trolling with plug/lures around rocky bays and inlets, where the monsters lurk in pursuit of tilapia, their main food source, although they are also cannabalistic. Live bait is also successful, especially in the river Nile below Murchison Falls, where the water is full of crushed weeds and hyacinth.

Tanzania authorities have banned commercial and local fishing around Rubondo Island, and this conservation measure has attracted many anglers from Africa and Europe, and it is there where the Nile perch seem to prefer large salmon flies. I am trying to persuade the authorities in Uganda to apply the same laws around the Sesse Islands.

Arthur De Mello
IGFA Representative Uganda.

# Appendix 1

# The Urgent Need for Formalised Training Facilities for Wildlife Management Personnel in the Africa of Today

by Major B.G. KINLOCH, M.C
(lately Chief Game Warden, Uganda, currently Chief Game Warden,
Box 1994, Dar es Salaam, Tanganyika)

*A paper presented to – 'The CCTA/IUCN Symposium On The Conservation Of Nature And Natural Resources In Modern African States' (The Arusha Conference – September 1961)*

Who has not heard of the 'wind of change' – the political 'wind' of nationalism that has been blowing across Africa with increasing strength in recent years, reaching gale force in many areas? But more than one 'wind' has been gusting across this great continent during the same period. A rising tide of worldwide interest and concern as to the future safety of the last great concentrations of the unique and varied fauna of Africa, has built up a high-pressure belt of public feeling. From this belt of high pressure another 'wind' has started, a wind of urgent enquiry and investigation; of intensive, though unfortunately still limited and localised scientific research; and of expressions of local public concern at the apparent lack of action and interest by the authorities concerned. This penetrating 'wind' had done much to blow away the fog of misunderstanding and ignorance that has hitherto hidden the true value of Africa's great wildlife resources, and has lifted the mists of misconception to reveal the vital role that the great game animals can play in the development of this continent and the advancement of its peoples.

But the clearing of these clouds has also revealed on the horizon, in stark reality, the dangers with which the survivors of Africa's previously apparently boundless herds of game are faced. The pessimists have already thrown up their hands in despair and described the present time as 'the twilight of the great beasts', but the optimists, and those determined to fight to the last ditch, are convinced that there is still time to avert disaster – given adequate material and moral support for the battle.

You can be cynical and say these are merely melodramatic words wrapped up in flowery phrases, but we cannot afford to be cynical at the present critical time, and if this dramatic version of a technical document will bring home to those in a position to help and act, the urgency of the situation better than the clinical phraseology of cold-blooded officialdom, then the writer is willing to face the scorn of the unconverted!

'Granted, the situation is serious, but what has all this got to do with staff and staff training, and in what connection is help needed?'

This is a question you may well ask. What is the answer? Obviously everything finally turns on adequate funds, or appropriate help in kind, but funds for much needed transport and equipment and additional staff will be of limited value unless both existing and extra staff can be properly trained. Such staff need to be taught up-to-date techniques of wildlife management, the degree varying with rank. At present full value is not being obtained from even the inadequate numbers of existing personnel because of the continuous lack of formalised training facilities.

We have no reason to decry the work done in the past by that rapidly vanishing race the sportsman-hunter-naturalist. Without their efforts at preservation there would now be little or no big game left to worry about. But they were working during less complicated times when there was little pressure on the land, the term 'nationalism' had hardly been heard of, and the issues in regard to game were apparently straightforward. Game was regarded as an attractive sporting asset, and a convenient fresh meat supply on safari, where there could be no other possible use for the land it occupied, but it was uncompromisingly condemned as a direct obstacle to development in virtually all other areas. Thus the Game Wardens of the day had the straightforward problems of total preservation of game in certain areas from which humans were completely excluded; the supervision of licensed hunting regulated by laws based on a traditional code of sporting ethics; and the destruction of all species of game in areas where they came into conflict with man's use of the land. The tempo of life was slower, game was plentiful, and the consequence of mismanagement of the land and its resources had hardly started to become apparent. Under these conditions the Game Wardens and their senior officers had time to spare to train their subordinate staff in their undoubtedly arduous but otherwise simple duties; and this they did with painstaking efficiency and thoroughness.

However, this golden age did not last. More and more land was cultivated or destroyed; wildlife was killed out to eradicate tsetse fly and encourage the keeping of rapidly increasing herds of useless scrub-cattle; game populations were decimated to provide meat for famine relief, meat for the war effort, and cheap meat for employers of labour; and the less resilient and adaptable species began to disappear with alarming rapidity along with the destruction of their essential habitat.

Now we have reached an era of involved issues and problems of extreme complexity, when our decisions and actions can have repercussions which are far-reaching and often difficult to foresee. On the brighter side, wildlife is at last beginning to be officially regarded as a natural resource in its own right, and even more important as a natural resource of potentially great economic value capable of being utilised on a sustained yield basis in a variety of ways, if properly managed. Yet despite this complex modern picture we are still relying on largely inexperienced, virtually untrained, and often unreliable and untrustworthy junior staff. In fact, they are now in general less well disciplined, trained and supervised than they were in the past, for the present day Game Ranger no longer has the carefree, paper-free life of his predecessor; he is a harassed, frustrated individual with an impossible task and insufficient time to do it in!

It is clear that the time is long overdue for wildlife management to be regarded in Africa as a true branch of natural science comparable with forestry and agriculture. It has long been so treated on the North American continent, why not here? The foresters and agriculturalists have always considered it necessary to have a high percentage of both scientifically and technically qualified officers; why should we continue to consider that those responsible for managing our wildlife resources are in a different category? Furthermore, it has long been regarded as important to require intermediate and junior staff of the departments of Forestry and Agriculture to undergo formalised training in a properly organised establishment; therefore, are we right in continuing with our present somewhat haphazard methods while in sight of us are impressive schools of forestry and agriculture?

Surely the answers to the above queries are obvious, but more recently a new factor has emerged which has injected an element of even greater urgency into the problem. I refer to one of the main and oft-declared aims of the architects of African nationalism – 'rapid Africanisation of the civil services.' This means that not only are we faced with having to introduce the long over-due properly organised formal training facilities for intermediate and junior wildlife staff, but we now also have the problem of having to locate, attract, train and establish suitable African officers in the senior posts in the immediate future, instead of progressively and steadily as had hitherto been foreseen.

The problem is aggravated by three major factors. Firstly, there is no obvious or ready source of recruitment of suitable educated Africans with a leaning towards working with wildlife; secondly, the number of graduates in natural science which can be expected from African Universities such as Makerere during the next few years is very limited; and thirdly, at present a career in wildlife management in Africa does not offer the same attraction and material advantages as a career for a qualified officer in the forestry, agriculture or veterinary services, yet it is with these services that we must compete not merely for the best but, for some time to come, the only available candidates.

Our staff problems do not end there. We have yet another – an unbalanced hierarchy in the wildlife departments of both Game and National Parks, for the middle ranks, considered to be the vital backbone of all disciplined armed forces and civil services, are to all intents and purposes missing. At the top we have well-educated, experienced and/or qualified Game Rangers. At the bottom we have the ranks of Game Scouts who form the bulk of the field staff; tough, usually loyal by their own rights, but poorly educated or illiterate and exposed to many forms of temptation, graft and corruption. In the middle there is a virtual vacuum, although in recent years some wildlife departments have introduced a few ranks of Game Assistant and Assistant Game Ranger. The difficulty has not only been financial; just as important has been the lack of training facilities required to produce men of the right calibre for these vital posts.

All this means that our recruitment and training problems fall into three groups as follows:

a  The attraction of Africans suitable for advanced technical and scientific training in wildlife management for the existing senior posts, and the organising of such training at suitable institutions;

b  The attraction of appropriately educated and physically and temperamentally suited Africans for training for the missing middle ranks, and again the organising of the requisite formal training;

c  The attraction of better educated, but still physically and temperamentally suited young Africans to the junior ranks, and yet again the establishment of formal basic training facilities.

We should now consider these groups separately in rather more detail:

a  *Senior Posts*

To attract the right material for this group we must offer the same terms of service as are enjoyed by qualified officers in other services which are responsible for the care and development of natural resources.

Training arrangements must be designed to cover the training of selected Africans with suitable academic qualifications, and mental and physical attributes for the more senior posts such as Game Ranger/Warden, and for that matter National Park Warden also. Such training could best be carried out in the USA and/or Canada where the Africans selected could do a four year degree course in 'Wildlife Management' or in some cases a shorter diploma course in the same subject, under suitable scholarships or grants managed by such institutions as the African-American Institute, or the African Wildlife Leadership Foundation. The former has expressed interest and willingness to co-operate in this matter, while the latter has already started on these lines – a most laudable and encouraging development.

The reasons for selecting the USA and Canada are, I think, obvious; they are the only countries who have really specialised in wildlife management and recognised it as a science of equal status to other branches of natural science; they have big populations of a variety of the larger mammals to conserve and manage in the face of human competition for other uses of the land involved; they have a hunter-pressure problem; and they have properly organised training facilities directed to both the theoretical and practical under-graduate and post-graduate training of students in the science of wildlife management.

Since the majority of the really critical wildlife problems in Africa today concern the preservation of the large mammals, particularly ungulates and carnivores, it is felt that some of the universities located west of the Mississippi River appear best suited to training these special students. These institutions are in areas of ungulates and range problems more closely allied to the problems in Africa than the eastern universities (Michigan State University being a probable exception to this general rule). It is also suggested that preference should be given to those universities, some of the members of whose staff have themselves had practical experience of wildlife management problems in Africa, eg, those who have carried out wildlife research in Africa under Fulbright or similar arrangements.

It must be stressed again that we have little hope of getting more than a very few African University graduates with natural science degrees during the foreseeable future, and certainly not enough to meet all our present needs, let alone any possible future expansion. All this virtually rules out post-graduate training, and in consequence I suggest that we should adopt the following emergency procedure. First select a few chosen Africans who have a Higher School Certificate or a good School Certificate pass, and who are in addition both physically and temperamentally suited to work with the departments of Game and National Parks. This primary selection to be followed by a short 'weeding out' period with the departments concerned, the successful candidates then being sent to a suitable University in the USA or Canada for a four year degree course in 'Wildlife Management'. The final stage to be a period of post-graduate 'on the job' experience with an established officer in the field of Africa.

To complete this Africanisation programme for existing senior posts, we would want to send at least six or seven African students to the USA or Canada per year for the next three years to meet the needs of the Tanganyika Game Department alone!

It has been suggested in some quarters that such training would be better carried out in Africa by arranging suitable facilities at say Makerere College. With this I cannot agree. Such facilities do not at present exist, wildlife management as a science is a very new idea in Africa, and time is too short to get it soundly established before the training must begin. Furthermore not only have the USA and Canada specialised in scientific and technical training in 'wildlife management' as a natural science of equivalent status to forestry, agriculture, etc, but the broadening of outlook, and the realisation of the value placed on wildlife by advanced countries, which would certainly result from prolonged study outside Africa, would be of tremendous benefit to African students. They would return to Africa with greatly enhanced status in the eyes of their fellows; their views and teachings would be respected; and their personal contacts with visitors of all races would be made easier.

I would like to stress that I have not forgotten or ignored the fine work being done by the Nature Conservancy in the United Kingdom in this particular field, but at the moment they only cater for university graduates, and it is a drawback that practical work with large mammals in the United Kingdom must perforce be confined almost entirely to one species of ungulate – the red deer.

b   *Middle and Junior Ranks*

For the sake of simplicity, and much needed brevity, I think we can deal with these two groups together. First of all, we cannot hope to attract and retain the right material, and we must now go for men of better education, unless we can offer terms of service at least as attractive as those enjoyed by other departments, and in particular the uniformed, disciplined and sometimes armed forces whose primary work is connected with law enforcement. I refer to the Police, Prisons and Customs Services. It should not be forgotten that the work of the rank and file in wildlife departments is usually arduous, frequently dangerous and at present largely misunderstood and unappreciated. On top of this their pay and prospects are poor while their temptations are great. This is not a situation which should be allowed to continue.

Training for these two groups must be formalised, standardised, properly organised, largely centralised and soundly administered with adequate equipment and facilities. It is clear that what is needed to meet these requirements is the organisation of 'Wildlife Management Training Schools' initially at least on a regional basis. Their primary task would be to train up the largely missing 'middle ranks' of the Game Assistant/Assistant Game Ranger level, but such schools could also cater for improving the standard of the more promising Game

Scouts etc, which in turn would both improve the efficiency of a service that has long been crippled by shortages of both staff and funds, and ensure that full value is obtained from such staff as exists. A plan for such a school to be based in the Arusha region of Tanganyika, and to serve the three East African Territories, has already been prepared in outline, but as always finance is the main stumbling block.

Space does not permit detailed description of the project here, but capital expenditure on buildings, vehicles and equipment would be not less than £70,000, plus the costs of common services depending on the site selected, and annual recurrent expenditure would amount to £12,000 or more, depending on the extent of external technical aid. Courses at this school would last for some 18–24 months and it would cater for 75–100 students at a time.

It has been suggested in some quarters that the whole idea is too grandiose, and that a start should be made by organising training in a small way in temporary tented or bush camps for short periods of two or three months. I would like to conclude this paper by countering that point of view, which I feel is dangerous since it over-simplifies the problem.

As I have stressed earlier in this paper, in the past game in Africa has generally been regarded mainly as an obstacle to development rather than as a valuable economic resource worthy of being conserved, developed and utilised. There has been a big official swing towards the latter view in recent years, but we (the wildlife departments) are severely handicapped by being the last to jump on the 'financial bandwagon!' We are still trying to catch up from the period when the finance allotted for game conservation was based almost entirely on the requirements for the protection of crops from wild animals, and the minimum effort needed to enable the territories to comply with their moral obligations under international agreements based on aesthetic interest. However, among the African territories Tanganyika in particular is a poor country and has a very shallow purse. Therefore to rob what the electorate regard as important essential services (such as education, health, agriculture etc) in order to boost game conservation would antagonise the majority of public opinion, and the long term future of wildlife depends on strong public support and co-operation. On the other hand, the world in general has, in recent years, brought considerable pressure to bear on the East African territories to take adequate measures to preserve their unique wildlife resources, which are valued highly by the outside world. The territories concerned now appreciate the value of this wildlife resource, and would like to be able to conserve it properly, but being relatively poor countries they just have not got the necessary money to do so. It would seem logical therefore to expect international aid if the world in general wishes to see the unique fauna of Africa preserved in Africa for the benefit of the world, as well as for the benefit of the people of Africa. Furthermore, I think it is fair to regard this world interest as not entirely altruistic, in view of the tremendous pleasure so many people obtain nowadays from visiting this continent to see, photograph, study and even hunt the great mammals of Africa in their beautiful natural surroundings.

My reason for stressing this all important financial aspect is that for too long the Game Departments and National Park Organisations in East Africa have had to try and operate efficiently on a 'shoe string'. Apart from the obvious consequences there are also less obvious, but equally important ones. For example, the indigenous peoples, seeing that wildlife conservation requirements are given low priority by those who are governing the country, are led to think that there can be little real value in conserving game, while the better educated ones are discouraged from choosing a career in a field which appears to be regarded as the 'poor relation'. African and Asian peoples in particular are impressed by pomp and ceremony and signs of prosperity – in fact 'window dressing' pays full dividends with them. Thus to run a wildlife management training 'school' under temporary camp conditions, while almost next door is a flourishing forestry school and a large agricultural school both with good buildings, equipment, etc, is a bad start psychologically, for it must be remembered that we are not dealing with enthusiastic and dedicated European and American students, but African students with a very different background and outlook who have to be conditioned, steered and encouraged.

The short two or three months course proposal is very much in line with what we, in Tanganyika, already arrange from time to time on a 'Range' basis for Game Scouts. It is useful but it is not enough since it does not even start to solve our main problem of building up a balanced hierarchy, with a solid central core of technically well-trained and disciplined 'middle ranks' and an 'upper crust' of scientifically trained officers of good calibre. With the African such training takes time. It cannot be rushed, otherwise the requisite knowledge, sense of discipline and genuine interest in the work itself will not be properly absorbed or developed, and consequently will not be retained. We need adequate financial and technical help from international sources, and this is not asking for charity. The results will not only help the advancement of the countries of Africa, but will be to the indirect benefit of the world in general.

# Appendix II

# Thirty Pieces of Silver

*The following tale is an eye-witness' version of the marlin fishing story which I have already told in Part One, but this version was published on the Internet by Roddy Hays, skipper of the big game fishing craft M.V. 'Margarita'*

July 21st, 1993 – it is 6.14pm in the late afternoon and we have achieved the impossible. We are trolling slowly homewards at the end of Major and Mrs Bruce Kinloch's two-day charter. It has been both a celebration of fifty years of marriage, and a quest to find a blue marlin for the Major, who – despite some forty years of service on the African coast in various civil positions – has never caught one before. With some trepidation we have earlier put the sprightly 72 year-old angler into the chair at just past 1.00pm, firmly attached to a lively fish on 130lb gear.

After some fancy boat work and plenty of black smoke we had the marlin alongside the boat after 35 minutes for the customary tags and measuring. The 450lb fish had swum off into a dull afternoon and an angler's cherished dream had come true. We celebrated with an extensive lunch, and Richard and I quietly congratulated ourselves and considered a difficult job well done. It is Richard's first season as a deckhand, and although he has yet to actually wire a marlin, he is proving himself extremely capable and efficient on the boat, a fact I remind him of often as he is both older and stronger than me!

It is now 6.15pm, and we are 30 minutes away from home. The weather has deteriorated and the afternoon is now grey and cold. Small white waves thud against the hull as we slowly head along the last of the drop-off. I look down at the sounder, see 69.8F, and look back into the two contented faces of the Major and his wife, huddled up against the cold. Richard is also looking forward, grinning from ear to ear. Over his shoulder I see a huge black hole where the right rigger lure should be and feel the outrigger thud slowly as if in shock. I scream 'FISH!' at the startled faces a mere two yards away from me and gun the boat. Even as Richard reels back with surprise and drops

*Well hooked!*
*The author's 475 lb Blue Marlin fought like this for nearly an hour.*

down into the cockpit – the good Major and his wife following more slowly – I sense the fish is solidly hooked, and immediately put the boat into idle. I can see the Dacron curving across the wake, slowly moving to the left. I yell at Richard not to panic and to bring the other rigger line in first – I can then go stern-first after the fish before it takes too much line for the poor Major. I instinctively feel that the fish is big and I am acutely aware that darkness is only 60 minutes away. As we start to chase the line astern I become aware of a fish jumping heavily out past the bow, but do not pay attention as I am making sure the two flat-lines are clear of the propellers before I, too, descend the ladder for the cockpit controls.

Amongst the confusion in the cockpit I stop and stare. The good Major has decided that fifty years of marriage is repayable in kind, and he has ushered his 67 year-old wife into the chair. Richard is clipping her up to the 80lb outfit, shaking his head as he does so. Fifty yards behind her, a huge blue marlin is sliding away from us into the gloom of the afternoon, her back and dorsal clear of the dark water. I curse and run for the VHF at the inside helm-station.

*Anguilla* is already back in harbour and within 10 seconds I have raised Jonno and explained the situation. He literally drops the VHF and goes off the air without stating his intentions. Puzzled and somewhat annoyed I return to the cockpit and make a determined effort to stay as close as possible to the fish and for twenty minutes we manage to miraculously keep her within 100 yards of the boat as *Margarita* barrels astern into a slowly increasing chop. Thankfully the marlin remains on the surface, and each time she shows herself Richard and I shout with excitement and awe, our teeth jarring in our heads from the severely cavitating propellers. Elizabeth Kinloch is winding for all she is worth, and we encourage her as much as we can. As could be expected of a woman who has sturdily born the tribulations of colonial life in Africa, she grits her teeth and manfully winds and pumps as she has seen her husband do some hours before. The fish takes line in sudden bursts, ripping it noisily off the reel, but each time is slows again, seemingly unbothered by the pressure and we continue to regain whatever line we lose.

*Having been brought alongside 'Margarita', the author's 475 lb Blue Marlin was first carefully measured, then tagged and finally – released.*

After 45 minutes I can see a small inflatable far away in the distance, leaping from whitecap to whitecap, and I realise what Jonno has done and that help is close at hand. Suddenly the small boat stops, and for two minutes it remains motionless in the water as we back down further away from it. I start to fear that they have run out of fuel, but suddenly it is up running again. Incredibly, the sea-conditions are changing. The wind dies away within minutes, and the surface of the water takes on a slow deep-troughed appearance. We have entered the strong currents off Ponta da Cruz, and *Margarita* starts to wallow as she continues astern after the huge fish.

Jonno and his crewman Myles finally catch up with us, and Myles puts the inflatable against the bow of *Margarita*, an act unseen by everyone else aboard. Jonno climbs on board with some effort and as he steps down past me into the cockpit from the fore-deck I realise he is dripping wet. He explains quietly that a huge wave had catapulted him out of the inflatable and he goes down below to quickly change into dry clothes. Within seconds he reappears and I quickly explain the situation to him. I tell him that the fish is somewhat over 1000lbs in weight and he grins with excitement and starts setting out tag sticks and gloves. Elizabeth is in a sweating world of her own, still steadily reeling when able, but it is only now that she notices Jonno and with a start she imperiously demands to know where he has come from! The Major is balanced precariously on the fly-bridge ladder with a camera and continues to encourage her in his soft Scottish accent.

*Margarita* continues to go astern in the waning light, Myles and the inflatable off to one side. The swell grows steadily.

At 8.15, just before the light goes, Jonno has a hand on the trace as *Margarita* pours astern at six or seven knots, the boat shuddering with the strain. The fish is parallel with the boat, her huge tail churning white water, but is there for the tagging. Jonno wraps once and heaves. The fish surges out of the water and everyone shouts with excitement, except for Jonno, who grunts with effort. He wraps once more, and the fish starts to finally recognise the extra pressure. She jumps again and in mid-flight Richard and I unbelievably each manage to put a tag in her at full stretch, almost simultaneously. The fish immediately starts to jump across the stern of the boat in slow motion, each splash of water soaking Jonno. We are still going astern in a pall of black smoke and as Jonno is dragged around the transom to the opposite corner we can see the lure and one hook hanging out of the far side of the fish's mouth.

*Elizabeth playing her record Blue Marlin which weighed in at 1300lbs
on her Golden Wedding Aniversary*

Poor Jonno reaches the corner of the cockpit and the fish accelerates away, leaving him pinned against the covering board. Almost in slow motion the wraps leave his hand with reluctance and the fish is gone, the reel screaming as the marlin goes deep for the first time. It is at this moment that Jonno breaks a bone in his left hand, but he says nothing until much later.

Until now, Elizabeth has done everything according to IGFA rules apart from Richard putting the rod into the chair for her. Having tagged the fish though, some of her strength goes, and now Richard is forced to help her back and forth in the chair for another forty minutes. The angler cannot weigh more than 110lbs, and has difficulty in pulling back against the weight of the fish. During that time, the fish heads south away from land in the growing darkness, seemingly content to stay at a depth of 60' or so. We fire up the generator and the two halogens on the hard-top flood the cockpit with light.

Outside in the night, we can hear Myles puttering along with us, facing a dilemma of his own. His fuel is low, and in the rush to reach us neither he nor Jonno had time to grab a light of any sort. Worried, he struggles to maintain a safe position alongside us as we continue astern at a steady pace, spray flying into the cockpit. The seas build up again in the darkness, and *Margarita* pitches and rolls steadily. Twice more, we have the trace up to Jonno's hands, but the fish is still green and each time she effortlessly slips away. Several times I turn the boat to change the angle and to try and raise the fish from ahead but this only seems to annoy her and we settle back into a stern-first chase.

By 9.30pm, Elizabeth has been in the chair for over three hours, and this 67 year-old woman decides that she has done enough. She climbs stiffly down and Richard settles into the vacated harness and bucket. Amusingly, she is furious with Jonno at having let go of the fish, but she recovers her strength quickly and joins her husband on the fly-bridge. Jonno also decides that something is seriously wrong with his left hand and tries to take the glove off. His hand is badly bruised and very swollen and I give him the cockpit controls as I don a pair of dry and undamaged gloves and prepare to get seriously wet. Steadily the lights of the city of Funchal slip into the distance as we race backwards in the black night.

Over the next thirty minutes, Jonno manages to give me the leader three times. Each time I wrap as tight as possible and pull the fish up a few yards, her ghostly form faintly lit with phosphorescence down deep behind the transom. It is a frightening but hugely exhilarating experience to be attached to such a great glowing fish in the middle of a dark ocean, screaming backwards into a smooth but regular six-foot sea, and the marlin is impossibly heavy to lift further. Each time she simply shakes her massive head, jerking me against the covering-board, and each time I cannot hold her as she powers her way back down into the depths. We are all distraught and are desperate to release the fish before the now heavily strained reel-line gives way, trapping her with the full length of leader and the lure. The seas are growing in size, and as loose gear starts to fall inside the boat I decide we are playing a dangerous game and acknowledge that enough is enough. The fish is too strong still and the night is blacker than ever.

At 10.10pm the trace comes to hand once more, and I wrap for the last time. Jonno leaves the controls and stands behind me, the boat still trundling steadily astern. As the swivel appears over my shoulder, he cuts it off with scissors. If the fish escapes now, the lure will fall off the leader. I heave again, and wrap another yard. Behind me, Jonno chops that off. Each time I lift the fish up, Jonno cuts the leader available to him. The cockpit is littered with small lengths of heavy mono. The fish and I reach a stalemate forty seconds later. My hands are swollen grotesquely inside the gloves, and I have no feeling in them. I can feel the great fish travelling steadily along, her huge body swaying with each beat of that enormous tail, and I have no more strength left to wrap with. Richard has dropped the rod and is now by the controls. Jonno leans over and helps me lift the fish another yard with his one good hand. Snip. Once more, snip. Then we can see the fish clearly, glowing green down in the wake. Suddenly, she increases speed and heads down. As Jonno holds me, my legs buckling with effort, we look at my gloves in the overhead lights, the wraps glistening slowly as they peel off. In a sudden rush they are gone and I am left with the memory of the last final inch of line slipping through my fingers. Richard puts the boat out of gear, and in the pitching sea Jonno and I look at each other.

For me, it is one of the most elemental moments in my life, and Jonno and I suddenly grin in unison. We have left the fish with 12" of leader and a small 10/0 hook in her cheek. We feel we have done the best we could for her, and suddenly we are all cheering wildly, the Major and Elizabeth perched on the ladder, Richard at the controls. In the same instant afterwards, the night goes very quiet and in its soft silence we are aware that very close by there is a soft but awesome exhaling. Suddenly, around the boat are four huge sperm whales, one of them glistening faintly on the very far edge of the light. The boat seems very small, far from land in the black of night, and we all feel exposed. Within seconds though, they are gone in gentle surging individual wakes of phosphorescence and we then hear Myles calling out through the gloom. A minute later the inflatable roars through the darkness and nearly comes aboard over the transom as *Margarita* goes downwards in a deep trough. He climbs aboard, exhausted and cold after being alone in a small boat in a pitching sea for four hours, and tells us of his own exhilarating experience with whales.

We slowly head home, towing the inflatable (which has a cupful of fuel left in its tank), each of us glowing softly with the cold but chattering excitedly. In the soft light of the instrument lights I can see Elizabeth explaining how she feels and I realise that this woman had done something very special. As we roll slowly through the darkness, she explains in a strong voice what she feels. She apologises for not staying in the chair, but then recounts that other factors had a part to play. Amazed, we learn that this woman has had two hip operations, been run over by a car, has fought and recovered from cancer, and suffers sorely from arthritis and rheumatism. In addition she has quite likely caught the largest blue marlin ever hooked by a female angler. I am lost for words and hope that if I live to her age, then I will have the courage to do what she has done. Back in harbour, Jonno and I put the fish down in the log at 1300lbs and we celebrate gently into the early hours of the morning, all of us totally and utterly exhausted.

We all hope the fish lives.

Roddy Hays

# Appendix III

# The Mystery of the Wandering Chinthe

In Chapter XIII, entitled 'The Elusive Sambar', I mentioned briefly, that in September 1944 I was posted as Second in Command of the 4th Battalion of the 9th Gurkhas Rifles. I also mentioned that, at that time, this Battalion formed part of 111 Brigade in Major General Orde Wingat's 'Special Force'.

When Wingate formed his 'Special Force', designed to operate behind Japanese lines, he chose as their symbol a Burmese 'Chinthe', the mythical, dog-like dragon, giant stone images of which stand guard, in pairs, at the entrance of all Buddhist temples in Burma. Hence, all members of Wingate's 'Special Force' became known as 'Chindits', with their shoulder emblems proudly displaying a golden Chinthe on a royal blue background.

A couple of months after I joined 4/9GR my new Commanding Officer was very seriously injured, both his arms being shattered by the premature explosion of a faulty demolition charge. My CO was then rushed into hospital, while I myself was immediately given the temporary rank of Lt-Colonel and ordered to replace him. So, when in August 1945 America brought the war with Japan to an abrupt end (by dropping atomic bombs on Hiroshima and Nagasaki), I was still in command of a Chindit battalion.

Sadly, two years later, the old Imperial Indian Army, with its proud history and famous traditions, ceased to exist after having been divided between the new, independent India and the newly created country, Pakistan. For myself it was the end of my chosen career, so I resigned my commission and started searching for 'pastures new'!

Once again in my crowded life 'Lady Luck' smiled on me, but this time she did not merely smile, she literally beamed! I had written to the Colonial Office in London, applying for a post in the Colonial Administrative Service, and this had resulted in an interview at which I was offered a job as a District

Officer in (wait for it!) the Crown Colony of Kenya, the country which has long been far and away the favourite destination of 'Africaphiles'!

Believe it or not, this was still not the end of my good fortune, for when my wife Elizabeth and I arrived in Mombasa in January 1948 and reported to the Government Coast Agent, I was told that I had been appointed to assist the District Commissioner of the District of Kilifi, in Kenya's beautiful Coast Province.

Kilifi District has a coastal sub-district called Malindi, and some months after our arrival in Kilifi, one evening Elizabeth was strolling alone, on Malindi's beautiful beach, when she noticed a small object tumbling over and over in the waves at the tide line. Out of curiosity she picked it up only to find – to her utter astonishment and almost total disbelief – that in her hands, dripping with sea water, she was holding a skilfully carved, six inch

*A miniature Chinthe (carved in teak) which was found by Elizabeth Kinloch on the beach at Malindi (in Kenya) in September 1978*

tall, teak model of a Burmese Chinthe – thousands of miles away from the country of its origins!

Where it had come from and how it had reached Malindi is a complete mystery. But this salt soaked miniature model of a Chinthe, with its strong Gurkha cum Chindit connections, now has a place of honour among my most treasured personal relics.